WITHDRAWN

D1068363

W. D. HOWELLS
and Art in His Time

W. D. Howells

AND ART IN HIS TIME

CLARA MARBURG KIRK

RUTGERS UNIVERSITY PRESS *New Brunswick, N.J.*

To

RUDOLF KIRK

in appreciation

"Though your Lordship hath many troubles, great cares, and much business in your particular affairs, yet you are pleased to peruse my works, and approve of them so well as to give me leave to publish them, which is a favour few husbands would grant their wives."

Margaret, Duchess of Newcastle
Preface to *Philosophical Opinions* (1663)

Preface

In the Preface to *W. D. Howells, Traveler from Altruria, 1889–1894,* the story of how that book came to be written is told in some detail. The present study is, in a way, a companion volume of that earlier exploration. *W. D. Howells and Art in His Time* focuses more on Howells' relation to the movements in art during his life as a writer than on the social background that was another important aspect of his outlook as a novelist. Students of William Dean Howells are accustomed to the fact that his quiet, sensitive mind played in and out of all the major movements of the last quarter of the nineteenth century—religious, scientific, and social as well as literary and artistic. Hence it will be no surprise to them to discover that Howells' views on social questions and his attitudes toward the various art theories of his day were interrelated.

As far as I know, Howells has never been studied as a critic of art and as a novelist whose style of writing was influenced by his close association with artists. Many critics have dismissed Howells as one who was definitely unresponsive to pictures, statues, architecture, and all artistic values not related to the written word. An avowed amateur in art, Howells, in fact, was fascinated by the artistic technique of men and women in every field of creative expression. The very fact that he always considered himself an amateur in artistic questions makes his response to the art exhibitions of his time, to the plans for Washington Square in New York, to the glories of the Chicago Columbian Exposition, of more than ordinary value, for they define the views of the educated but nonprofessional group of his day. "There *is* no acknowledged authority on art in this country," said Howells. Why should he not speak?

As always, I wish to acknowledge my indebtedness to Rudolf Kirk, who not only is a patient reader of manuscript but also an amused explorer of art collections, library files, and even of small New England towns, such as Ashfield, Massachusetts, where some of the material for this book was gathered. Professor W. W. Howells and the trustees of the Howells Collection in the Houghton Library, Harvard, kindly granted me permission to quote from the manuscript letters in their possession. The Rutgers University Library accorded me the kind of hospitality I wish all scholars could enjoy, and the Rutgers Research Council gave me a grant that helped me to circumvent various practical problems.

C. M. K.

San Marcos, Texas
7 January 1965

Contents

Introduction

When William Dean Howells wrote *Years of My Youth* in 1916, he tried to recall his earliest conscious sense of beauty. He was then a novelist and critic of seventy-nine years, comfortably seated in the "Easy Chair" of *Harper's Monthly*. In attempting to recall the barefoot Ohio boy of pre-Civil War days, Howells clearly remembered his

> aesthetic devotion to a certain gas-burner in the window of a store under the printing office. It was in the form of a calla-lily, with the flame forking from its tongue in its white cup; and I could never pass it, by day or night, without stopping to adore it.

The printing office was that of his father, William Cooper Howells, who, assisted by his sons, edited the Dayton *Transcript* in 1849. Howells, a boy of twelve, hurried back and forth to the family printing office that was henceforth his only "school" and paused briefly to admire the flaming lily before mounting the stairs.

Howells remembered, too, as he mused in his New York apartment on Fifty-seventh Street or in his office in Franklin Square, the arrival in Dayton of the "great painting" of Adam and Eve, by the French artist, Claude Marie Dubufe, which created in many small towns as great an excitement as the arrival of the circus. Howells saw himself standing fascinated before the enormous canvas, entitled "Adam and Eve in a State of Innocence," which was once displayed in Dayton in a huge tent. The experience came back to him with its attendant emotions:

> The large canvas was lighted up so as to throw the life-size figures into strong relief, and the spectator strickenly studied them through a sort of pasteboard binocle supplied for the purpose. If that was the way our first parents looked before the Fall, and the Bible said it was, there was nothing to be urged against it, but many kind people must have suffered secret misgivings at a sight from which a boy might well shrink ashamed, with a feeling that the taste of Eden was improved by the Fall.[1]

Howells' secret misgivings at this "awful novelty of the nude," thus set before "untravelled American eyes," were merely those of his own generation; what is remarkable is that he remembered the canvas of Adam and Eve and the name of the artist over an interval of many years. Had it not been for the fact that Howells, by nature an artist, associated with painters, sculptors, craftsmen, and architects all of his life, that he spent four years in Venice as a young man, that he married an artist who was the sister of an architect and of a sculptor, and that his two children followed the family tradition, he might easily have forgotten his early introduction to painting, and given us, as a consequence, a more limited interpretation of "realism" in his novels and critical essays.

These youthful aesthetic perceptions were enlarged by Howells' consulship in Venice, where he learned to enjoy color, light, and form in the public squares, as well as in the museums and churches. The interest Howells felt in the sculptors and artists he met in Venice, as well as in the studio of his brother-in-law, Larkin Mead, then spending the winter in Florence, he carried home with him when in 1866 he returned to Boston as assistant editor of the *Atlantic Monthly*. Through the young Henry James, whom he soon engaged to write art notes for the *Atlantic,* Howells grew to know William Morris Hunt, John La Farge, George Fuller, and many other artists of the early Impressionist group.

Howells' resignation from the *Atlantic* coincided with the rise of the *Century Magazine,* which, under the direction of Richard Watson Gilder, was engaging the best artistic talent of the day and thus challenging the leadership of the less venturesome *Atlantic*. When Gilder learned that Howells intended to collect material for *Tuscan Cities* while traveling through Italy in the winter and spring of 1883, he sent Joseph Pennell to journey with Howells from Florence to Siena, to Pisa, to Fiesole, sketching the churches, the bridges, the piazzas, and clock towers about which Howells wove the peculiar blend of history, anecdote, and artistic appreciation that enchanted and educated his generation.

On Howells' return to this country the following July, he found himself drawn into the New York circle of writers, painters, architects, and sculptors, partly through his association with Gilder and partly through that with his brother-in-law, William Rutherford Mead, a member of the architectural firm of McKim, Mead, and White. Though he did not actually assume his position on the staff of *Harper's* until 1886, Howells frequently went to New York, then the literary and artistic center of the country, to confer with his agent, James R. Osgood, and to enjoy the sights and sounds of the metropolis.

When Howells moved with his family to New York for a few months in the winter of 1888, it was the lively interchange between the "young painting and writing fellows" that inspired him to write to Thomas Sergeant Perry, his Harvard friend and advisor, that "Boston seems of another planet." Howells found "immensely interesting" the "bigger life" of New York; here artists, actors, newspapermen, and musicians mingled in drawing rooms and restaurants in a manner that brought to the transplanted editor from Boston a lively sense of fresh literary and artistic movements. Though Howells expressed some doubt to Perry as to whether a man of fifty-one could "catch on" to the stimulating life of the metropolis, so "lordly free," [2] he at once plunged into a study of the artistic life about him. The year after his arrival, he introduced one of "the painting fellows" into *A Hazard of New Fortunes,* "the first fruits" of his New York life. Furthermore, he seems to have sensed the relationship between his own technique as a writer and that of a painter. Henry James, in commenting on Howells at this time, wrote, "I know of no English writer of our hour whose work is so exclusively a matter of painting what he sees." [3]

Certainly from his varied experiences in the enjoyment and understanding of the arts, Howells enriched and deepened his concept of literary realism. These ideas he attempted to define in the essays that began to appear in the "Editor's Study" in 1886, many of which were later collected in *Criticism and Fiction* (1891). Howells found support for "our hope with regard to the unity of taste in the future" in John Addington Symonds' new book, *The Renaissance in Italy* [4] (1886). Symonds' conclusion, that "the perceptions of the enlightened man" are sufficient to discern "the truth, sincerity, and natural vigor" in a work of art, was, Howells believed, as "applicable to literature as to the other arts." On this premise Howells built his critical theory of the relation to a democratic society of all the arts working in harmony to form the "culture" of the new country.

Howells' two-page Preface to *Criticism and Fiction* suggested to the reader at once that the art of fiction is closely related to the plastic arts, that, in fact, the unity of the arts must be felt and understood before one can grasp the meaning of any one of them. He asserted, too, that it is of immense importance to society, especially to a democratic society, that the arts should be enjoyed by all men, even the most "common." Abandoning "all sentimental or academical seekings after the ideal," we must "comprehend with more instinctive certitude what is simple, natural, and honest, welcoming with gladness all artistic products that exhibit these qualities."

Howells found the Chicago Columbian Exposition in 1893 of immense interest as an example of the democratic arts effectively united. The spectacle of thousands of men and women from farms and country towns casting "the glance of the common eye" on the wonders of the "White City" created by our foremost artists, sculptors, and architects reinforced his belief in the importance of art for the ordinary man. These ideas Howells incorporated at once into "Letters of an Altrurian Traveller," [5] in which he voiced, not only his own social concepts of art, but those of many of his generation concerned with the future of a country increasingly controlled by business interests.

During the last decade of the nineteenth century, Howells became a member of the Century Club of New York, where he was in contact with artists and writers, lawyers and businessmen, many of whom shared his growing hope for democratic art; and in this milieu he greatly extended his knowledge of the social and artistic movements of the day. Largely from the membership of this club were drawn the men who, in 1898, established the Institute of Arts and Letters, and who, a few years later, organized the American Academy. Howells was active in this movement to raise the standard of taste in the country and to make culture a part of the lives of ordinary men and women.

By 1900 Howells' views of the current exhibitions were of real interest to New Yorkers. At that time he was invited by the National Sculpture Society to address the group on "the art and true principles of art criticism." His speech was given a prominent place in the New York *Evening Post* of May 16, 1900, under the title, "A Novelist on Art." Few readers today know what Howells had to say on art, nor do they realize that, through his association with artists, sculptors, and writers, he played a role in the civic and artistic growth of New York City itself during the last two decades of the nineteenth century.

In order to understand Howells' frequent references to the arts in his essays and novels, one must trace, through his own words, the development of his aesthetic appreciation from the days of his boyhood, through his four years in Venice, to his Boston sojourn, to his final move to New York. In following Howells' artistic evolution, one recovers an almost forgotten chapter in the history of our national sense of art, from the introduction of lectures on art at Harvard College in 1874, through the exhibition of impressionism at the Chicago fair in 1893, to the establishment, in 1900, of the American Academy of Arts and Letters, of which Howells was the first president.

In the course of a long career, William Dean Howells wrote over forty novels, as well as many columns of essays and reviews for the *Atlantic Monthly* and *Harper's Magazine,* in which he illustrated and defined the new interest in realism. Many critics have successfully related the realistic movement in literature to the mid-century interest in science; no one has pointed out that the literary movement was also related to the various artistic movements of the day in painting, sculpture, and architecture. Howells, sensitive to every wave of thought and feeling of his era, presents a remarkable example of the interplay of literature and art. In a sense, he was a sounding board for the views of many artists and writers who, at the turn of the century, confidently looked forward to a renaissance on these shores that would affect the lives of "the common man" and leave a permanent mark on American civilization.

NOTES

1. See *Years of My Youth* (1916), p. 40. Claude Marie Dubufe (1790–1864) was a pupil of Jacques Louis David's and was known for two canvases, "Adam and Eve in a State of Innocence" and "The Expulsion from Paradise," both of which were exhibited far and wide in Europe and in this country. The London *Illustrated News* of January 2, 1858 (Vol. XXXII, p. 22), tells us something of the rumors that grew up around these famous paintings: "According to one report the originals were accidently burnt in a fire in New Orleans; according to another report the copies were burned, and the originals are now in Australia. At all events, Messrs. Gambaert [art dealers] commissioned Mr. Dubufe to paint another pair from the original sketches, with a view to engraving. Hence the reapparition of an 'Adam and Eve' of Dubufe. The one picture represents the primitive types of humanity in the Garden of Eden, surrounded by a luxuriant landscape—fruits and flowers being abundant but not overdone. The Serpent is slightly indicated as using a pernicious influence, Eve is in all her youth and beauty holding the fatal fruit, and Adam is irresolute on the eve of the great Lapse." The other picture, entitled "The Expulsion," represented Adam and Eve leaving the Garden in a great storm.

2. April 14, 1888. Mildred Howells (ed.), *Life in Letters of William Dean Howells* (1928), II, 413.

3. "William Dean Howells," *Harper's Weekly,* June 19, 1886.

4. Reviewed by Howells, "Editor's Study," *Harper's Monthly,* LXXV (November, 1887), 963–965.

5. *Cosmopolitan,* XVI (December, 1893), 218–232. Clara and Rudolf Kirk (eds.), *Letters of an Altrurian Traveller* (1961). See also Clara Marburg Kirk, *W. D. Howells, Traveler from Altruria, 1889–1894* (1962).

PART

ONE

· 1 ·

Education in Art

If there was any one living in 1860 who had given himself more entirely to literature, Howells wrote of himself in 1894,[1] he would not know where to find him. As a reporter on the *Ohio State Journal,* the young Howells had already become the unofficial literary editor for his paper. More than that, he had in 1860 published, in collaboration with another young reporter, *Poems of Two Friends.* Though but twenty-three years of age in 1860, Howells was considered by William T. Coggeshall worthy to be included in *The Poets and Poetry of the West*—perhaps because four or five of his poems had already appeared in the *Atlantic Monthly.* During this period of "high literary exaltation," Howells knew himself to be a successful journalist, but he hoped that he might also become a poet. The "literary interest, the aesthetic interest," [2] remained long after the journalistic interest had begun to wane. During these two years in Columbus, 1857–59, Howells' poetic ambitions were so strong that his "veins might well have run ink." [3]

Fortunately, Howells' newspaper work kept him so busy that he could pursue his elusive poetic muse only in stolen moments. "I could find time for poetry only in my brief noonings," [4] he wrote, "and at night after the last proofs had gone to the composing room, or I had come home from the theatre or from an evening party." Reviews, translations, paragraphs of comment, as well as dinner parties, charades, and whist in the hospitable homes of Columbus, effectively distracted the brooding poet, who was, at the same time, as gay, sociable, and worldly as his slender earnings would permit. Looking back many years later on these years of his youth—the happiest period of his life—Howells remembered that "everywhere there were the talking and the laughing and the singing which fill the world with bliss for youth." This too-literary reporter was led by the friendliness of the little Ohio capital from the unreal poetic dream world that he had built after years of lonely reading of Pope, Goldsmith, Heine, and others. Howells had yet to find his own idiom.

The verses that Howells had submitted to the *Atlantic* were, indeed, so Heinesque that James Russell Lowell had laid them aside for a time lest they should prove to be translations. When he found that "Andenken," "The Poet's Friend," "Pleasure-Pain," and the others were merely the effusions of a lonely youth who had wandered too long in the fields and woods of Ohio with Heine in his pocket, Lowell published them, advising their author to "sweat the Heine" out of him and to write in a vein more natural to himself.[5] The gentle melancholy that suffuses these verses is clearly imitative and certainly not painful. With what pleasure the young poet must have read them aloud to his fellow writers, over midnight oysters at Ambos' in High Street, or to one or two of the pretty girls with whom he talked "literature" on the wide porches of Columbus. Surely it was "pleasure" rather than "pain" that moved the young Howells to write:

> Through the silent streets of the city,
>   In the night's unbusy noon,
> Up and down in the pallor
>   Of the languid summer noon,

I wander and think of the village,
    And the house in the maple-gloom,
And the porch with the honeysuckles
    And the sweet-brier all abloom.

My soul is sick with the fragrance
    Of the dewy sweet-brier's breath:
Oh, darling! the house is empty,
    And lonesomer than death!

When one remembers that Howells' own home, standing in "the maple-gloom" of the village of Jefferson, Ohio, was at the time overflowing with the vitality of seven brothers and sisters, one smiles somewhat at these stanzas:

If I call, no one will answer;
    If I knock, no one will come;–
The feet are at rest forever,
    And the lips are cold and dumb.

The summer moon is shining
    So wan and large and still,
And the weary dead are sleeping
    In the graveyard under the hill.

One can imagine Howells penning this wanly melancholy poem —this "psychological lemonade," to use his own phrase—in his third-floor room in the old medical college of Columbus after a hard day's work on the *Journal*. One pauses reflectively over the last two verses:

The old, old dreams of childhood
    Come thronging my weary brain,
Dear foolish beliefs and longings;–
    I doubt, are they real again?

It is nothing, and nothing, and nothing,
    That I either think or see;–
The phantoms of dead illusions
    To-night are haunting me.

Fortunately for Howells, these "phantoms of dead illusions," these ghosts of the poetry of others, could never, in the nature of things, haunt him for long, not only because of the necessity of earning a living, but also because of his own essentially cheerful, eager, and friendly temperament.

Not only did Howells enjoy lively discussions of the new books of George Eliot, Charles Reade, and Nathaniel Hawthorne, for instance, in the friendly parlors of "the amiable little town" of Columbus, but he also came into contact with those whose interest in the arts was akin to his own but quite different, too. Thomas D. Jones,[6] a sculptor who planned to complete a collection of busts of the notable men of the West, became Howells' friend upon his arrival in Columbus. When the young journalist made his acquaintance, Jones had set up his studio in the Neil House, a hotel directly across the square from the State House, where much of Howells' day as a reporter was to be spent. As a break in the daily routine, he enjoyed dropping in on Jones during his lunch hour and watching the sculptor at work on a bust of Salmon P. Chase, the governor of Ohio, whose kindly hospitality had been extended to the reporters of the *Ohio State Journal*. The bust, according to Howells, was "admirable as a likeness, and of a very dignified simplicity." The sculptor, in turn, enjoyed being seen modeling it—"I can see him yet," wrote Howells, "stepping back a little from his work, and then advancing upon it with a sensitive twitching of his mustache and a black censorious frown." The governor posed in the pleasant studio of the hotel where Jones lived rent free, as Howells supposed, for "he was threadbare poor." No doubt, in those days when "many good things seemed without price," the management tolerated him for the sake of the curious onlookers, such as Howells, who were fascinated by the spectacle of an artist at work.[7] Soon Jones left Columbus, in pursuit of other "notable men of Ohio," and Howells wrote disconsolately to John J. Piatt, fellow reporter and poet, "Dear old Jones is gone to Cincinnati, and I don't haunt the Neil House any more. It is quite lonesome without him." [8] At this point in Howells' career, when journalism was beginning to pall, he learned from Jones the lesson of how a sculptor can transform "real life" into art. Howells himself was determined to become an artist, too, but unlike the indigent sculptor whom he admired, he had no intention of remaining threadbare.

Early in 1860 Howells and his friend Piatt published together a charming little book of poetry. *Poems of Two Friends,* so neatly bound in brown cloth and embossed with a wreath of flowers in gilt, must have seemed to the two young poets a happy omen of their literary futures. Of far greater practical use to Howells, however, was his campaign life of Abraham Lincoln, which appeared in June of that year. Hardly known in the East, this rather hastily composed account of Lincoln and his running mate, Hannibal Hamlin, was widely read in the West, for into this volume Howells, the journalist, poured his feeling for Western men and the cause of abolition.

Soon after the publication of Howells' *Life of Lincoln,* his "young publisher"—as resourceful and hopeful as Howells himself—suggested that the author use the hundred and seventy-five dollars he had earned from the book on a trip east, supposedly for the purpose of gathering material for another book the publisher had "imagined." This one was to be concerned with "the operation of the principal manufacturing industries" of the East, and, though Howells inwardly abhorred the project, he was "eager to see the world," and gladly agreed to spend the money he had earned in furthering the interest of the publisher, as well as of himself. Strongly "confirmed" in his belief in his future as a poet, Howells, nevertheless, knew too much of the literary world to think that he could earn a living by poetry alone and shrewdly looked to plain prose as a means of support until he should become famous as a poet.[9]

Willing as he was to use his pen for practical purposes, Howells was refused admission to the first iron foundry he approached and made no further attempt to ferret out the secrets of other manufacturers; instead, he saw Niagara Falls, which, he wrote, "did not with-hold its glories from me in fear of the publicity which I gave them in my letters to the Cincinnati *Gazette*." [10] Though he had every intention of carrying out the behest of his publisher when he set out on his pilgrimage, Howells, in fact, soon gave up all thought of investigating factories, and, instead, began several series of letters to Ohio papers,[11] one of which, "Glimpses of Summer Travel," ran in six issues of the Cincinnati *Daily Gazette* from July 21 through

August 9, 1860. These letters were signed "Chispa." [12] Readers of Ohio knew, however, that they were written by Howells, whose pseudonym had, for several years, been familiar to them. Moreover, "Glimpses of Summer Travel" were soon reprinted in the family paper, the Ashtabula *Sentinel,* with the note that they were written by W. D. Howells, "now on a trip to the New England states." [13]

Howells' first few "Glimpses of Summer Travel," described in his opening letters, were of "the broad sweeping meadows of old Ashtabula," of "near-lying" Lake Erie seen "through the foliage of the trees," and of "pretty trim farmhouses," behind which farmers were cutting their wheat. In the next letter Howells was very much in need of "someone to burst forth to," for by then he had seen Niagara Falls. Though "in the real presence of the Cataract" it was "a divine rapture to remain dumb," nevertheless Howells soon broke into poetic speech that filled more than a column of the *Gazette.* Since he found himself, he wrote, unable to speak "against the tumult of his own soul" while gazing at the Falls, silence seemed "wisest, and humblest and best." Howells could only "stand still and look at that divine Revelation, and feel the truth of God." Speechless though he claimed to be, effusions soon burst forth:

> Ah, no words can tell it, no pigment can counterfeit it, that magnificence of whirling, knolled, bewildered, mad, white plunging water . . . How it cries aloud with the strong voice of its agony to the Everlasting.

And how, indeed, the bewildered traveler agonized in his search for words with which to express his overwhelming emotion—until the shouts and laughter of his companions restored him to his more rational self. For "there were two women down there, with parasols, and irrepressible skirts, and pretty feet," accompanied by two gentlemen to assist them over the slippery rocks; and these the future writer of romance felt able to describe to his readers in spite of the tumult of his feelings.

When Howells returned to his "pleasant room in the Cataract House" and consulted his guide book, he discovered that he should have begun his inspection of the Falls from Prospect Point, rather than from Goat Island. Desiring to repair his error, if possible, he retraced his steps to Prospect Point, there to reflect upon "the inadequacy of human life and human affairs," while disconsolately watching "a battered tin cup" and "an old castaway boot" float by in the rushing waters. He returned again to his hotel, "weary with splendor and magnificence—too weary to glow in the mention of Prospect Point." Leaning from his window, Howells moodily beheld "the rapids, dark and headlong"; and, snatching his notebook, he wrote, "on the heavy air rises hoarsely the thunder of the cataract. Peace! O feeble pen." At this point Howells' column broke off—to begin again the next day, after a sound night's sleep and a hearty breakfast.

In the morning all was changed to sunshine and cheer again, for Howells, when he returned to the Falls, had the good fortune to encounter artist Godfrey Frankenstein. Under his guidance Howells "did" Goat Island once more, this time "thoroughly, and subtly, and profoundly." The artist, Howells explained to his Ohio readers, like the haymaker, works best in sunny weather, "and this forenoon, when some light clouds had dimmed the sun, my painter-friend put up the beautiful sketch which he was making of the Canada Falls," and made, with the reporter, "the circuit of the island." Aided by his new friend, Howells saw during this walk what he had failed to see the day before. Having trained himself for years to view the world through the eyes of the poets, he enjoyed a much-needed lesson in how to see nature directly, without the medium of words, through the eyes of the painter. Of his artist-friend he wrote in the Cincinnati *Daily Gazette* of July 24:

> Ah! if this man could waste his time as guide, how gloriously the public could see Niagara. For I penetrated with him all manner of inscrutable thickets and secret nooks, commanding unknown views of the cataract—places that only an artist's eye could discover. He taught me, too, to see some of the beautiful tints of the water and mists—delicious purples, and greens and crimsons—that escape the greedy, common eye, which gulps and bolts the whole thing, as it were, untasted.

Howells' eye, we may assume, was learning not to "gulp" and "bolt" the beauties of Niagara (as his "greedy" eye had doubtless done the day before), but rather to chew and savor the colors and tints of the Falls—to prolong Howells' unfortunate metaphor! Sixteen summers at Niagara had made Frankenstein, it seemed to his young friend, "in some sort the genius of the place, and worthy, if any one is worthy, to paint it." Howells gladly followed the artist's lead. "He takes you down a narrow path," wrote Howells,

> steeply dropping through the hillside cedars, where it seems that the only thing you can do is to fall off without expostulation, and lo! the Falls as they appear in one of his pictures. Here, in a space not two feet wide, hanging half way down the precipice, he or his brother John stands to paint. Above the suspension bridge, on a narrow strip of land, that juts into the rapids, I saw his brother at work this morning, on a very successful sketch of the great tumult before him. And wherever Niagara is beautiful and grand (and that is everywhere) the Frankensteins have transferred as much beauty and grandeur as paint can fix upon the canvas.[14]

On July 20 Howells said good-bye to the Frankensteins, "commended the cataract to their keeping," and caught the steamer bound for Toronto. Eager for experience of every sort, Howells gazed at groups of travelers on the deck of his boat up the St. Lawrence, and seized opportunity to leave the ship in order to investigate historic monuments and battlefields along the route. Like the Ellisons of *A Chance Acquaintance,* this Midwesterner delighted in the crooked streets of Quebec and listened patiently to the droning of guides in cathedrals while casting glances at the darkened paintings above the altars and at shadowy stone images in dim corners. The "impressions" of the day, both serious and frivolous, were promptly written down and mailed to the newspaper at home. These "Glimpses of Summer Travel" [15] reflected not only the young journalist who, in his account of his simple adventures, caught just the right tone of ironic banter, but also the future writer who was reaching out for a whole new area of experience—that of the practicing artists intent on actually "seeing" what lay around them.

In his essay, "Niagara First and Last," Howells reflected upon his brief friendship with the Frankenstein brothers. For these two artists who guided the adventuring young newspaperman about the Falls freely questioned his "literary position" in relation to the wonders of nature and introduced him to their own "artistic position." As Howells recalled thirty years later:

I made the acquaintance of no one in the hotel, but by a sort of affinition [*sic*], which I should now be at a loss to account for, I fell in with two artists who were painting the Falls and the Rapids, and the scenery generally, and I used to go about with them, and watch them at their work. They were brothers, and very friendly fellows, not much older than I, and because I liked them, and was reaching out in every direction for the materials of greater and greater consciousness, I tried to see Niagara as actively and pervasively iridescent as they did. They invited me to criticise their pictures in the presence of the facts, and I did once intimate that I failed to find all those rainbows, of different sizes and shapes which they had represented on the surface of the water everywhere. Then they pointed the rainbows out with their forefingers and asked, Didn't I see them there, and there, and there? I looked very hard, and as I was not going to be outdone in the perception of beauty, I said that I did see them, and I tried to believe that I saw them, but Heaven knows, I never did. I hope this fraud will not be finally accounted against me. Those were charming fellows, and other pictures of theirs I have found so faithful that I am still a little shaken about the rainbows. My artists were from Ohio, and though I was too ignorant then to affirm that Ohio art was the best art in the world, just as Ohio money was the best, still I was very proud of it, and I suppose I renowned those invisible iridescenses in my letter to the Cincinnati paper.

We walked all about the Falls, and over Goat Island, and to and from the Whirlpool, and it was a great advantage to me to be in the artists' company, for they knew all the loveliest places, and could show me the best points of view.[16]

Howells had "schooled himself for great impressions" before he set forth on his trip, nor did he "mean to lose one of them," for "they were all going into that correspondence which I was so proud to be writing, and finally, I hoped, they were going into literature: poems, sketches, studies, and I do not know what all."

But Howells "had not counted upon the Rapids taking [him] by the throat, as it were, and making [his] heart stop." [17] Nor had he counted on meeting two artists who insisted that he should be made to observe the "facts" of those "rainbows of different sizes and shapes." The effort to see what his artist-friends claimed to perceive encouraged him to describe more exactly his own perception of the "supreme beauty" of Niagara. "If one looked steadily at any part of the cataract," he remarked, "the descending floods seemed to hang in arrest above the gulfs below." With carefully chosen words, he wrote:

> Those liquid steeps, those precipices of molten emerald, all broken and fissured with opal and crystal, seemed like heights of sure and firmest earth, and the mists that climbed them halfway were as still to the eye in their subtler sort. This effect of immobility is what gives its supreme beauty to Niagara, its repose. If there is agony there, it is the agony of Niobe, of the Laocoon. It moves the beholder, but itself it does not move.

The result of Howells' excursions with the Frankensteins was that he was challenged by their insistence on the importance of actual observation to say more exactly what seemed true to his perceptions, if not to theirs.

> I spent a great deal of time trying to say this or something like it, which now and always seemed to me true of Niagara, though I do not insist that it shall seem so to others. I could not see those iridescences that everywhere illumined the waters to my artist friends, and very likely the reader, if he is a person of feeble fancy, small sympathy and indifferent morals, will find nothing of this Repose that I speak of in Niagara. I imagine him taking my page out into the presence of the fact, and demanding, Now where is the Repose? [18]

Howells' trip to the East, which began with an attempt to investigate factories, soon turned into an endeavor to study the tints and colors of Niagara Falls. Since his visit was paid "in the midsummer of the year, and in the midsummer of [his] life," when "all nature was rich and beautifully alive," [19] he was able gayly to respond to the challenge of two young artists and to take his "page out into the presence of the fact," which happened to be Niagara Falls.

Without the aid of an interpreter, Howells studied the New England towns—Portsmouth, Haverhill, Salem, and others—through which he journeyed on his way from Canada to Boston. Tree-lined streets, old graveyards, town commons, dignified mansions surrounded by gardens—all spoke directly to his "young Western consciousness" and brought home to him "the fact of a more complex civilization" than he had ever known, where "family" was taken seriously as a matter of "vital import." Pausing in Salem for a day, Howells was struck by "those fine square wooden mansions, of a tasteful architecture, and a pale dull-color, withdrawing themselves in quiet reserve from the quiet street," which gave him an impression of "family as an actuality and a force," familiar to Easterners but unknown to Westerners.[20] When Howells at last reached Boston, which seemed to him "a seething vortex of business, as well as a whirl of gayety," he was as eager to climb Bunker Hill, explore the narrow streets behind the State House, discover Faneuil Hall and the Hancock House, as to meet the literary characters, Lowell, Longfellow, Holmes. Buildings and men alike were parts of the dreams of the young poet-journalist from Ohio.

"I think that I did not try to see Cambridge the same day that I saw Lowell," Howells wrote in retrospect. But the next day after his talk with the older poet, Howells returned to Cambridge to enjoy the "elmy quiet" of the streets, and to linger before "the yellow colonial houses, with their white corners and casements and their green blinds, that lurked behind the shrubbery of the avenue" that he traversed on his way to Mount Auburn. The monuments in this historic graveyard Howells "viewed with a reverence" that "their artistic quality did not merit," for the literary young journalist was determined to enlarge his aesthetic sense. "The Gothic chapel of the cemetery," he observed, "unstoried as it was," gave him a very real emotion, which the Acropolis, Westminster Abbey, and Santa Croce in one, failed to give him later. "I tried hard for some aesthetic sense of it," he admitted, "but the truth is that I had no taste in anything but literature." [21]

When Howells returned to Columbus after his "pilgrimage to New England," he found the Ohio capital distracted by rumors of war, which did not prevent him from "going the rounds of the friendly houses" of Columbus. "Of all the winters this was the gayest," [22] wrote Howells many years later; nor did the "general mood" change as "the hours passed and the days and the weeks and the months bringing us forever nearer the catastrophe" [23] of the Civil War. Immediately after "the fateful shot was fired at Fort Sumter," Columbus was inundated with volunteers from the towns and farms of the surrounding area. "Our pretty Goodale Park," Howells wrote, was used for a camp and here these red-shirted boys "shouted the day and shouted the night away" in "the wild hilarity of their young vision." Howells, for his part, observed these Union soldiers and meditated a possible novel in which he would pluck out "the heart of the matter" and lay it "throbbing before the reader." As an older man looking back at his youthful self, Howells observed that a better novel might rather have been concerned with "the more subjective riddle of one who looked on, and baffled himself with question of the event," [24] for Howells had not yet learned to value the "things of fact" so highly as the "things of fiction."

Aloof as the young Howells was from the boisterous farm boys who were swaggering about the town and pushing "the willing citizens from the pavement," he was very much aware of a gifted sculptor, J. Q. A. Ward, seven years his senior, who came to Columbus in the winter of 1860 in the hope of a commission from the legislature for a statue of Simon Kenton, the old Indian fighter, "known to every small boy of Ohio." When Ward arrived in Columbus, he was already respected for his many busts of famous men, among them one of Hannibal Hamlin, whom Howells had just included in his campaign life of Lincoln. Ward was given a "handsome room with a good light, in the State House," where he was to model a figure of Kenton "in his hunting shirt and squirrel-skin cap." Here Howells used to visit Ward, "trying to imagine something of art, then a world so wholly strange to me, and talking about New York and the aesthetic life of the metropolis."

Though Ward lived much to himself in Columbus, Howells saw a great deal of him, for they "had no want of things to talk about" with their common interest in questions of art. As Howells remembered him later, Ward "was in the prime of his vigorous manhood" at that time, "with a fine red beard, and a close-cropped head of red hair, like Michelangelo, and a flattened nose like the Florentine's, so that I rejoiced in him as the ideal of a sculptor." [25] Goodale Park remained in Howells' mind, not only as the park where the young volunteers were encamped, but more especially as the wooded area where he "used to walk and talk with the sculptor, Ward, and try the athletic feats" in which Howells was easily beaten.[26]

The "Kenton" was never completed, for "the cloud thickened over us, and burst at last in the shot fired on Fort Sumter." [27] The legislature at once appropriated all available funds toward the cost of war, "and Ward's hopes vanished as utterly as if the bolt had smitten his plaster model into dust." All during the winter of 1860–61, after the election of Lincoln and before the outbreak of the conflict, Ward had been "hopeful of an order from the state for his 'Simon Kenton,' " [28] and Howells had been equally hopeful of "poetic pre-eminence," which never really came to him then or later. The careers of both men were interrupted by war and so also was their fruitful friendship, which had grown and prospered under the very shadow of the impending struggle.[29] Many years later they met again in the metropolis where both men moved in the art circles that they had discussed in Columbus; they then resumed a desultory relationship that lasted until Ward's death in 1910. "I still think him, for certain Greek qualities, the greatest of American sculptors," [30] Howells wrote in 1916 of this artist who, like Howells himself, infused a classical beauty into our native material.

Both Howells and Ward lived in New York during several decades before and after the turn of the century, meeting not infrequently at the homes of mutual friends.[31] Late in the 1890's, Howells recorded,[32] he went to dine with the sculptor in his great "yawning studio" in order to gather material for *Stories of Ohio* (1897). Ward had become famous for his statues, "The Freedman," shown in the Paris Exposition of 1867, "The Indian Hunter" (1868) and "The Pilgrim" (1885), both in Central Park, as well as for statues of Horace Greeley (1890), Henry Ward Beecher (1891), and many other monuments well known to New Yorkers. Howells' account of Ward, and of the sculptor's way of working, showed both his interest in native American art and his respect for the realistic technique of a fellow craftsman.

J. Q. A. Ward seemed to Howells "a sculptor who, if not the

greatest American sculptor," was the one who had achieved in his art "the most American things ever done in it." Ward, he wrote, was of old pioneer stock, Ohio-born, "in a region remote from artistic influences," just as was Howells himself. Ward, again like Howells, "felt the artistic impulse in his boyhood." Ward's

> earliest attempt was a figure modeled in the wax which one of his sisters used in making wax flowers, and which he clandestinely borrowed. Then he made a bas-relief of the first train of cars he ever saw, but this he did in clay at the village potter's; and he also modeled in clay the head of a Negro, well-known in the place, which all the neighbors recognized. A few years later he was sent to school in Brooklyn, where he used every day to pass the studio of the sculptor, H. K. Browne, and long for some accident which would give him entrance. The chance came at last; he told the sculptor the wish of his heart, and Browne consented to let him try his hand under his eye. From that time the boy's future was assured.[33]

Howells, too, had learned from fellow printers, as a boy in Jefferson, not only how to set type, but also how to read and enjoy Cervantes, Shakespeare, and Goethe. He was perfectly prepared to understand the village training Ward availed himself of as a sculptor. Nor did Howells ever forget, in his later years, the lessons he had learned from Ward and other practicing artists whom he encountered in Ohio during his early days as a journalist with lofty artistic ambitions of his own.

When, in 1897, Howells wrote for children a small book called *Stories of Ohio,* he devoted several pages to the artists of Ohio, many of whom, such as J. Q. A. Ward, he knew personally either at this time of his life or later, in Rome, Florence, or New York. Hiram Powers,[34] for example, "was the first American sculptor to give us rank in Europe. Longworth, who loved the arts as well as the industries, helped him to go to Florence from Cincinnati, where he had begun by modeling wax figures for a local museum." James H. Beard, portrait painter, Frank Dengler, sculptor, and painters Frank Duvaneck and Kenyon Cox were among the "gifted Ohioans" whom Howells briefly commented upon in his telling the story of his native state.[35] From talking with artists, watching them at work, studying their paintings and statues in galleries, Howells learned something of the interrelation of the arts. These ideas, implanted in his youth, became a part of his own approach to writing and contributed to his sense of a philosophy of the creative process.

Perhaps of even more importance to Howells' growing understanding of the arts, was his meeting, during that last gay winter in Columbus, with his future wife, Elinor Gertrude Mead, who was herself an artist and a member of a family of artists. Howells wrote later, "she became with her unerring artistic taste and conscience my constant impulse toward reality and sincerity in my work." [36]

NOTES

1. *Literary Friends and Acquaintance* (1900), p. 1.
2. *Years of My Youth* (1916), p. 182.
3. *Literary Friends and Acquaintance,* p. 2.
4. *Years of My Youth,* p. 152.
5. *My Literary Passions,* pp. 172–173.
6. See *Ohio State Journal* (Jan. 14, 1859), pp. 135–136.
7. Mar. 4, 1859, *Years of My Youth,* pp. 216–217.
8. *Life in Letters,* I, 23.
9. *Years of My Youth,* p. 207. A somewhat different account of these money transactions is given in "Niagara First and Last," *The Niagara Book* (1893), p. 2.
10. *Ibid.*
11. A second series of letters, "En Passant," appeared in *Ohio State Journal* concurrently (July 23 to Aug. 7, 1860). Much of the same material was used for both of these series.
12. See *My Literary Passions,* p. 39, for an explanation of "Chispa."
13. William M. Gibson and George Arms (eds.), *A Bibliography of William Dean Howells* (1948), Item 60–26.
14. John Frankenstein was the author of a book entitled *American Art: A Satire* (1864), in which he presented Thomas D. Jones, Esq., under the pseudonym of "Tremendous Dead Bones, Esq. Sculptor."
15. Not all of Howells' contributions were printed. This he noted in "Niagara First and Last," *The Niagara Book* (1893), p. 3.
16. *Ibid.,* pp. 6–7.
17. p. 4.
18. p. 10.
19. p. 23.
20. *Literary Friends and Acquaintance* (1900), p. 18.

21. *Ibid.*, pp. 30–31.
22. *Years of My Youth*, p. 222.
23. *Ibid.*, p. 227.
24. *Ibid.*, pp. 234–235.
25. *Ibid.*, pp. 215–216.
26. *Ibid.*, p. 235.
27. *Ibid.*, p. 216.
28. *Ibid.*, p. 219.
29. "Overland to Venice," *Harper's Magazine*, CXXXVII (November, 1918), 837–845. See also "Letter from New York." Cincinnati *Gazette*, LXXVII (Nov. 25, 1865), 1.
30. *Ibid.*, p. 216.
31. In 1863 Ward became a member of the National Academy of Design and was made president in 1874. In the same year he became president of the National Sculptors' Society. In 1899 Ward was elected to the American Academy of Arts and Letters. Howells was associated with all of these organizations. See Part Four, Chapter 4 of this book.
32. *Years of My Youth*, p. 219.
33. *Ohio Stories* (1879), p. 269.
34. For further comment on Hiram Powers and other artists in Rome, see Howells' review of *Passages From the French and Italian Notebooks of Nathaniel Hawthorne*, "Recent Literature," *Atlantic Monthly*, XXIX (May, 1872) 625, Appendix I of this book.
35. *Ohio Stories*, pp. 274–275.
36. *Years of My Youth*, p. 225.

· 2 ·

Artists in Italy

Fortunately for Howells, his art education, both at home and abroad, had progressed beyond the rudimentary stages before he married Elinor Mead. This talented young lady from Vermont was never without her sketchbook; indeed, sketching was for her and for her two older brothers, Larkin and William Rutherford Mead, a necessary form of communication. On the table of the Mead sitting room in Brattleboro there always lay "a piece of gamboge, a cake of Prussian blue, and one of crimson lake, so that any member of the family could pause in passing through the room to do a little painting, and when they wished to describe anything very clearly to each other, they always drew it." [1]

Whether Howells and Elinor became engaged before he sailed to Venice in November, 1861, or whether the affair was arranged by an exchange of letters during Howells' first lonely year in that bewilderingly beautiful city, is not known. In any case, Howells and Elinor were married before the end of the following year. Larkin

Mead accompanied his sister across the Atlantic and was present at her marriage to Howells, which took place in the Legation library of the American Embassy in Paris at three o'clock in the afternoon of December 24, 1862. The "charming little affair" was described by the bridal couple in a joint letter written on their wedding day to Elinor's parents in Brattleboro, Vermont. It is clear from Howells' paragraph that his art education, under the tutelage of Elinor and Larkin, went gayly forward. Immediately after the ceremony, he wrote, "the happy couple and the adjacent brother went to see churches and things, all looking remarkably like Elinor." Howells ended his portion of the letter with greetings from one who now viewed himself "in the light of an universal brother and son-in-law." Elinor explained to her mother that since "Mr. Howells" had discovered that the train for Venice did not depart until 8 o'clock the following evening the three were under "the painful necessity" of spending the next day visiting the Louvre. However, "Lark behaves splendidly—is *wild* over the Louvre, talks most remarkable French aided by frantic gestures and enjoys himself hugely," so all was merry. "To tell you the truth, I'm in love with—Paris," she signaled happily to her parents in Vermont.[2]

Soon the three were on their way to Italy, Larkin to study art in the studios of Florence and the Howellses to begin housekeeping in Venice. During his first year in Venice as United States consul, Howells had occupied single rooms on various back streets; now all was changed. Once settled in their apartment in the Casa Falier on the Grand Canal, the couple had little amusement other than that of exploring the museums, churches, market places, and the ancient gardens of that romantic but subdued little city. For Venice, then under Austrian rule, was a city in mourning for its lost freedom, with nothing of its old carnival air; what pleasure the Howellses found, they made for themselves. Several months after their arrival, Howells wrote a long letter to his father [3] in which he reported that he had bought Elinor a new sketchbook, for she proposed to "unite sketching with boating." She had, indeed, already set up her painter's stool on one of Venice's many bridges, with Howells hovering near by to protect her from the inevitable crowd of curious observers. Since the letter to William Cooper Howells was dictated by his son to Elinor, we may suppose that the humorous description of the first sketching expedition was written for her benefit:

> Yesterday she made her first sketch in public, presenting a birdseye view from one of the bridges of "A fisherman mending his coat." The subject was quite unconscious and sat still for a long time, in spite of the eager and applausive multitude scuffling about the elbows of the artist for the best view of her creation.

But soon the fisherman changed his position in order to reach for his knife; to the noisy disgust of the Venetians, Elinor suspended her labors, too. "The crowd," Howells observed, "is the only drawback on these occasions," and he hoped the difficulty would not prove too great:

> But I find that it is quite impossible for a short man like myself to stare starers out of countenance, when he can only bring his eyes to the level with their shirt bosom, and I must confess that the crowd is a sore trial to my spirits.

When he wrote this letter, Howells had already mailed the first of his "Letters from Venice" to the Boston *Advertiser;* [4] his experiences as Elinor's protector supplied the young consul with the very material needed for the success of these letters.

Not only did Howells watch, with an amused eye, Elinor at work surrounded by expressive Italians, but he also was quick to see how further knowledge of art in general might be made to supply additional "Letters" to the Boston *Advertiser.* After a description of "the usual monotony of our Venetian Sundays," Howells spoke of the zeal with which he and Elinor were enlarging their understanding of the art treasures around them.

> As for the rest, we spend most of our time now in reading up the history of art. I had no idea that I could come to feel so great an interest in the matter as I have done. But in Venice the influences of art pervade the whole atmosphere and it is hard not to inhale something of them. The intellectual life of the place is dead. All that remains are the triumphs of past genius, but these are everywhere. So our talk is a jargon, more

unintelligible on my part and less so on Elinor's, of Titians and Tintorettos, of paintings and sculptures and mosaics, of schools and of manners, and our reading naturally takes that direction, too.

But the elder Howells, working long hours on the family newspaper in Ohio, must not be allowed to suppose that his son was wasting his time exploring this new field of interest. "I do not think the time lost, either, that I spend in this way," Howells hastened to add, for he had both "a general view of the usefulness of looking at art a little," and also a "particular purpose." This double intent he explained to his father in the same long letter of March 15. "I don't know how it is with others," he wrote, "but some part of every study that I have pursued with honesty has been of use to me at one time or other." Moreover, he admitted that his "intellectual muscle" actually needed more exercise.

So much for "the general view of the usefulness of looking at art a little." A "particular purpose," he wrote, was "to make some biographical sketches of the Venetian schools, for the bookseller here, who wants me to do it, and who only hesitates about the price I want him to pay me for the work." Apparently these sketches were not sold to the dealer, though Howells did persuade the bookseller to pay him for a translation of a small German guidebook to Venice.[5] For his work he received the equivalent of $75, and with this sum he purchased a gold watch, a chromo of St. Barbara, and "Kugler's Italian Art." [6]

Howells' "intellectual muscles" were further developed in May of that same year by "a jaunt to Florence" to visit Larkin Mead,[7] then established in his own studio. Here the Howellses saw the King review his troops, made the rounds of the galleries and museums, and, with Larkin, visited the studios of various artists and sculptors.

The Howellses were soon back again in Venice, Elinor happily sketching and Howells scribbling poetry, reading up on art, and writing his "Letters" to the *Advertiser* during the hours not claimed by his consular duties. But in spite of his expenditure of effort, both in writing verses and in gathering material for his "Letters" from Venice, he felt both "ashamed and discouraged," after two years abroad, that he had made such "halting progress" toward establishing his claims as a writer. He lamented to his friend and fellow poet, Edmund Stedman,[8] that

> The Novel is not written; the Great Poem is hardly dreamed of; I think Dante "somewhat grimly smiles" when he regards . . . my halting progress through his Divine Comedy. Nothing written, nothing read.

But Howells' "exile" in Venice, as he called it, was now shared with Elinor; he was, therefore, neither lonely nor homesick for long, as he had been during his first year as consul. In his letter to Stedman, Howells soon turned from his literary discouragement to his domestic happiness:

> Since we talked together, I have married—most happily, need I say? Witness, content that I never knew before! In every way the union seems perfect—certainly esthetically, for my wife is an artist, in all but the profession of art. She is making some sketches which are to illustrate my poem. Imagine the life we lead in Venice!

One aspect of the life the Howellses led in Venice had to do with welcoming American friends to their apartment and accompanying them on their rounds of museums and art galleries. "I just left Henry Ward Beecher in the Academy of Fine Arts, one limp and helpless mass of enthusiasm and perspiration," Howells noted before he closed his communication to Stedman.

A letter to his sister Annie [9] written September 17, 1863, spoke eagerly of a proposed visit of Elinor's sister, Mary, who had been invited to spend the winter with them; it also announced that the editor of *Harper's* had at last accepted a poem by Howells, with the illustrations by Elinor to which Howells had referred in his note to Stedman. "The poem is called Saint Christopher, and the illustration represents an old gateway and statue in Venice, not far from where we live." [10]

However, it was not until Howells had received a letter from Lowell the following August praising his studies of Venetian life and accepting an essay for the *North American Review* [11] that Howells felt he had at last discovered the direction that his writing would take. These sketches, printed first in the Boston *Advertiser* [12] and later collected and published as *Venetian Life,* had "grown earnester in style, and solider in matter" as he proceeded. Howells had learned to combine his interest in passing street scenes with his enlivened appreciation of art, both old and new, into something fresh to American readers of his day—a travel book, which was both readable and instructive.

Lowell's letter, which many years later Howells referred to as marking a "turning point" [13] in his life, called forth a long, retrospective reply, in which Howells looked back over the discouragements of his stay in Venice, as far as his writing was concerned, and then glanced "light-heartedly" ahead to the book he was envisioning, based on his Venetian sketches. "I shall have to change the printed matter very little," he wrote, since he had composed the Venetian studies "laboriously enough." But he planned to add several chapters of new material, one of them on Venetian painting before Titian. Howells' belief in "the usefulness of looking at art a little" was clearly vindicated by his new-found confidence in himself as a critic.

The growing habit of studying carefully the work of painters affected the way in which Howells himself "painted" in words the scenes he presented in *Venetian Life.* When Lowell [14] reviewed the collected sketches in the October, 1866, issue of the *North American Review,* he remarked upon the painterly quality of Howells' writing and referred to him as "the artist":

> The artist has studied his subject for four years and at last presents us with a series of pictures having all the charm of tone and the minute fidelity to nature which were the praise of the Dutch school painters, but with a higher sentiment, a more refined humor, and an airy elegance that recalls the better moods of Watteau.[15]

Before the appearance of this book, Lowell observed, "the hitherto unfamiliar name of Mr. Howells" was known only to a small circle of readers, and to them rather as a poet than as a writer of prose. That such delicacy and finish could be "a product of the rough-and-ready West" appeared to this Bostonian as interesting a phenomenon of "our shaggy democracy" as it had ever been his fortune to encounter. Lowell, in this review, expressed his astonishment at "the natural gift" of Howells, who had had "no advantage of college training" and had passed "from the compositor's desk to the editorship of a local newspaper." Howells must have been his own "faculty of the humanities," Lowell concluded, thinking perhaps of Howells' essay on "Modern Italian Poets," which appeared in the same issue of the *North American Review*,[16] as well as his chapters on the great painters of Venice in *Venetian Life*.

When Lowell wrote this faintly patronizing essay on his younger friend, he did not take into account the fact that Howells had not only become thoroughly imbued with the language and literature of Italy during his four years in Venice but had also become absorbed in his avowedly amateur study of the arts of Italy under the guidance of his wife and brother-in-law. For, in spite of consular duties and a new baby (born December 17, 1863), Howells traveled extensively in Italy, exploiting to the full his experiences in the gay and familiar style already established in his earlier travel-letters to the papers of Ohio. In November, 1864, for example, Howells and his wife left their home in Venice, and took "the longest road to Rome," which led them to Padua, Ferrara, Bologna, Genoa, and as far south as Naples before they at last reached their goal. Like all "sentimental travelers" from the days of Laurence Sterne, they enjoyed casual conversations in hostels along the way, as well as the sudden vision of a great Cathedral across a sunny piazza. "What is Rome, after all, when you come to it?" asked these nonchalant travelers, who saw "art" as only a part of the general scene,[17] to be enjoyed by the amateur (or the "common man") as well as studied by the scholar.

As practicing artists themselves, however, both of the Howellses had a professional interest in watching other artists at work and talking with them as they sketched or sculptured. In Rome they visited the studio of the aged American sculptor, John Gibson, whose tinted figures had been adversely criticized in artistic circles. Howells, who had recently studied the fragments of ancient statuary in the museum at Naples, did not feel that Gibson's works were in the least preposterous. Indeed, Howells wrote later in his *Italian Journeys,* "I am not ashamed to say that they gave me pleasure."

When the Howellses visited the studio, they found Gibson himself working on a bas-relief of Psyche and the Zephyrs in a small area opening into the roomy studio, where workmen were completing several large figures. Gibson paused in his labors to greet his visitors "very simply and naturally." Howells "touched the right spring" when he praised the tinted figures, and the old man talked "with visible delight" on his favorite theme, the color of antique statuary.[18]

On another afternoon in Rome, the Howellses were taken by "some artistic friends" to the studio of the great German painter, Johann Friedrich Overbeck. With his usual sympathy for artists at work, Howells felt an "illogical pleasure" in studying the romantic drawings of this painter, who sought his themes in "the twilight of the Romish faith." After several hours of reflective study, however, Howells quietly concluded that the weirdly beautiful paintings of Overbeck were expressive of "the sentiment of no time" and that they were akin to the poetry of the romantic Germans, "without relation to any world men ever lived in." [19] Romanticism in painting seemed as distasteful and false to Howells as romanticism in literature, and for the same reason—because it was unrelated to the world of normal human beings.

The Howellses, "fully armed" with art equipment—he with notebook and she with sketchbook—were sympathetic but critical observers of their fellow artists. They also not infrequently strolled through the various gates of Rome and took their joy of dusty roads and wild meadows, pausing on their way to sketch or write—or to converse with a shepherd-boy returning with his flock in the late afternoon. Howells, at least, could speak a fluent, colloquial Italian, which the shepherd-boy and Mrs. Howells could readily understand. Both of the Howellses, before their years in Italy drew to a close, in July, 1865, became so harmoniously attuned to Italian life that always thereafter they dreamed of returning there to relive the happiness of those years. Though the dream remained unfulfilled, at least the nostalgic yearning found expression in a series of novels written on his return to the United States—*A Foregone Conclusion* (1875), *Lady of the Aroostook* (1879), *A Fearful Responsibility* (1881), and finally *Indian Summer* (1886), the hero of which, in middle life, gave up his newspaper work and returned to Florence in quest of his lost youth.

Howells' immersion in Italian art left him with a fondness for Europe as "a place of wonder and delight," far removed from Cambridge, Massachusetts, to which he was soon to return as assistant editor of the *Atlantic Monthly*. Four years in Italy so modified his views of the Old World, that, when, in 1866, he found himself an editor and the owner of a white "salt box" of a home in Cambridge, he sought to escape from the limitations of the New World by evoking a vision of Italy. This dream he conveyed to his readers in an essay, "At Padua" which appeared in the *Atlantic* of July, 1867. Not as an art critic or a scholar, but as an appreciative amateur, Howells described the Chapel of Annunziata in Padua to his untraveled readers: "You reach it by passing through a garden lane bordered with roses," he wrote,

> and a taciturn gardener comes out with clinking keys, and lets you into the chapel, where there is nobody but Giotto and Dante, nor seems to have been for ages. Cool it is, and of a pulverous smell, as sacred places should be; a blessed benching goes round the wall, and you sit down and take unlimited comfort in the frescos. The gardener leaves you alone to the solitude and the silence. . . . Through the half-open door falls, in a pause of the rain, the same sunshine that they [the artists] saw lie there; the deathless birds that they heard sing out in the garden trees; it is the fresh sweetness of the grass mown six hundred years ago that breathes through all the lovely garden grounds.

Howells, seated at his desk in Cambridge, imagined himself on the bench in the cool interior, and meditated again on the New World and the Old, America and Europe, youth (he was then thirty!) and immortality. "How mistaken was Ponce de Leon, to seek the fountain of youth in the New World!" he wrote.

> It is there—in the Old World!—far back in the past. We are all old men and decrepit together in the present; the future is full of death; in the past we are light and glad as boys turned barefoot in the spring. . . . We are not only young again, we are immortal. It is this divine sense of superiority to fate which is the supreme good won from travel in historic lands, and from

the presence of memorable things, and which no sublimity of natural aspects can bestow. It is this which forms the wide difference between Europe and America—a gulf that it will take a thousand years to bridge.[20]

To discover, at its very source, the perennial freshness of art, expressed in painting, statues, or village chapel, was to feel a deeper sense of the relation of his own efforts as a writer to that of other artists, and to make Howells realize, too, that all art grows from the soil in which it is planted.

Feeling so aware of the impact of Italy, not only on his writing, but on his whole life thereafter, Howells turned with particular interest to Hawthorne's *Italian Notebooks*. Soon after he became editor, Howells devoted a four-column review to Hawthorne's book, in the May, 1872, issue of the *Atlantic Monthly*.[21] Alternately amused and amazed by the responses of this "exquisite genius" to the cold, the squalor, the poverty in Rome—not to mention the "droll rascality and mendicancy with which a foreigner's life in Italy is enveloped"—Howells could only account for his lack of humor by remembering that Hawthorne's nature was "peculiarly New Englandish"; one need hardly be surprised, then, he wrote, that "the moral disrepair, like the physical decay, continually offended him beyond retrieval by his sense of its absurdity." Unlike the more adaptable Howells from the Middle West, Hawthorne "confessedly remained an alien in Italy," abhorring a beggar as much as he detested a painting by Giotto or Cimabue. But even the limitations of a man like Hawthorne were interesting to Howells, who rejoiced in Hawthorne's frankness. "Most of us are, by the will of heaven, utterly ignorant of art," Howells admitted, and it is "vastly wholesome" to read Hawthorne's candid descriptions of the "vile streets" of Rome, and the dreary thirteenth-century frescoes in the cold churches, even though Hawthorne's conclusions were often erroneous. Moreover, "Hawthorne's doubt whether he was not bamboozling himself when he admired an old master, is one which has occurred, more or less remotely, to most honest men," including the reviewer, as Howells freely confessed.

More interesting to Howells than Hawthorne's errors in artistic judgment was his predecessor's account of his visit to the studio of the American sculptor, Hiram Powers, whom Howells also admired. Still more significant to Howells was Hawthorne's sense of the relationship between art and character. Since Howells, too, was using his own experiences in Italy in the stories and sketches he was writing, he was fascinated by Hawthorne's description of Praxiteles' faun in the Capitoline Museum and the steps by which "the romancer" transformed the ancient statue into the character of Donatello in *The Marble Faun*. Apparently, Hawthorne at first intended to write nothing more than a short story "with all sorts of fun and pathos in it," and no shadow of tragedy. "Afterwards, how the idea expanded and deepened and darkened!" marveled Howells.

By the time Howells wrote this review of Hawthorne's *Italian Notebooks,* his own response to Italy had been expressed in two books, *Venetian Life* (1866) and *Italian Journeys* (1867); in the course of the next ten years his feeling was to deepen, if not to darken, and at last find expression in four or five novels with Italian settings. During Howells' four years in Venice he had exercised his "intellectual muscle" to advantage; he had studied the great works of art around him and, through his wife and brother-in-law, he had become familiar with artists in their studios in Venice, Florence, and Rome; he had contemplated the further dimension in the presentation of character that artists offer the novelist.

NOTES

1. The oldest member of the family, John Noyes Mead, died while still at Harvard. According to his niece, Mildred Howells, he drew and painted well. Larkin G. Mead, Jr., was a sculptor. He made the Lincoln statue at Springfield, Ill., and the statue of Ethan Allen in the Capitol at Washington. William Rutherford Mead, architect, became a partner in the firm of McKim, Mead and White. *Life in Letters,* I, 11.

2. *Ibid.,* I, 63.

3. *Ibid.,* I, 64–67.

4. The date line of the first letter is Mar. 2, 1863. It appeared in the Boston *Advertiser* of Mar. 27, 1863. The editor at that time was Charles Hale, the brother of Edward Everett Hale.

5. See "Howells' Guidebook to Venice," Rudolf and Clara Kirk. *American Literature,* XXXIII, No. 2 (May, 1961), 221–224.

6. By Franz Theodor Kugler (1808–1858). Inasmuch as Mrs. Howells did not read German, the Howellses probably used the *Handbook of Paint-*

ing, The Schools of Painting in Italy translated by "a Lady" (Mrs. Margaret Hutton) and edited by Sir Charles L. Eastlake. London: J. Murray, 3d edition, 1855.

7. Larkin Mead married Marietta da Benvenuta on February 26, 1866, and lived happily with her in Florence until his death in 1910. See James L. Woodress, Jr., *Howells and Italy* (1952), p. 18.

8. Aug. 16, 1863. *Life in Letters,* I, 70–72. Also see Woodress, pp. 34–35.

9. *Life in Letters,* I, 75–76. Mary Mead remained in Italy until the How-ellses returned to the United States in July, 1865.

10. *Harper's,* XXVIII (December, 1863), 1–2. See Howells' reply to Lowell on August 21, 1864 in *Life in Letters,* I, 84–87.

11. "Recent Italian Comedy," *North American Review,* XCIX (October, 1864), 304–401.

12. See Howells' letter to Charles Hale, editor of the *Advertiser,* Oct. 25, 1863. *Life in Letters,* I, 77–78.

13. *Harper's Bazaar,* XLIV (March, 1910), 165–166. Moncure D. Conway was at this time trying in vain to find a publisher in London for Howells' poetry. Also at this time, Frank Foster was procrastinating about pub-lishing "Disillusion" (later called "No Love Lost"), Woodress, p. 35.

14. This essay is ascribed to C. E. Norton in the marked index of the *North American Review.* Woodress, p. 58. Howells continued to study the works of the Italian painters all of his life. In "The Editor's Easy Chair," *Harper's Monthly Magazine,* CXIV (February, 1907), 480–481, he wrote:

> But for good or for evil it is impossible that artists should not imi-tate one another, so long as one is born earlier and another later. As far as this goes, there is no such thing as originality in art. From Cimabue and Giotto we have Botticelli, from Mino da Fiesole we have Donatello, from Giovanni Bellini we have Titian, Tintoretto, Paolo Veronese, and so on, all measurably, none entirely, like his master. It is so in the literary arts, as, for instance, Dryden—Pope, Cowper—Wordsworth, Keats—Tennyson, Goldsmith—Irving, George Eliot—Mrs. Humphry Ward, Zola—Mr. George Moore, Miss Edgeworth—Miss Austen, Sterne—Heine. There is occasionally an author so overwhelmingly himself, after a certain time of being some one else, that he cannot be imitated except for a very short time and in a very few things, and it would not be easy to couple with another name the name of Shakespeare, or Dickens, or Thack-eray. But probably no authors have so widely affected or infected authorship as these.

In "Eighty Years and After," *Harper's Monthly Magazine,* CXL (De-cember, 1919), 21–28, he wrote:

> Titian outlived his ninety-nine years and kept on painting almost to the last. I have not found any critic to say how well he continued to paint, though I dare say there is more than one such critic. I

can well believe that he wrought as greatly then from his exhaustless soul as in his prime. At ninety-nine he was working hard at Venice, in the intimacy of another Venetian master, the great sculptor and architect Sansovino, who was, however, only ninety-three. I used to view his Renaissance work with as great pleasure as my subservience to Ruskin's Gothic tyranny would let me, but I did not try to distinguish the later work in it from the earlier, and I cannot say from my personal knowledge that his mastery held out to the last. It is only now that from the Encyclopedia Britannica I have learned that "his masterpiece, the bronze doors of the sacristy in St. Mark's," was done when he was eighty-five, and that at eighty-eight "he completed a small bronze gate with a graceful relief of Christ surrounded by angels." Titian and he lived in great jollity together, and were of a gaiety which is rather characteristic of the old, though their younger friends are apt to think otherwise. Sansovino was not of his friend's unfailing health, but he knew how to ward off an attack in his latest years, when Vasari tells us "he retired to a dark, warm place," and remained there till perfectly restored. It seems worth trying.

15. CIII, 611.

16. October, 1866. Lowell was then coeditor, with Charles Eliot Norton, of the *North American Review*.

17. *Italian Journeys* (1867), p. 1.

18. *Ibid.*, pp. 169–170.

19. *Ibid.*, pp. 170–171. Fryckstedt writes that Howells' treatment of Rome in *Italian Journeys* "is remarkable for what he omits rather than for what he considers worth reporting. Most apparent is his lack of appreciation of art," p. 61. Fryckstedt fails to appreciate the fact, obvious in all of Howells' books on Italy, that though he was always a declared amateur in art appreciation, he was throughout his life so fascinated by art that it influenced his own theory of writing. See Olov W. Fryckstedt, *In Quest of America, A Study of Howells' Early Development as a Novelist* (1958).

20. *Atlantic Monthly*, XX (July, 1867), 27–28.

21. *Passages From the French and Italian Notebooks of Nathaniel Hawthorne*, "Recent Literature," *Atlantic Monthly*, XXIX (May, 1872), 624–626. Appendix I of this book.

· 3 ·

Toward a Theory
of Aesthetics *

When Howells returned to New York in August, 1865, after four
years as United States consul in Venice, Charles Eliot Norton made
a place for him on the newly established *Nation*.[1] Norton, together
with E. L. Godkin, F. L. Olmsted, and J. M. McKim, had launched
the weekly journal to maintain standards in politics, literature, and
art, in the period of confusion after the close of the Civil War. As
coeditor, with James Russell Lowell, of the *North American Review,* Norton was quite familiar with Howells' charming and in-
formative essay on "Recent Italian Comedy," [2] and, like many other
delighted readers, he, too, had been enjoying for several years
Howells' "Letters" from Italy as they appeared in the Boston *Advertiser*.[3] Norton had every reason to be pleased with the appoint-

---

* This chapter, somewhat expanded, appeared in the *New England Quarterly*
(Autumn, 1963) under the title, "Toward a Theory of Art: A Dialogue between W. D. Howells and C. E. Norton."

ment of this talented young journalist from Ohio to the staff of his new literary venture.

After his four years in Venice, Howells, for his part, was glad to grasp Norton's extended hand. Ten years Howells' senior and a regular contributor to the *Atlantic Monthly,* Norton had published essays on painting, sculpture, on Dante and on English country houses in the magazine since its founding in 1857.[4] Since the interests of the two men were so closely related, and as Howells himself was aspiring to a position on the *Atlantic,* he must have read Norton's essays with particular pleasure. Even before he set out for Italy in 1861, Howells' imagination must have been caught by Norton's long essay on "The Manchester Exhibition," [5] for example, which presented, in picturesque terms, Norton's interpretation of the place of art in the modern industrial world. "Smoke, steam, coal-dust, blackened walls, and bare fields lie outside the Exhibition," he wrote—"and now let us go within." Paintings from "many a famous country-house" of England, from Blenheim, Wilton House, and Warwick Castle, were displayed on the walls of the quiet interior. Norton's meditative walk through the Exhibition brought him to the conclusion that "the times in which we are living are not fitted to develop and confirm the qualities on which the best results of Art depend." [6] Howells, then, was as familiar with Norton's general views on art in modern society when he joined the *Nation* as Norton was with those of his younger colleague—which he considered, on the whole, "light," [7] in spite of their charm and learning.

After a few months on the New York weekly, Howells was invited to become assistant editor of the *Atlantic Monthly.* He soon found himself living in a small Cambridge house, secured for him by Norton, not far from the beautiful Norton home, "Shady Hill," where Howells was always a welcome guest. To Howells, recently returned from Europe and living in "the Carpenter's Box" on Sacramento Street, the white, colonial mansion in which Norton had been born and reared must have seemed reminiscent of the great houses Howells had seen in his travels. Set in a wooded tract of fifty acres not far from Harvard Square, Shady Hill was lined with bookshelves and hung with paintings, some of them brought back from Italy. Norton's description of the English houses from which the paintings in the Manchester Exhibition were borrowed reminds one that Shady Hill was an American example of the British tradition.[8] "Who does not remember as one of the most delightful recollections of England," Norton wrote in his essay for the *Atlantic,*

> Who does not remember the drive from the little country town to the old family place, up the long avenue under its ancestral trees, the ferny brook crossed by the stone bridge with its carved balustrade, the deer feeding on the green slope of the open park or lying under some secular oak, the heavy white clouds casting their slow shadows on the broad lawn, the dark spreading cedar of Lebanon standing on the edge of the bright flower-garden—the old house itself, with its quaint gables and oriels, the broad flight of steps leading to the wide door,— the cheerful reception from the prim, but good-natured house-keeper,—her pride in the great hall, and in the pleasant, home-like rooms; in Vandyck's portrait of the beautiful countess, and in Holbein's of the fifth earl,—the satisfaction with which she would point to the pictures and the marbles brought two centuries ago from Italy . . .[9]

Though Norton's sentence by no means stopped at this point, enough has been quoted to suggest that the tradition of the great house as a perfect repository for great art was deeply felt by Norton, who made of his inherited home in Cambridge just such a haven of culture. For more than forty years Howells came and went freely in this hospitable home, reading Dante aloud with his host before the fireplace, or conversing with him in his book-lined study. Long letters exchanged during absences, reviews and comments on each other's books, messages relayed through mutual friends such as James Russell Lowell and Henry James kept the relationship always warm and lively.

Like all well-nourished friendships, however, the temperamental harmony between Howells and Norton was strengthened by politely sustained disagreement. Beneath the genuine cordiality, one is aware of recurring argument between the two friends and colleagues on the question of art, civilization, and the "common man." Their divergence of views is foreshadowed by two early contributions to the *Nation*—Norton's scathing editorial on America, "The Paradise of Mediocrities" (July 13, 1865),[10] and Howells' four-column essay, "A Little German Capital" (January 4, 1866).

No doubt inspired by the published purpose of the *Nation*—to uphold standards in politics, literature and art—Norton declared, in "The Paradise of Mediocrities," that "there are very few first-rate things in America." Because of our "low standard of taste, of morals, and of intellectual performance," he asserted, our country "has become the happy home of flourishing mediocrity." Howells, who had just agreed to write for the *Nation,* probably read this pronouncement with interest. Having recently returned from his travels abroad, he must have been both amused and surprised to learn how differently Norton felt about Boston on *his* return to that "little city" after years of study and travel in Europe. "The good Bostonian," wrote Norton, "who when he dies goes to Paris," will, on his homecoming, "be surprised to find how long he had been contented with the commonplace and dull excellence of the greathearted little city."

Not only did Howells still look upon Boston as a center of culture, but he had already discovered the literary value of "the commonplace" about which Norton wrote so disdainfully. To Howells, who never lost touch with his simple, Midwestern origins, Norton's remarks, that "we are still in the era of rail fences," that we lack culture because we live in "the land of railroads, common schools, and an instructed democracy," must have seemed peculiarly harsh. He must have read with a smile or a sigh Norton's questions as to why Boston women did not preside over salons, and why, in that center of refined learning, he found so few gentlemen of "cultivation" and "breeding." Howells could hardly have sympathized with Norton's conclusion that "where education and property are universally diffused, where there is no hereditary lower class, there must be a larger proportion of the intelligent mediocrities than in any other country." Since Howells personally had profited by the general diffusion of education and property in this country, and since he then had every expectation of making a place for himself in the inner circles of Boston and New York, he surely read with a pang Norton's final remark that "the average man in America is not up to an appreciation of the best things; he does not want them."

While still in Italy, Howells had recorded his first impressions of the civilization of Europe, which were in direct contrast to those suggested by Norton's editorial. This essay, "A Little German Capital," he offered to the *Nation,* perhaps as a reply to Norton's assertion that Americans lived in "a paradise of mediocrities." Apparently, Howells pointed out, Germany furnished another and more glamorous "paradise" for even more objectionable "mediocrities."

The little German capital of Howells' essay was Stuttgart, where he had spent several days late in November, 1861, on his way to Venice. "It is quite a wonderful little city," Howells wrote to the "Dear Folks at Home." It was "full of palaces, full of pictures, and I saw everything." [11] Then the capital of a small German principality, Stuttgart was equipped with a stout, grandfatherly king, a royal palace hung with paintings and tapestries, a venerable—and cold—church, an opera house open every evening, royal ponds stocked with ducks and swans, and public promenades where beplumed ladies strolled arm in arm with red-coated officers in the approved style of Thackeray's *Vanity Fair.* Howells, at the age of twenty-four, regarded the scenes before him with a critical eye; a "democrat of the crimson and combustible," he was both amused and disgusted by the artificiality of European society. One had to go to Europe, he wrote in his article for the *Nation,* to learn that the Old World was still "a civilization of classes," whereas the New World was "the civilization of individuals." The art of Stuttgart was, therefore, tame and dull, because it was class culture. Howells' first stroll through the royal gardens on a Sunday afternoon in autumn, when the feeble November sun fell aslant the numerous statues, convinced him that these figures, which "dealt with fables and feelings as dead to that people [the Germans] as the stone from which they were hewn," were tangible evidence of a decadent feudal culture.

When Howells visited the royal palace, he hardly knew which caused him the more poignant suffering, the chill of the endless corridors or the portraits lining the walls, most of them of plump nudes, "perfectly executed" but "coarsely and simply sensuous in purpose." The youthful Howells recorded an "instinctive repugnance" and "felt no need to change the views [he] had adopted from Hawthorne concerning the nude in modern art." [12] Not that the gazer "received any hurt" from contemplating the "lavish charm" of the king's mistresses, both past and present, for they were "muscular merely, and soulless." But the paintings did give one "a bad opinion of the sort of civilization which produced them." "For my part," he wrote, "I like not over-ripe sausages and far-smelling cheese, nor their principles as developed in morals and aesthetics." To Howells, who was rapidly forming his views on the relation of art, morals, and civilization, the "decent amenities of our American life" were distinctly to be preferred.

A short time before Howells wrote down his views of the paintings and statues of Stuttgart, Norton had issued a small book, *Notes of Travel and Study in Italy* (1860), in which he expressed his views of Americans abroad for the first time who dared to judge European art. "We come abroad utterly ignorant of Art, and, with natural and national self-confidence, at once constitute ourselves judges and critics of paintings and statues." [13] Norton's *Notes* were written after two years of "travel and study"; no doubt he had had ample time to observe American travelers abroad as well as the art they examined. "The majority of American travelers have yet to learn," he wrote, "that some previous knowledge is to be acquired before one can be a judge even of the externals of Art; that it is not the eye alone that needs cultivation, but the heart and the intellect as well, by those who would understand and enjoy the works of the great masters." During Norton's two years abroad he had met John Ruskin for the first time and had absorbed from him an attitude of awe and respect for the study of art, which only deepened as his friendship with Ruskin developed.[14] At this time he wrote in his *Notes,* "If you are unwilling to accept the authority of others, it is well to remember that the only independence of judgment that deserves the name is that which rests upon a basis of humility, and of desire to learn how to judge correctly."

Soon after Howells joined the staff of the *Atlantic Monthly,* his "Letters" from Italy were published in a charming volume entitled *Venetian Life.* Norton immediately reviewed it for the *Nation,*[15] pronouncing it "a delightful and excellent book," abounding in "genial humor," play of fancy both "graceful and original," and marked by "the pleasant flavor of individuality." Though "travelers are still, for the most part, little better than ignorant barbarians, with little power and less disposition to comprehend sympathetically and understand intelligently the lives of a foreign race," Howells, Norton pointed out, was an exception. For "Mr. Howells possesses . . . the penetrating insight of a poetic temperament, together with good common sense and sound moral feeling." His perceptions were, therefore, "fruitful" and not subject to "that bondage of habit, custom and use which controls most men as with the authority of an absolute law of nature."

Norton's generous review of Howells' little book was a tribute to the breadth of the older man's critical insight. In spite of the fact that Howells exclaimed at the end of one of his chapters, "Thank God! that the good old times are gone and going! One learns in these old lands to hate and execrate the past," Norton gave it his wholehearted approval, observing that "no better book about Venice has been written." It was "a rare pleasure," he wrote, "to be able to recommend it unreservedly to those of our readers who have any disposition to visit or revisit the unique picturesqueness, the unrivalled beauty, the strange grandeur of Venice."

No doubt Norton, with his customary forbearance, attributed the author's casually irreverent comments on Ruskin, scattered throughout *Venetian Life,* to Howells' humor and gayety, and excused it on the score of pleasant lightness. Humorous though these remarks undoubtedly were intended to be, they also indicated a divergence of attitudes between the two men that was to become more marked as they grew older. "Ruskin," wrote Howells, "is undoubtedly the best guide you can have in your study of Venetian painters"; but "after reading him, and suffering confusion and ignominy from his theories and egotisms, the exercises by which you are chastised into admission that he has taught you anything cannot fail to end in a humility very favorable to your future as a Christian." [16] But "even in this subdued state," Howells distrusted the method Ruskin used to relate aesthetic truths to "certain civil and religious conditions." He questioned still more Ruskin's assertion that Tintoretto "genteelly disdains . . . to paint well any person baser than a saint or senator." [17] In fact, Howells repudiated the "loose general principles" of art set down by Ruskin and other art critics, as well as the aristocratic attitudes lurking behind their words.

Since these were the very assumptions that Norton in his long and distinguished career continued to uphold, he and Howells must tacitly have agreed not to discuss art when they met at Lowell's home for dinner, or at Professor Francis Child's tea table.[18] When *Venetian Life* appeared as a book, Howells did not hesitate to add paragraphs expressing his views of Tintoretto, for he was in quiet re- bellion against the standard guides and teachers that told the traveler how to look at art. Howells' four years in Venice had emboldened him to assert that

> without any guide, I think, these painters may be studied and understood, up to a certain point, by one who lives in the atmosphere of their art at Venice, and who, insensibly breath- ing in its influence, acquires a feeling for it which all the critics in the world couldn't impart where the works themselves are not to be seen. I am sure that no one strange to the profession of artist ever received a just notion of any picture by reading the most accurate and faithful description of it.[19]

And as for Ruskin, Howells wrote, "Just after reading Mr. Ruskin's description of St. Mark's Church, I, who had seen it every day for three years, began to have dreadful doubts of its existence."

Venetian Life proved so popular that a second American edition was immediately planned. Since this edition was to be printed from new plates, Howells wrote to Norton and asked for any corrections or suggestions he might have to offer. In spite of Norton's laudatory review in the *Nation,* Howells was quite aware of the reservations Norton must have felt about the style and tone of the book. "Do- mestic troubles," wrote Howells to Norton, on September 17, 1866,[20] had combined to keep him confined to the Carpenter's Box on Sacramento Street. But, he wrote to the landlord of Shady Hill, "between the hours of washing the breakfast dishes and of putting on the roast for dinner, I find a little leisure, and this I employ in correcting my book, of which Messers. Hurd and Houghton, having sold the first edition, wish to issue the second at once." Howells then came to the point of his letter: "As you now know the book and may possibly have some objections to its style or diction, will you not kindly give me the benefit of your criticism now when it can avail me? I ask this favor supposing you may have some points in your mind, and not wishing to burden you at all with the matter."

Though Norton probably offered a number of minor verbal changes to Howells for his second edition of *Venetian Life,* and though Howells added several new sections, the spirit of the book remained the same. Norton himself recognized that Howells represented a new post-Civil War generation and that his view of literature and art was not that of Norton's generation. "Those of us who lived by artistic impulses expected great things in literature and art after the war," Howells said many years later. He added, "We lived in a poetic period, we felt that after the great social upheaval would come flashes of great genius . . . In sculpture, in painting, in literature, we expected great strides after the social convulsions of war." [21]

Howells' own way of regarding art, and especially civic manifestations of the decorating impulse, was reflected in an article he addressed to "the common man" as soon as he became assistant editor of the *Atlantic* in April, 1866. The following month, in an essay entitled "A Question of Monuments," Howells brought to bear his recent European experience on the "question" of what sort of Civil War monuments should be erected in all the small towns and villages of the North. Howells had had ample opportunity to observe the inappropriateness of the statuary in the royal gardens of Stuttgart; his essay for the *Nation* expressed the fear that American sculptors, in their misguided quest for culture, might be led to fill public parks with monuments in the classic style. "I wonder if when the sculptors begin to look for the statues that are to adorn our public places in America," he wrote at that time, "they will find nothing in the blocks of marble but the trite Greek celestials, who seem always to be lying in wait there to spring out on a bewildered modern public. Ambrosia is good, but it is hardly a drink to the present taste."

In his article for the *Atlantic,* the new assistant editor proposed to consider "the present taste" and its relation to civic life. The Civil War being over, he pointed out, "for the first time in history, as a people, we seem to feel the necessity of art," as an expression of the country's "universal desire to commemorate its heroes by the aid of art." Fortunately, the initial "aesthetic sensation" immediately after "the fall of the first and greatest of its dead," had been forgotten. Since time has been granted for a second thought, why should the public not resolve to look to American, rather than European artists, for its memorials? J. Q. A. Ward's statue of the Freedman, Howells pointed out, was "the full expression of one idea that should be commemorated"; in its simple truthfulness, it was superior to the bas-reliefs of battles on government buildings, the equestrian statues of officers designed for village greens, or the draped figures of classical goddesses called "Liberty" proposed for city parks. Indeed, why should imagination be limited to statues? In that decade of postwar prosperity, the country could afford to erect beautiful gateways to parks in memory of the dead, design handsome fountains, and build schoolhouses as fitting memorials, wrote the editor of the *Atlantic* in defiance of the notion that art must always be associated with the aristocratic, the ideal, and the classical. Every town and village in the country, Howells declared, should know that "it is bound to the arts and to itself not to build ignobly in memory of its great." This was "the rare occasion" meant for the plastic arts to supply our need of beautiful architecture and sculpture, by expressing "something of the new order" in America. Howells' essay was an appeal to American citizens to commemorate the heroes of the Civil War, and, at the same time, to improve the appearance of the villages, towns, and cities of the country.[22]

In 1868 Norton gave up his editorship of the *North American Review* and sailed for Europe, where he remained for five years. "I went to-day to say good-bye to some friends about sailing for Europe," Howells wrote on June 27, 1868, to an acquaintance in Ohio,[23] "Mr. Norton (of the *North American Review*) and his family. He advanced me the money to buy the house in which I live, and has helped me with every kindness during my life in Cambridge, and of course their going away is a great loss to us. He is a man of almost ideal purity and goodness—one of those incomprehensible beings who are always looking about the world, and seeking occasion to be useful and comfortable to somebody. I shall not only miss sadly his personal friendship, but his literary sympathy which has attended me in every undertaking, here."

Another expression of Norton's "literary sympathy" for Howells' writing was the review of *Italian Journeys,* which, a few months before he surrendered the editorship, Norton invited their mutual friend, Henry James, to write for the *North American Review* of

January, 1868. In this review, James sought and found the truly
literary quality of Howells' presentation of an older civilization.
His two books on Italy, said James, "belong to literature and to
the center and core of it,—the region where men think and feel,
and one may almost say, breathe, in good prose, and where the
classics stand on guard." He described the author of these studies
as "not an economist, a statistician, an historian, or a propagandist
in any interest; he is simply an observer." Many of the best passages
of *Italian Journeys,* wrote James, "bear upon the common roadside figures which he met," for "Mr. Howells is by no means indifferent . . . to the human element in all that he sees." On behalf of the simple people, Howells observes "a vast number of
small things; and he ignores, for their sake, a large number of great
ones. He is not fond of generalizing, nor of offering views and opinions." Howells felt no urge to educate the lower classes, nor did
he gaze upon them from the heights of his superior understanding;
on the contrary, he was touched, amused, pleased, interested, surprised, and annoyed by the small dramas of the roadside. "Mr.
Howells is in fact a sentimental traveler," James remarked in conclusion.

James himself sailed for Europe soon after the departure of the
Nortons and returned in 1870 to find his friend Howells a university
lecturer at Harvard. Though Howells' subject was "New Italian
Literature," what he actually discussed, according to James, was the
"general culture and literature of Italy." James enjoyed listening to
Howells and described his pleasure in a letter to their mutual friend,
Grace Norton.[24] "Howells is lecturing very pleasantly on Italian
literature," he wrote. "I go to the lecture room in Boylston Hall,
and sit with eyes closed, listening to the sweet Italian names and
allusions and trying to fancy that the window behind me opens out
into Florence."

James returned to England the following year, and there mingled
once more with Norton's "international set," with Ruskin, George
Eliot, the Rossettis, and others, imbibing Norton's own attitude
toward European culture, which set its mark on all of James's
novels.[25] To James, Norton was to be admired as a "representative
of culture" who nobly fulfilled his "civilizing mission" to this country. Both James and Norton returned to Boston in 1873 to find

Howells in full charge of the *Atlantic Monthly*—whether or not in furtherance of the cause of "culture."

Norton, having severed his connection with journalism before leaving for Europe, turned to teaching on his return to Boston. In 1874 he established, at Harvard, the first continuous university course in the history of the fine arts ever offered by an American university, and the following year he became professor of the history of art.[26] Norton announced his course as the history of the fine arts "as related to social progress, general culture and literature"; he aimed to point out, he said, in broad terms the abstract, spiritual beauty of all creative expression. As a missionary of civilization, Norton demanded, "Are we bound to sacrifice all that is best and highest in America on the altar of the common mediocrity and wane of culture?" [27]

Howells' casual comment in the letter to Henry James of December 5, 1873,[28] suggested something of the younger man's feeling for this "apostle of culture," who was, at the same time, his beloved friend. "I haven't fairly got used to the Nortons' being at home," Howells wrote, "and I haven't seen Charles more than twice. He is better in health, but he comes home with a dreadfully high standard for us all. We may attain it as blessed spirits a thousand years hence." To Howells, the here and the now—not to mention the mediocre and the common—held an irresistible attraction, especially since he had achieved a measure of success by exploiting just such material in his novels, which were soon recognized as examples of the new "realism."

A suggestion of the underlying difference in outlook of the two was reflected in a letter from Norton to Lowell written on February 6, 1874,[29] just after Norton's return from a visit with Longfellow, in the course of which Howells had come to dine. Howells, Norton wrote, has grown "plump and with ease shining out from his eyes." He felt that Howells "has passed his poetic stage, and bids fair to be a popular American author." With *Their Wedding Journey* and *A Chance Acquaintance* to his credit, as well as his two books on Italy, and, finally, the editorship of the *Atlantic,* Howells had, indeed, surprised his older friends and advisors. Norton, however, withheld his full approval in his letter to Lowell, then wintering in Italy. "As for art in American letters," he wrote, "recent numbers of the 'Atlantic Monthly' forbid one to think of it. There are no artists left but Emerson and Longfellow and you!" [30]

Two weeks later Norton wrote again to Lowell and again commented genially though patronizingly on their astonishingly prolific and successful protégé. "I thought Howells would be here to-night to read me part of the new novel he has just finished," Norton wrote, referring, presumably, to *A Foregone Conclusion.* "It is a pleasure to see him now-a-days," Norton continued; "he looks much at ease, and his old sweet humour becomes ever more genial and comprehensive." Norton then touched on his general disapproval of the new trends in art and literature as exemplified by the *Atlantic Monthly* and its editor. Howells, Norton observed, "is in just such relations to the public that he makes the very editor needed for the 'Atlantic' "; but, he added, "there is not much in the magazine that is likely to be read twice save by its writers, and this is what the great public likes. There must be a revival of letters in America, if literature as an art is not to become extinct." [31]

Would Norton have written so disdainfully of the quality of the literature appearing in the *Atlantic* had Howells appeared that evening with the manuscript of *A Foregone Conclusion* under his arm? Norton, no doubt, would have been amused enough to recognize Howells himself in the role of a leading character, Mr. Ferris, painter, American consul in Venice, and hero of the novel. In the opening chapter Don Ippolito called upon the consul, and saw through an open door "the paraphernalia of a painter's studio: an easel with a half-finished picture on it; a chair with a palette and brushes, and crushed and twisted tubes of colors . . . 'The Signor Console amuses himself with painting, I see,' said Don Ippolito courteously. 'Not at all,' replied Mr. Ferris, putting on his gloves; 'I am a painter by profession, and I amuse myself with consuling,' " [32]—precisely as Howells, a writer by profession, liked to assume that he was only incidentally a consul.

It is doubtful whether Norton would willingly have followed the subtleties of Howells' unfolding story of a painter's peculiar insight into character; certainly Norton would not have relished Howells' ironic smile at "the good folks who get themselves up on Ruskin and try so honestly hard to have some little ideas about art." [33] To Howells it was obvious that both painters and writers attempt to see beneath the surface of things into "reality," which is only to be seized by means of the symbol, whether painted on canvas or suggested on the printed page. In this story the painter fixed in a sketch the particular look of proud rebellion on the countenance of the heroine, a glance that precipitated the crisis of the novel. Norton could hardly have been expected to catch, in this psychological study of the intuitive perception of an artist, a suggestion as to a possible theory linking both literature and art. In any case, as Norton wrote to Lowell, Howells did not appear at Shady Hill that winter evening to put to the test his friend's understanding of a new and fresh way of writing. Howells, by then, had acquired the habit of seeking Norton's comment on his writing. "Whether you like it or not," he wrote Norton, "you are always one of the half score readers I have in mind when I write: I don't write *at* you but *for* you; and no doubt you sometimes save me from myself." [34] Though Howells was never in sympathy with Norton's aristocratic theory of art, he nevertheless sought the older man's counsel and advice until Norton's death in 1908.

NOTES

1. The first issue of the *Nation* is dated January 6, 1865.
2. *North American Review,* XCIX (October, 1864), 304–401.
3. The "Letters," under various headings, appeared in the Boston *Advertiser* between May 2, 1863, and May 3, 1865.
4. See Kermit Vanderbilt, *Charles Eliot Norton, Apostle of Culture in a Democracy* (1959), pp. 70–75.
5. *Atlantic Monthly,* I (November, 1857), 33–46.
6. *Ibid.,* p. 45.
7. In July, 1864, Norton, then making up the next issue of the *North American Review,* wrote to Lowell requesting him to send Howells' essay, "Recent Italian Comedy," to the printers at once. "I wish it to stand as the second article in the October number. . . . I mean that the October number should be a lighter one than that for July." Quoted by Vanderbilt, p. 87.
8. See Henry James, "An American Art Scholar, Charles Eliot Norton," in *Notes on Novelists* (1914).
9. *Atlantic Monthly,* I (November, 1857), 35.
10. See also Norton, "Waste," *ibid.,* II (March, 1866), 303; "Good Manners," (May, 1866) p. 571.
11. *Life in Letters,* I, 43.

12. Hawthorne expressed some of these views in *The Marble Faun* (1860), a novel that Howells very much admired.

13. P. 179.

14. See Norton (ed.), *The Letters of John Ruskin to Charles Eliot Norton* (1904).

15. *Nation*, III (Sept. 6, 1866), 189. Howells wrote to Norton, June 14, 1866, telling him that the English edition of *Venetian Life* had been favorably reviewed and requesting Norton's support of the forthcoming American edition. "You and Mr. Lowell have both kindly offered to notice it in the N. American—could you not divide your forces so as to take possession of the Nation also?" Letter, Houghton Library, Harvard. See also Lowell's review of *Venetian Life* in *North American Review*, CIII (October, 1866), 610–613.

16. All of the quotations from *Venetian Life* in this paragraph are from Chapter XI. See also "Eighty Years and After," *Harper's Monthly*, CXL (December, 1919), p. 25.

17. Norton owned a Tintoretto that Howells took his brother-in-law to see. *Life in Letters*, I, 133. See also Howells' reference to this painting in his essay, "Charles Eliot Norton: A Reminiscence," *North American Review*, 198 (December, 1913), 840.

18. *Life in Letters*, I, 109–111.

19. While in Venice, Howells translated *Venice, Her Art-Treasures and Historical Associations* by Adalbert Müller, from German into English. With the money earned by this translation, he bought Franz Theodor Kugler's *Handbook of Painting, The School of Painting in Italy*, commonly called "Kugler's Italian Art." See "Howells' Guidebook to Venice," pp. 221–224. Norton referred to this book in *Travel and Study in Italy* (1860), p. 178.

20. Letter, Houghton Library, Harvard.

21. "Mr. Howells Talks About Fiction and Fiction Writers." New York *Times*, Sunday, Apr. 30, 1905.

22. More than twenty years later, Howells reverted to the question of appropriate war memorials for small American towns in *Annie Kilburn* (1888). The home committee had, after the close of the Civil War, written to Annie, then in Rome with her father, asking her to purchase "something fit and economical" for a memorial to the soldiers of Hatboro'. "She accepted the trust with zeal and pleasure; but she overruled their simple notion of an American volunteer at rest, with his hands folded on the muzzle of his gun, as intolerably hackneyed and commonplace. Her conscience, she said, would not let her add another recruit to the regiment of stone soldiers standing about in that posture on the tops of pedestals all over the country; and so, instead of going to an Italian statuary with her fellow-townsmen's letter, and getting him to make the figure they wanted, she doubled the money and gave the commission to a young girl from Kansas, who had come out to develop at Rome the genius recognised at Topeka. They decided together that it would be best to have something ideal, and the sculptor promptly imagined and rapidly executed a design for a winged Victory, poising

on the summit of a white marble shaft, and clasping its hands under its chin, in expression of the grief that mingled with the popular exultation." When, after the death of her father, Annie returned to Hatboro', she saw the Victory in its position on the town square, she was so humiliated that she could not speak. "It seemed as if she could not take her eyes from the figure; it was such a modern, such an American shape, so youthfully inadequate, so simple, so sophisticated, so like a young lady in society indecorously exposed for a *tableau vivant*. She wondered if the people in Hatboro' felt all this about it; if they realised how its involuntary frivolity insulted the solemn memory of the slain." *Annie Kilburn* (1888), Chapter III, pp. 13–15

23. To J. M. Comly, June 27, 1868. *Life in Letters*, I, 130–131.

24. May 20, 1870. Leon Edel (ed.), *The Selected Letters of Henry James* (1955), p. 38.

25. See Malcom M. Marsden, "Discriminating Sympathy: Charles E. Norton's Unique Gift," *New England Quarterly*, XXXI (December, 1958), 463–483.

26. Perhaps Norton's lectures were inspired by Ruskin's Oxford *Lectures* (1870–1879). See Vanderbilt, p. 124. See Norton's letter to Ruskin, Feb. 10, 1874. *The Letters of Charles Eliot Norton*, I, 34.

27. Letter, June 4, 1870. Houghton Library, Harvard.

28. *Life in Letters*, I, 182.

29. *Letters of Charles Eliot Norton*, II, 33.

30. *Ibid.*

31. *Ibid.*, Feb. 23, 1874, pp. 35–36.

32. *A Foregone Conclusion* (1875), p. 14.

33. *Ibid.*, p. 104.

34. Letter, July 4, 1880. Houghton Library, Harvard.

· 4 ·

Art and the
Atlantic Monthly

When Howells became editor-in-chief of the *Atlantic,* in April, 1871, he immediately took steps to brighten the magazine by bringing the whole question of modern art before his readers. He did not, however, invite Charles Eliot Norton to express his ideas on art; instead, he turned to Henry James, who had recently appeared in Cambridge after a year in Europe, and invited him to contribute his views on paintings to be seen at the exhibits on Tremont Street. On February 4, 1872, James wrote to Norton: "Howells is making a very careful and businesslike editor of the *Atlantic.* As proof of his energies—he has just induced me to write a monthly report of the Fine Arts in Boston!" [1]

The first of James's articles appeared in the January, 1872,[2] issue of the *Atlantic*—the same month that the new editor commissioned Thomas Sergeant Perry to write the notices of French and German books for the department called "Recent Literature." Just as Perry was to enlarge the American taste for European literature in his reviews, so James, in his notes on art, was to alert the *Atlantic* readers to the new tendencies in European painting, especially among the French. "There has lately been an exhibition in Boston, at the rooms of Messers. Doll and Richards," James reported in his first article, "a small but remarkable collection of French pictures." They suggested, wrote James, something of the potential wealth and taste scattered through "our supposedly sordid American community." These paintings were interesting evidence of "the admirable aesthetic gifts of the French mind"; they were interesting, also, for "the reciprocal light" they shed on the new Barbizon school of painters, represented in the exhibition by Delacroix, Decamps, Troyon, Rousseau, Dupré, Diaz, and Daubigny. The new school was that of the early French Impressionists, important to James both in themselves and as offering hints to experimental writers in the use of color, light, and design.

James's description of a painting by Troyon indicated, more clearly than any theorizing on French art could, the sympathy felt by an advocate of "the new way of writing," such as James, for the early Impressionist's sense of light and space, which combined to give the viewer a firmer sense of solidity. The painting, wrote James, was "of a cluster of magnificent forest oaks," at the edge of a wood, "seen on a dampish day in September." The trees seemed to James a "perfect achievement," solid and dignified, spreading their mighty limbs against a vast background, which they by no means crowded. The picture, indeed, might have represented the opening of a James novel. The noble trees were "only part of the great landscape beyond and beside them; they seem really, as we may say, to irradiate atmosphere and space." As clearly as words may be said to apply both to a description of painting and writing, James's words on the Troyon painting could be felt as a comment on "the tone" of his own writing: "The tone of color in this work is extremely subdued, yet consummately sustained—sober and brilliant at once; a powerful harmony of gray and gray-green relieved with quiet russet and brown."

His discussion of the painting of Delacroix in the same essay showed the extent to which James had identified the problems of painting and writing in the new mode. Delacroix viewed his scenes, said James, "in a ray of light that never was on land or sea—which is simply the light of the mind." [3] Delacroix's merit, according to James, was that he had an eye for "the *mystery* of a scene," and this enabled him to fuse "its general expression and its salient details . . . into the harmony of poetry itself." Just as James caught hints for his own writing from the painters, so he used literary concepts in discussing their canvases.[4]

James paused, as he circled the small room of Doll and Richards' on Tremont Street, before a large landscape called "Paradise Valley," painted by John La Farge, which he considered the most important of "the three or four American pictures lately visible in the same rooms." It represented "the view of a deep seaward-facing gorge, seen from above, at Newport," particularly pleasing to James as an example of American impressionism by a friend whom he had known during long summers at Newport.

> This is in every way a remarkable picture. It is full of the most refined intentions and the most beautiful results, of light and atmosphere and of the very poetry of the situation. We have rarely seen a work in which the painter seems to have stored away such a permanent fund of luminosity.

Gazing at La Farge's painting of "Paradise Valley," James must have been taken back more than a decade to the several summers he had spent with his family in Newport, when that small seaport was a village of frame houses strung along a beautiful but lonely rocky coast. William Morris Hunt, a follower of Millet and the Barbizon school of painting, had established his studio near the quiet harbor when he returned from France in 1856. Here during the summers of 1858 and 1859 Henry James, his brother William, John La Farge, and Thomas Sergeant Perry [5] tried their hands at painting in Hunt's studio while discussing, among other things, the new literature from Europe or reading aloud the stories of Balzac and Turgenev. La Farge—the only real painter among them—who sketched "at the Glen" with the Jameses, remarked many years later to his biographer [6] that Henry James, indeed, had "the painter's eye" but did not so much see an object as think about it, a remark that many have made of La Farge himself, who had been deeply affected by his preoccupation with the poetized painting of the Pre-Raphaelites.

During these experimental summers at Newport, La Farge met George Bancroft, the historian, who introduced to La Farge the new scientific concepts of optics, by means of which the artist anticipated the effects of Monet and other Impressionists. As La Farge later remembered that period of his life, he and Bancroft "plunged into the great questions of light and color which were beginning to be laid out by the scientific men and which later the painters were to take up." All his work after that time was modified by those summers of optical study, "and the last realistic painting which may have shown it is the 'Paradise Valley,' which belongs to the '66–'67–'68's." This painting, over which James paused when he saw it in the exhibition of 1872, was emphatically modern in its impressionism; it was, according to the artist himself, "both novel and absolutely 'everydayish.' " To Henry James, such paintings were suggestive of the particular kind of realism he was discussing in Newport with Perry and later in Cambridge with Howells.

La Farge, like the writers of the new school, wished to free himself from the old "recipes," and to "paint from nature a portrait" free from any personal interpretation. "I aimed at making a realistic study of painting," he said, "keeping to myself the designs and attempts, serious or slight, which might have a meaning more than that of a strict copy from nature." [7] For "sheer accuracy," he felt a painting should rival a laboratory experiment; it should reflect "the exact time of day and circumstance of light" and should scorn any conventional arrangement of the subject to be painted. "I had it placed for me by chance, with any background and any light" in order to avoid the atmosphere of the studio. The "luminosity" that James found in La Farge's painting of "Paradise Valley," [8] and the "beautiful results" achieved by the use of light playing on ordinary objects was akin to the quality of poetic realism for which James was searching in his prose.[9]

In spite of La Farge's success in Boston, his paintings were rejected by the National Academy of Design in New York.[10] This early failure to understand the meaning of impressionism in painting and to encourage those artists who were experimenting in this direction led to the organization of the American Art Association in New York, on October 29, 1877, in opposition to the old National Academy of Design, which had been founded in 1802.[11] Six or eight artists met together in revolt against "the prejudices of Academicians," [12] who, they felt, were "jealous of young artists" and no longer represented "the truest and freshest impulses in art." Among the charter members were John La Farge, Augustus Saint-Gaudens, Helena Gilder, Francis Lathrop, Julian A. Weir—all friends and associates of Howells' and James's.

The demand for "more elbow room" on the part of the charter members grew from the fact that many of their own paintings had been refused a showing by the Academy on the ground that they were "studies" rather than finished works. However, as their spokesman, G. W. Sheldon, pointed out, "Studies being made directly from their subjects, and (in the case of landscapes) in the open air, have their own peculiar charm of freshness and brightness. They differ from completed works as conversation differs from written discourse." Such sketches were "simple, vigorous, original, sparkling"; they deserved recognition, for they frequently reflected the quick imaginative grasp lost in the "faithful reproduction" of the more "finished" painting. The French painter Corot produced "a poem" in each of his paintings, which were often hardly more than sketches. "The outward facts—a distant farm house, a bare heath, a country road, a pool by its side, some ordinary trees—are lifted into the soul and transfigured, and then set down on his canvas, clad 'in the light that never was on sea or land' . . . He is a poet." American painters were only beginning to learn that the artist must strive to catch the impression of reality, suffused with light and color, as it appears to his inner eye. Technical skill without imagination was the weakness of American art, and "Mr. Story has taken the trouble to come all the way from Rome to tell us that our principal fault is 'literalness.' " The American Art Association was organized to combat this deadening concept of art. Inspired by "some clever artists" in Paris, "notably the so-called 'Impressionist School,' " who "open annually an independent show," a group of young American artists resolved to set up their shows in opposition to the National Academy of Design.

Reflecting this new interest in impressionism, Howells immediately introduced into a little drama he was writing for the *Atlantic* the character of Bartlett, a young artist who was intent on catching his own impression of the autumn foliage of New Hampshire. Since Howells was then more skilled as a storywriter than as a playwright, *A Counterfeit Presentment* (1877) opened, not with a dramatic dialogue, but with a prose passage describing scene and characters.

> On a lovely day in September, at that season when the most sentimental of the young maples have begun to redden along the hidden courses of the meadow streams, and the elms, with a sudden impression of despair in their languor, betray flecks of yellow on the green of their pendulous boughs—on such a day at noon, two young men enter the parlor of the Ponkwasset Hotel, and deposit about the legs of the piano the burdens they have been carrying: a camp-stool, namely, a field-easel, a closed box of colors, and a canvas, to which, apparently, some portion of reluctant nature has just been transferred.

Though the artist had gone to the mountains for the autumn in order to work face to face with nature, and though he thought he was conveying his own *impression* of the yellows and greens and reds of the maples to his canvas, he nevertheless admitted to his friend, Cummings, that, if there was any greatness in him, it would be in terms of the paintings of Meissonier or of Corot. In other words, Bartlett, with his quick eye, his "full brown beard," and his dark hair that fell "in a careless mass" over his white forehead, was strictly within the tradition of impressionism as it was conceived by a conventional young painter of the nineteenth century.

As the weeks passed and Bartlett proved to be more successful in his love affair with Constance Wyatt (who also sketched) than in his paintings, he determined to give up imitating the small canvases of the early Impressionists and to attempt to catch the beauty of Ponkwasset in an enormous canvas such as that used by Albert Bierstadt. "I must have room," he told his friend Cummings, "like the Yellowstone and Yosemite fellows." Cummings, merely "an art-cultured fellow," tended both to sentimentalize and—what was still more offensive to his avant-garde companion—to moralize his paintings. "If there's anything that makes me quite limp," Bartlett told him, "it's to have an allegory discovered in one of my poor stupid old landscapes." However, Cummings bestowed a sentimental title, "The First Gray Hair," on one of Bartlett's paintings, and thus managed to catch the public fancy in a Boston show room some weeks later and to sell the canvas.

As editor of the *Atlantic,* Howells was sensitively aware of the change of taste in art, parallel in a sense to a shift in taste in literature. As editor, he felt it desirable to spend a week studying in detail the Philadelphia Centennial.[13] Recognizing the possibilities in a fresh, casual quality in magazine writing, he had, in the January, 1877, issue of the *Atlantic,* inaugurated the "Contributors' Club" in order to break away from the formality of another generation. "We begin our Contributors' Club in January," he wrote Mark Twain, on October 10, 1876. "Do send me at least a paragraph, spitting your spite at somebody or something. Write it as if it were a passage from a private letter." [14]

Since all contributions to the Club were anonymous, it is not known whether Twain responded to this appeal. However, in the columns of the "Contributors' Club" of July, 1877,[15] a paragraph of comment appeared on the portrait of Clemens by Francis Davis Millet and on that of Charles Dudley Warner by Frank Duveneck, which were to be seen in the Spring Exhibition of the Academy of Design of New York. The unidentified writer filled the remainder of his space with a comparison of the paintings of William M. Chase and Duveneck on exhibition at that time; and he gave his approval to the former, because, in Chase's portrait of a boy, "the plush looks tangible; the rug, against which the boy is leaning, is real drapery, capable of being folded."

That Howells was aware of the dangers of such criticism, even before the organization of the American Art Association, is suggested by the fact that, in September, 1877,[16] he wrote to one of his own New York contributors, W. H. Bishop, and invited him to treat "the aesthetic interests of that city in a monthly paper in the *Atlantic.*" In describing to Bishop what the editor would exact from the writer of such a monthly paper, Howells made it clear that he did not wish a routine covering of the New York cultural season; he wished the writer to adopt a lighter, more sophisticated tone. "I do not mean," wrote Howells to Bishop, "that he shall *report* literary, social, dramatic, musical and artistic events, but that he shall somehow express or distil the vital essence of these subjects, and give us that in the casual, touch-and-go manner of a French *chro-*

nique." Howells knew, as well as James, that the new literary and artistic style was French in origin—so why not enliven the columns of the *Atlantic* by catching something of this tone? "Several have tried this," Howells warned Bishop, "but they have all been put to death for their failure . . . but if you would like to try it, I should be glad. I know it makes a man heavy to charge him to be light, but your success will largely depend upon your volatility." Before he closed his letter, Howells added, "Also, for your own sake, be unknown; that alone can render you free."

So well did Bishop preserve his anonymity that one cannot trace his art "chroniques" in the *Atlantic*. Apparently Bishop contributed a paper on the National Academy of Design Exhibition of 1879, referred to by Howells in a letter but never printed in the *Atlantic*. This essay seems to have caused Bishop's "death, with confiscation," for in it Bishop failed to mention Howells' friend and neighbor at Belmont, the artist George Fuller, whose paintings were included in the Exposition. "I have had one great disappointment in your paper," Howells wrote to Bishop on April 12, 1879, "namely, that you have said nothing of Fuller's paintings: *The Romany Girl* and *She Was a Witch.*"

> I like his work far better than that of any other American; it seems to me beautiful and interesting, with a soul as well as body. These two pictures especially charmed me. Didn't you think them good; or do you object to his methods, or did you merely pass them in carelessness or weariness? If you like them well enough to send me a page of manuscript about them, I should be glad. Fuller is one of the painters who feel and think; and most of them seem to do neither.[17]

Howells was at that time living in "Red Top," his country home in Belmont, on a wooded slope near the studio of George Fuller, who had recently painted the portraits of Mrs. Howells' father and mother. This shy and sensitive farmer-painter from Deerfield, Massachusetts, had come to know Howells' brother-in-law several years earlier when Fuller was studying art in New York and, for a few years, had joined the group of artists and writers who lived on the hills of Belmont. Rutherford Mead, of McKim, Mead, and

White, made frequent trips to Belmont at that time, for it was he who designed the Howellses' hilltop house.

Howells had first met Fuller in 1876 at an Exhibition of Impressionists in Boston and had conceived for Fuller, as he said, "an instant affection." [18] Fuller, then emerging from the seclusion of his Deerfield farm, had caught the popular taste with his dreamy pictures, described by his critics as "painted poetry." That Bishop should have failed to comment on the two new Fuller paintings that had recently been sent down from Boston to the New York Exhibition of 1879 was enough to doom him in Howells' eyes. The editor of the *Atlantic* had, indeed, frequently stopped in at Fuller's Boston studio on Tremont Street and observed the progress of these two paintings. Painter and writer exchanged few words on these occasions; however, Howells recorded, Fuller asked him to suggest titles for the pictures as each was completed. The paintings still carry the titles given them by Howells—"The Romany Girl" and "She Was a Witch." [19]

The affection Howells felt for Fuller seemed to be his "chief warrant" for contributing, after Fuller's death in 1884, to a handsome, privately printed memorial volume entitled *George Fuller, His Life and Works* (1886), edited by Josiah B. Millet. Howells' "Sketch" of the life of Fuller is an introduction to a series of essays by Francis D. Millet, William J. Stillman, and others, that are enhanced by steel engravings of Fuller's paintings by Timothy Cole and William B. Closson. Much as Howells enjoyed the paintings of his friend Fuller, he never looked upon himself as other than a writer sympathetically interested in all the arts, especially in painting. Hence his contribution to the volume is in no sense a critical appraisal of Fuller's work; it is, rather, a collection of personal information supplied by Fuller's wife and sons and linked together by the painter's letters and journals.

Most of the Fuller manuscripts with which Howells worked in preparing his essay referred to the year 1860, which Fuller spent in Europe visiting the galleries of Paris, Rome, Brussels, Amsterdam, and London. Many of the letters, addressed to Fuller's family and friends at home, were reproduced in Howells' "Sketch" with the comment:

I believe that no one who has truly felt or thought, or has the desire to do good work in any art, can fail to be encouraged by these expressions of a genius which was not awed, but exhalted to serene self-trust, by the great works of other geniuses.[20]

Howells himself had grown "by the great works of other geniuses," both in literature and in art, and welcomed the thought that Fuller had learned, not by the imitation of other artists, but rather by the contemplation of their work. He, like the Impressionists who came after him, had especially admired "the mystery of color and the poetic suggestiveness" of "The City Guard" by Rembrandt, "the shadows of white dresses" in the paintings of Velasquez, the luminous atmosphere of the great paintings of the Pre-Raphaelites. These painters, Fuller wrote,

have merit to be great despite their name and peculiarity, and they have done me great good . . . The great pictures have grown on me at each visit, and I have grown with them.[21]

Fuller, who was, in a sense, an American Pre-Raphaelite, knew and talked with Rossetti, Holman Hunt, Millais, Ruskin, developing his own individual talent by his study of "the great works of other geniuses."

Since Howells' own concept of writing was growing at this time by the study of European writers such as Turgenev, Björnson, Pérez Galdós, and many others, and since he, too, believed that the techniques of European writers could be grafted onto native material, he was especially interested in observing Fuller's solution of a similar problem in the realm of painting. Though Howells often paused to watch Fuller in his studio, he modestly disclaimed the right to speak of Fuller's pictures in terms of painting. "Of his work I think myself unqualified to speak," Howells wrote, "except in its literary side, which, however, was full." Fuller's paintings all "had something to say," and, "like all good pictures, could speak clearly to the least technically instructed." He added, modestly, "Even I could not go into that little gallery of Doll's on Tremont Street, and find myself amid the delicate glow of the canvases with which he had hung it around, and not feel their exquisite, their authentic and singular charm." [22] The pictures, Howells pointed out, were "the slowly ripened fruit of fifteen years"; they recorded "the beloved faces of his own household," as well as "the scarcely less beloved features of the Deerfield landscape."

When he visited Fuller in his studio, Howells found himself in quiet sympathy with the painter and was content to forego conversation as he watched the artist mix his paints and bend over his canvas, half-forgetting his visitor. "It was my good fortune," Howells wrote, "to see some of his famous pictures wane and wax again under his brush." Now and then words were exchanged between the two, words which turned Howells' thought to his own problems of expression in another medium. Little was actually said during these visits, but the communication was curiously real; "it was not that he talked so much," Howells remarked, "but that he never talked unwisely." Fuller once observed to Howells, "It is often what you leave out that makes your picture." Howells added, that "with a lenient silence, a sparing comment," Fuller expressed "more than other men with words." [23]

In his own experiments in prose, Howells was learning the value of "the lenient silence," and "the sparing comment"; unlike Fuller, however, he was moving away from the poetic in his writing and into "the strong, full light of day," which was reflected in his first important novel, *A Modern Instance* (1881). But Howells was always fascinated by the poetic vision and continued to write poetry long after he had learned that his real gift lay in another direction. Fuller's paintings were "all poems," he wrote, "and I had the same pleasure in them that poetry gives." Howells then mused on the sort of painting he would have done, had he been an artist.

> I suppose that if I had been a painter I should not have wished, even if I could, to do those faces and figures and landscapes often teasingly withdrawn into their glows and mists; my liking, in literature at least, is to the strong, full light of day, to visages unsparingly distinct, to scenes in which nothing is poetically blinked. Yet I enjoyed Fuller's work as I did Carpaccio's, or Botticelli's or Tadema's. If it had not the earthly reality which I love, it had a heavenly sincerity, which is perhaps the celestial translation of reality.[24]

Into his paintings went "all the lovely, wise single-heartedness of the man," Howells concluded; Fuller's "soul expressed itself there in all its richness and truth."

Though Charles Eliot Norton was at the height of his popularity as a lecturer on art at Harvard when Howells was visiting Fuller's studio, it was not from Norton that Howells learned to understand the new movement in impressionism that was affecting both art and literature, for "Norton in teaching about art seemed to renounce modern art, especially American art." [25] Indeed, both critics and teachers tended to support "the vested interests of criticism," Howells declared from the "Study" of *Harper's* soon after the death of Fuller; they attempted to teach the artists, and the writers as well, "to compare what they see and what they read, not with things that they have observed and known, but with the things that some other artist or writer has done." So strongly had Howells come to feel the importance of a direct relationship with the life "known to us all," that he made this "Editor's Study" the second section of *Criticism and Fiction* (1891) and basic to all that followed.

Association with artists and experience in studying painting had taught Howells that "the seeds of death are planted" in those who do not trust their own native observation and that "they can produce only the stillborn, the academic." James, too, insisted that the writer, like the artist, is one who is capable of receiving a direct impression,[26] and it was James, whose interest in painting was closely related to an interest in writing, to whom Howells appealed when he became editor of the *Atlantic*. Not only had James been a student in the Newport studio of one of the first American Impressionists, William Morris Hunt, but he had also recently returned from a visit to the salons in Paris at the very time when early exhibitions of the new movement in art were to be seen in Boston. Howells was quick to see the meaning for literature of the new impressionism in art.

Venetian Life, in which Howells had described what he had seen "by the light of the piazza," rather than by the instruction of the guide books, was reissued in 1891, the same year in which *Criticism and Fiction,* addressing itself more directly to writers and critics, upheld the superiority of all creators to that "lowly caterpillar," the critic. "Sometimes it has seemed to me that the crudest expression of any creative art is better than the finest comment upon it," [27] wrote Howells, who, in his own work, identified himself with all creative spirits.

Armed with this fundamental belief in the arts, which he had discovered through his own experiences both as a writer and a student of art, Howells was ready to profit by his association with the active group of artists, architects, sculptors, and actors that he encountered when he began, in 1886, his association with *Harper's Monthly Magazine,* and the "larger life" of New York.

NOTES

1. Letter, Houghton Library, Harvard.

2. *Atlantic Monthly,* XXIX (January, 1872), 115–118. Reprinted as "French Pictures in Boston, 1872," in *The Painter's Eye* (1956), John L. Sweeney.

3. See James's contribution to the *Atlantic,* XXXV (March, 1875), 376–377. Here James enlarges on what he thinks the French painters have to teach to Americans.

4. See *The Ambassadors,* Book XI, Chapter II, for a synthesis of the painter's and the novelist's view of a river scene in France. Here Strether reminisced on a small painting by Lambinet, which he had seen many years earlier on Tremont Street and wished to buy.

5. John La Farge married Margaret Mason Perry, sister of Thomas Sergeant Perry, in New York in 1860.

6. Royal Cortissoz, *John La Farge, A Memoir and a Study* (1911), pp. 121–122.

7. *Ibid.*

8. See the *Atlantic Monthly,* XXXVIII (August, 1876), 251–252, for several columns of unsigned comment on "Paradise Valley" by Perry. The *Atlantic* of February, 1877, contained a review of twenty paintings by William Morris Hunt then being exhibited in Boston.

9. James frequently found hints for his own writing in paintings. After contemplating Tintoretto's magical use of light, he remarked, "I'd give a great deal to be able to fling down a dozen of his pictures into prose of corresponding force and color." Quoted by Leon Edel, *The Untried Years* (1953), p. 302.

10. See G. P. Lathrop comment in *Atlantic Monthly,* XXXIV (September, 1874), 379.

11. "The National Academy of the Arts of Design," *Harper's,* LXVI (December, 1882), 852–863.

12. G. W. Sheldon, "A New Departure in American Art," *Harper's,* LVI (April, 1878), 764–768.

13. See Howells' essay, "A Sennight of the Centennial," *Atlantic Monthly* XXXVIII (July, 1876), 92–107 in Appendix II of this book.

14. *Life in Letters,* I, 228.

15. *Atlantic Monthly,* XL (July, 1877), 105–106.

16. *Life in Letters,* I, 240–241.

17. *Life in Letters,* I, 267. La Farge's "Paradise Valley" was also shown in this exhibition.

18. Josiah B. Millet (ed.), *George Fuller, His Life and Works,* 1886. See *Atlantic Monthly,* XXXVII (May, 1876), 631–632.

19. Perhaps suggested by Emerson's poem, "The Romany Girl," *Atlantic Monthly,* I (November, 1857), 46. "She Was a Witch" is from Shakespeare. See *The Merry Wives of Windsor,* IV, 201.

20. *George Fuller,* p. 28.

21. *Ibid.,* p. 30.

22. *Ibid.,* pp. 48–49. In 1911 Howells visited in Spain the galleries mentioned by Fuller, *Life in Letters,* II, 305.

23. *Ibid.,* p. 50.

24. *Ibid.,* p. 48.

25. "Charles Eliot Norton: A Reminiscence," *North American Review,* CXCVIII (December, 1913), 836–848.

26. *The Art of Fiction* (1884).

27. Rudolf and Clara Kirk (eds.), *Criticism and Fiction and Other Essays by W. D. Howells* (1959), p. 25.

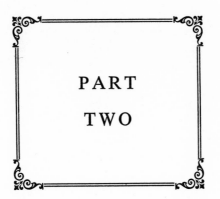

PART

TWO

· 1 ·

Writers, Artists,
and Publishers

Though Howells, as editor of the *Atlantic,* introduced art criticism
into his columns, he did not modify the austerity of the *Atlantic*
pages by the use of illustrations. Apparently Howells never attempted to bring about any such drastic change. A full-page ad-
vertisement [1] of the so-called Atlantic Portraits of Longfellow,
Bryant, Lowell, and Whittier by F. E. Baker, "one of the best
crayon artists in America," and available "to subscribers only for
$1. each" was the *Atlantic's* nearest approach to illustration at that
time. The striking fact that the more conservative *Atlantic* did not
follow the trend toward the illustrated magazine, which *Harper's,
Scribner's,* and other New York publications had made popular,
might have been one of the aspects of the more lively magazine
world of New York that influenced Howells, in the 1880's, to leave
Boston and move to the "immensely interesting" metropolis. Here,
he wrote to T. S. Perry, he found "lots of interesting young painting
and writing fellows" [2] with whom he enjoyed associating.

That Howells and James R. Osgood, publisher of both the *Atlantic* and Howells' novels, recognized the enlivening effect of the illustrator's pen, is evident; in 1871 and 1872, three of Howells' published books were adorned with clever sketches by Augustus Hoppin. Howells regarded the illustrator of his *Suburban Sketches, Jubilee Days,* and *Their Wedding Journey* as one of the most successful of all his many illustrators, no doubt because Hoppin, himself a writer of forgotten travel-books and novels, entered sympathetically into the humorous realism of the author. In the exchange of letters concerning the illustrations for *Their Wedding Journey,* Hoppin, indeed, went somewhat further than Howells in his zeal for realism. Unfortunately, a sketch of Mrs. March in her Pullman berth, therefore, had to be withheld from publication. Hoppin, in his letter of October 30, 1871, to Howells, sadly admitted that the sketch was not successful, though, at the same time, he showed an inclination to argue the point. "The scene where Isabel is represented in the sleeping car *is not a successful one*—I must try again," he wrote, "although I can't quite agree with you that she is treated with discourtesy—any woman with her dress off—& in the thumping & bumping of a sleeping car would lose a little of her 'tone' about *day-light*. I know—" [3]

When Hoppin died in 1896, Howells lamented not only the passing of the artist, but also the passing of the period, about which he always felt nostalgic. He wrote of Hoppin:

We have admirable artists of that sort now, but none who can more vividly suggest the fashion of his world. It was the gayer world, which thinks itself the greater, that Hoppin liked to deal with; and when he first began to portray its airs and graces, how stunning we youngsters of forty years ago thought his pretty girls and his handsome men! The girls were in swelling hoops, and the men had drooping whiskers and mustaches; and their fashion has long passed away but not the fashion of the artist. He had grace, he had chic, he had charm. Above all, he had distinction. [4]

Not only had Osgood been instrumental in bringing the popular new writer together with the very illustrator capable of presenting Howells' characters to the reader in the most lively fashion, but he also had acted as his young friend's host in visits to New York. Though Howells had been somewhat repelled by New York on an earlier visit, and though he always professed his preference for Boston, he was not slow to grasp, even in the early days of his editorship of the *Atlantic,* the importance of trips to New York, where he mingled with artists of all sorts, with actors, musicians, writers, and even politicians and financiers.

Howells fully and freely described these periodic forays into alien territory to his sister and father in Ohio. "My visit in New York was a wonderful round of dinners and breakfasts," he wrote to his sister Aurelia from the office of the *Atlantic Monthly* on May 7, 1872. He was there five days, he reported, and "never once dined alone." Osgood, as a well-known publisher, was a perfect host. He took Howells to the Union League Club, where he got "a glimpse of such club-life as you read of in Thackeray," and later gave a dinner for him at Delmonico's at which Howells laughed and talked with Joseph Harper of Harper and Brothers, John Hay, Bret Harte, Charles Dudley Warner, William De Forest, and his old friend, by then a well-known sculptor, J. Q. A. Ward. "The dinner was, of course, very elegant, and we had lots of fun," he added. So busy with engagements was Howells that he "missed a lunch which Mr. Harper wanted to give me." Then there was a breakfast with John Jay at the Knickerbocker Club—"one of the most aristocratic"— where Howells met "a new company of artists, literary men and *dilettanti*—including Harte and Ward again. It was if possible a little finer affair than the dinner, and it fitly crowned the visit." Howells ended his letter to his sister by confessing, "I enjoyed myself, but I like Boston best and Cambridge best of all. New York is large and jolly, but it's too much of a good thing." [5]

Howells' letters to his family continued to refer to his trips to the "large and jolly" city of New York, however. Though his visits were necessary to the business of an editor and writer—"I went to New York to be at a dinner the Harpers made for E. A. Abbey, the artist" [6]—they also included a good deal of "junketing" which was definitely a part of the business of a rising journalist-novelist and to Howells "lots of fun." On April 14, 1878, Howells described to his father his "ten days' stay" in New York, "all of which was taken up with continuous junketing." It began with a dinner for

Bayard Taylor at Delmonico's. "Next night Harper made a dinner party for me; next night Church of the late *Galaxy* dined me." Howells spent Sunday with relatives of his wife, only to resume his round of sociability the next day:

> Monday morning I breakfasted with Sedgwick at the Union Club, and went out to Shepard's for the night. Tuesday I lunched with Quincy Ward, and dined with Whitelaw Reid, at whose house I spent three days. Wednesday night, I dined at the Union League Club, meeting all the New York sages in politics, literature and finance, including Tilden, Bryant, and John Jacob Astor . . . That day Reid made a dinner party for me; Friday morning I breakfasted at Ward's . . . So you see what a round it was.

Howells assured his father that he "enjoyed it all for the novelty and excitement, and was glad to have it over."

In the course of this crowded week, Howells recorded briefly, he "met and made up all old sorrows with Dr. Holland, which I was glad to do." [7] Howells' adverse review of the poetry by J. G. Holland in the December, 1867, issue of the *Atlantic,* had precipitated one of the very few quarrels in which Howells, as an editor, had ever been a part. Howells was glad to heal the rift with this editor of *Scribner's Monthly,* who was soon to transfer his responsibility to his younger colleague, Richard Watson Gilder.

During the years that Howells was editor of Boston's leading magazine, his friend Gilder was associated with Holland as editor of *Scribner's.* In 1881, the same year that Howells resigned from the *Atlantic,* Gilder assumed the editorship of *Scribner's Monthly,* the name of which he immediately changed to the *Century.* Gilder was the writer and publisher who, perhaps more than any other, encouraged Howells to transfer his allegiance from Boston to New York, for the two men had, for many years, shared an interest in the surge of new ideas, social, literary, and artistic, which were discussed at just such breakfasts, luncheons, and dinner parties as Howells touched on in his letters to Ohio. Like Howells, Gilder was both an editor and a poet; like Howells' wife, Mrs. Gilder was an amateur artist [8] who occasionally illustrated her husband's books. Under Holland's editorship, Gilder had edited a department called

"The Old Cabinet" and had charge of "the art features" of *Scribner's;* deeply interested as he was in the development of magazine illustration, Gilder in 1881 renamed the publication the *Century Illustrated Monthly Magazine*. At the same time, Gilder reached out his editorial hand in the direction of his Boston friend and invited Howells to contribute to the magazine.

Sustenance for Howells' inquiring mind was to be found in many of the drawing rooms of lower New York besides that of the Gilders, with which he had been familiar for many years. Referring to the few months in 1865 when he had worked on the *Nation,* Howells said that he then renewed his still earlier acquaintance with C. E. Stedman and R. H. Stoddard, both of whom were poets and critics as well as journalists. Of the Stedmans, Howells wrote,

> I remember very well the lodging over a corner of Fourth Avenue and some downtown street where I visited these winning and gifted people, and tasted the pleasure of their racy talk, and the hospitality of their good-will toward all literature, which certainly did not leave me out. We sat before their grate in the chill of the last October days, and they set each other on to one wild flight of wit after another.[9]

Always sociable by nature, Howells also resumed his friendship with the Stoddards at this time.

> I believed that my lines were cast in New York for good and all, and I renewed my relations with the literary friends I had made before going abroad. I often stopped on my way up town, at an apartment the Stoddards had in Lafayette Place or near it; I saw Stedman, and reasoned high to my heart's content, of literary things with them and him.[10]

Returning to New York in the 1880's, Howells soon became a frequent visitor in the Gilder home, known as "The Studio," at 103 East Fifteenth Street, which was for many years a center of intellectual and artistic life in lower Manhattan where publishers, writers, and artists mingled with newspapermen, actors, musicians, and architects. It was here that Chase founded the Society of American

Artists in 1877 and Stedman in 1882 founded the Authors' Club, from which grew the American Copyright League, known later as the Authors' League.[11] Brander Matthews, John La Farge, Mark Twain, Augustus Saint-Gaudens, Kenyon Cox, Stanford White, William Chase, Jo Jefferson, Walt Whitman, William Rutherford Mead, and Herman Melville were among the interesting people who came and went in the Gilders' "charming reception room with a heavily lintelled fireplace and a staircase climbing, Japanese fashion, from the room itself." [12] Here Howells encountered many of the men, artists, and writers who compiled *Harper's Christmas* (November, 1882), to which special issue he contributed a play, *The Sleeping Car*.[13] This splendid holiday number was issued in the spirit of gayety by the Tile Club, in collaboration with Harper and Brothers, by writers, architects, and artists who worked together on more serious projects and convened over dinners at each other's homes.

The very title of the first Howells novel to appear in the *Century* —*A Modern Instance*—declared to the public that the magazine, under Gilder's editorship, was definitely interested in forward-looking ideas of all sorts in that post-Civil War decade. Before Howells' serial had run two months, the *Century* published a biographical-critical essay on Howells accompanied by his picture. Howells was invited to select his own biographer, and he chose Thomas Sergeant Perry,[14] his friend and associate on the *Atlantic*. He felt Perry best understood the true meaning of the realism for which he stood and clearly recognized it as an aspect of the scientific, democratic outlook of the younger generation to which Gilder was addressing the *Century*. As a part of the announcement of his platform, Gilder invited Howells to write for the following November a similar biographical-critical essay on Henry James, Jr., the third of the triumvirate that had so successfully scanned the horizon for the "new" in art and literature while Howells was still editor of the *Atlantic*.

When Howells, partly for reasons of health, definitely gave up his editorship of the *Atlantic* in February, 1881, he wrote to James R. Osgood that he wished to retain him as his agent. Since Osgood himself was at that time on the point of breaking with his partner in publishing the *Atlantic* and was planning to organize his own publishing company, he was glad to take all that Howells might write during those years of free-lancing and to put him on a yearly salary. *A Fearful Responsibility* and *Dr. Breen's Practice,* though both appeared originally in the *Atlantic,* were published as books under Osgood's imprint in 1881—before Howells, in July, 1882, finally "cut for Europe" to regain his strength after a prolonged and depleting illness that made him feel "like a diluted shadow." [15]

From England Howells wrote to Osgood to report that he and his family were established in "a very charming lodging" that Henry James had found for them; that he was already in touch with James Russell Lowell, Minister to the Court of St. James's, who seemed ready to open doors for him; that he had met Aldrich, John Hay and his wife, and many other "nice people." Before the month was out, Howells had met the portrait painter, "Mr. Herkomer," and written to his friend, Charles Fairchild, to introduce him to Herkomer, "the great painter who has taken all the honours in Europe, and made everybody talk of him here." [16] Bret Harte, Charles Warner, Clarence King, as well as Osgood, all met in London during the summer of 1882. According to his new friend, Edmund Gosse, Howells found himself enjoying a certain London fame because of *A Modern Instance,* which was still appearing month by month in the *Century.* Since Gosse had agreed to act as the English representative for *Century,* and since Osgood was attempting to arrange for the British publications of Howells' books, it was perhaps not surprising that the gay gathering of publishers, editors, artists, and writers should resume again in London.

Howells met many of these "desirable people" through Edmund Gosse, who had introduced himself to Howells by letter before Howells' arrival in England in July, 1882. Gosse at once wrote Howells a little note inviting him to his home on Delamere Terrace, overlooking Regent's Canal. "We shall probably be alone," he wrote, "except that we may have Alma-Tadema [17] and his wife with us, and that I am just writing to ask the much-engaged James himself if he will not come." Though people were beginning to leave town in August, the Gosse guest book, in which were inscribed the signatures of those who attended his Sunday evening parties, carried the names not only of the Howellses, but also of John Singer Sargent, du Maurier, Swinburne, the Rossettis, and many others who contributed to make this summer in London one of the happiest of

Howells' life. "In that season of 1882," Gosse wrote, "having dreaded London, and feared its unseen inhabitants," Howells found himself "something of a lion in London"; those he encountered at Lowells' receptions, in James's clubs, at Gosse's Sunday evenings, seemed to him, wrote Gosse, "angels moving in a golden glory because we were, as who could help being, enthusiastic and responsive" to his novels and plays, which were appearing in England as well as in the United States. Gosse reported that Howells, at that time, "enjoyed his literary fame with the most unaffected pleasure." He was, then, as always, "affable, gentle, and exquisitely responsive"; he also possessed "an aëry playfulness, a sort of roguishness which faded from him in years of anxiety and grief." [18] Such, at least, was the impression made by Howells on the London representative of *Century Magazine*.

Renewed sociability seems to have restored Howells' health and spirits in any case, as a merry letter to Mark Twain of September 1, 1882, attested. After describing a trip to Oxford with Osgood and Hutton, Howells suggested jovially that Clemens and his wife should join them in England. "Warner lunched with us on Tuesday," he wrote, "and is to return from Scotland for a big dinner that Osgood gives next Thursday. W. [Warner], Gen. Hawley, John Hay, Boughton, Aldrich, Tadema and W. D. [Howells]. How does that strike you as a time?" The artists, Boughton and Tadema, he declared delightful "above all," and he enclosed a card "by a wonderful painter, Herkomer, who is going to America next month." [19]

Osgood's "big dinner" on September 7 at the Hotel Continental in London proved a great success. Not only were all the guests about whom Howells had written to Twain present, but also many other old friends and new, among them Henry James, T. B. Aldrich, Edwin Booth, Laurence Hutton, Charles Dudley Warner, Bret Harte, Clarence King, and Moncure D. Conway. The menu, decorated by Edwin Abbey with a sketch of a merry little chef, half elf and half Frenchman, was preserved by Aldrich [20] and is interesting not only because of the signatures of the guests scrawled over the face of it, but also because of the bill of fare arranged for a truly festive dinner given by a publisher to his friends—and possible professional associates—on both sides of the Atlantic. That the affair was actually a matter of interest in far-away Ohio is suggested by a sentence from a letter that Osgood wrote to Howells several weeks later when Osgood had returned to the United States and Howells had fled the sociability of London. "Everybody is talking about 'the Osgood dinner,' " he wrote happily, on October 2, 1882. "I send you Conway's account of it copied into the *Advertiser* from the Cincinnati *Commercial*. I wish he had made it a little less sloppy." [21]

Howells realized by the end of September that in order to complete *A Woman's Reason,* the novel on which he was then working, he must leave London and seek a quiet retreat in Switzerland. Before leaving London, however, Howells met Whistler and Ruskin, as well as the popular artist, Lawrence Alma-Tadema, who became his personal friend. He also visited the exhibits at the Royal Academy and Grosvenor Gallery and become more aware of the new movements in art that he had followed, through Perry and James, during his editorship of the *Atlantic*. It was, however, to his old friend Norton that Howells wrote of his pleasure in his brief contact with the artists in London. "I seize myself in both hands at this last moment before leaving England," he wrote from London on September 14, 1882, "and send you any sort of line lest I should send you no sort." [22] The London sojourn had been "charming"; the Howellses had dined and lunched with "all kinds of desirable people."

> I must name Burne-Jones first among these; he came to a dinner with us at the Tademas, before I had the chance of making his acquaintance through your letter; and I had enough talk with him to feel his gentle and exquisite spirit, which had already delighted me in his pictures at the Grosvenor and the Royal Academy.

After a year spent in Switzerland and Italy, the Howellses made their way back to London in the early summer of 1883, pausing in Paris to call on "the Gerhardts." Gerhardt was a struggling young American sculptor who, with his wife, had been sent by Mark Twain to study for a year, and Twain had asked the Howellses to look in on the couple and to report to him. Howells wrote the following letter to Twain from the steamer, on his return trip:

S.S. *Parisian,* off the Straits of Belle Isle,
and about 180 miles from Greenland.
July 10, 1883.

My dear Clemens:

We saw the Gerhardts in Paris. I took a fiacre and drove literally hell-wards to the region of the Boulevard d'Enfer, near which they live, and found the little woman preparing asparagus for dinner in his studio. There was a stove in the middle of the room, a lounge-bed for the nurse and baby at one side, and a curtained corner where I suppose the Gerhardts slept. It was as primitive and simple as all Chicopee [Massachusetts], and virtuous poverty spoke from every appointment of the place. Gerhardt was off at work somewhere, but the next day they both came to see us at our hotel, and Mrs. Howells took a great liking to them. She thought Mrs. G. thoroughly good and honest and very ambitious for her husband, and she thought that he was looking a little worn with overwork. I should think he had used the time you've given him very conscientiously, and that he had studied hard; it seemed to me also that they were keeping a good conscience about living economically, in a city which seems to me rather more expensive than New York. I don't know how far your beneficence is to extend to them; but if you are still paying their way it wouldn't cost any more to let them run down into Italy for three or four months than it would to keep them in Paris— not as much—and Gerhardt needs some sort of outing, and he could learn while he was resting in Italy. He seems to be a man of delicate and refined genius; the little medallion which he exhibited of you in the Salon was full of this, and seized your best points; it was artfully concealed from the public in the catalogue as the portrait of "M. Marc Swain," but it was favorably noticed by the critics. You are those poor little people's god—I don't know but they'd like me to write you with the large G.[23]

This brief description of the Howellses' plunge into "la vie de Boheme" is all we know of their sojourn in Paris. By the middle of June they were again in London. As in the previous summer, Howells found a delightful company of artists, writers, and publishers, both English and American, willing to chat and dine with him and thus to enlarge and enrich his sensitive, responsive mind, rested and refreshed by a year of remarkable productivity. Brander Matthews, in *These Many Years,* recalled "the vision of a goodly company gathered in the private dining-room of the Saville when Gosse invited a group of his friends to do honor to Howells." [24] Of those present, Matthews could, in 1917, remember with certainty the names of the sculptor-poet Thomas Woolner, and the writers, Austin Dobson, George Du Maurier, Thomas Hardy, and William Black. From "the flotsam and jetsam which the dark tides of Time deposit on the shallow shores of Memory," Matthews wrote that he was able to bring back two topics of conversation—the first a discussion of *revenge* as a motive in fiction, and the second "a definition of the image called up in our several minds by the word *forest.*" Until that evening, Matthews wrote, he had never thought of the fact that such a word might take on different colors and different forms in the eyes of different men. Each guest, of course, summoned up the images associated with his earlier experiences:

> To Hardy "forest" suggested the sturdy oaks to be assaulted by the woodlanders of Wessex; and to Du Maurier it evoked the trim and tidy avenues of the national domain of France; to Black the word naturally brought to mind the low scrub of the so-called deer-forests of Scotland; and to Gosse it summoned up a view of the green-clad mountains that towered up from the Scandinavian fiords. To Howells it recalled the thick woods that in his youth fringed the rivers of Ohio.[25]

As Matthews listened to the evocations arising from the one word, "forest," he mused on the "inherent and inevitable inadequacy of the vocabulary of every language." Furthermore, he meditated, if such a divergence of imagery is produced by an ordinary concrete word, it must be "intensified in all discussions of art." No doubt Matthews brought forth some of these contemplations to be further refined by the interesting group sitting over coffee and cigars in the Saville Hotel.

At this dinner, Matthews, then at the height of his fame as a novelist, first met William Black, whom he encountered again "once or twice at one or another of the gatherings of The Kinsmen." It was at the meetings of this short-lived, but important organization that Matthews again met Howells and continued his cordial relations with him. Because Howells was either in another city or another country when the Kinsmen held their first five meetings,[26] he did not actually become a member of the Club until several years later. Laurence Hutton records, in *Talks in a Library,* that he suggested the name of the Kinsmen, the idea for which came from actor Lawrence Barrett. In the early months of 1882, these two men, with artists Edwin A. Abbey and Frank D. Millet, Columbia professor Brander Matthews, and journalist and art critic William M. Laffan, found themselves dining at the home of Hutton. Barrett proposed the idea that these five should attempt "to bring together the players, the writers, the sculptors, the painters, into some simple organization which should be select and fraternal." Before the evening was over, Matthews suggested further that the group should meet a few nights later at the Florence House, on the corner of Eighteenth Street and Fourth Avenue (105 East Eighteenth Street). There, on April 1, 1882,[27] seated about a round table, "the unique little society was formally organized." No constitution, no dues, no officers, were to mar the "good fellowship and the good times" of these five original members. The simple plan, as Hutton described it, was as follows:

> We were to breakfast, or dine, or lunch or sup, together; each member was to bring to each symposium a guest of his own choosing and of his own profession, whom he felt would be acceptable to the other members—the simple presence of such a guest making him a member of the club itself without any other form of choice or ballot; and in this way was the society to be increased with no limit except that of the proper fitness of congeniality and talent. All sorts of names were suggested for the organization, but none of them seemed suitable or sufficiently comprehensive until Barrett, in a neat little speech, alluded to the "amiable and convivial association of the kindred arts about our simple board." And that gave me the cue; Kinsmen, then, let us be!" And "Kinsmen" we are to this day.

With "the breaking of bread and the sipping of beer and claret" —the only initiation required—Mark Twain became a Kinsman at the second meeting of the group, a dinner at Hutton's home, at 229 West Thirty-fourth Street, on March 9, 1883. "Everything was going on beautifully and harmoniously," Hutton wrote, when an uninvited guest, James R. Osgood, drove up in a cab and demanded entrance as an old friend and publisher of all the members present. Osgood poured forth such a jovial flood of admonitions, advice, and exhortation when he found himself unexpectedly in such delightful company that Twain arose and proposed that the name of the Club should be immediately changed to "The Osgood Club." Osgood was thereupon voted a member and became the guiding spirit of the group. Under Osgood's cheerful influence, the club was soon enlarged to include kindred spirits in England, where the next two meetings were held.

Though Howells had returned from Europe by the time the fourth meeting was called in New York, in November, 1883, he was in Boston and therefore was not initiated into the group until April, 1884. Howells was soon swept into the current of writers, artists, actors, and publishers that eddied around the lively personality of Osgood. After the sudden failure of his publishing company in 1885, Osgood was officially attached to Harper and Brothers in 1886, the year Howells himself joined the staff and the year in which the last meeting of the Kinsmen was held in this country. From 1886 to 1890, Osgood was the London agent for Harper's, and was soon busily arranging the last two recorded gatherings of the Kinsmen (March 17, 1887; November 17, 1889) before his death in London in 1892. Howells' sense of the literary and artistic movements on both sides of the Atlantic was enormously enriched by his association with "the clever and good fellows" who lifted their glasses around the "groaning board" at the Kinsmen meetings over which Osgood frequently presided.

NOTES

1. Vol. XLII (January, 1879), p. 128. The portrait of Longfellow was first printed in 1875. See *Atlantic Monthly*, XXXVI (Dec., 1875), 762 for comment.

2. *Life in Letters*, Apr. 14, 1888, I, 413.

3. "Augustus Hoppin to William Dean Howells," Arthur A. Adrian, *New England Quarterly*, XXIV (March, 1951), 85.

4. *Harper's Weekly*, XL (May 2, 1896), 438. Many years after the death of Hoppin, Howells wrote to a friend who had lost his original copy of

Their Wedding Journey, that Hoppin was "the first of our illustrators to give the sense of actuality, and [the illustrations] were strictly of the time of the book." *Life in Letters,* II, 195.

5. *Life in Letters,* I, 168–169.

6. *Ibid.,* II, 1.

7. *Life in Letters,* I, 253.

8. Helena de Kay, a student of painting at Cooper Institute.

9. "My First Visit to New England," *Harper's,* LXXXVIII (May, 1894), 816–824.

10. "Roundabout Boston," *Harper's,* XCI (August, 1895), 438.

11. See Chapter III, *The Letters of Richard Watson Gilder* (1916), edited by Rosemond Gilder. See also Brander Matthews, *These Many Years* (1917), pp. 220–227.

12. Douglas Sladen, "New York as a Literary Center," *English Illustrated Magazine,* X (1892–1893), 136.

13. Other contributors were E. C. Stedman, T. B. Aldrich, Thomas Hardy, Mark Twain, and among the artists, F. D. Millet, E. Vedder, R. S. Gifford, C. S. Reinhart, E. A. Abbey, G. H. Boughton, C. Parsons, W. M. Chase, J. A. Weir, F. H. Smith, and Arthur Quartley. The Tile Club was formed by a group of eminent artists, each of whom presented a tile to the host of the evening. See *House of Harper,* p. 492. See also "The Tile Club Afloat," *Century,* February, 1882.

14. "William Dean Howells," *Century,* XXIII (March, 1882), 680–685. Also *ibid., "Two Notable Novels"* (August, 1886), 632–634.

15. Howells to Horace E. Scudder, Dec. 12, 1881. *Life in Letters,* I, 305.

16. *Ibid.,* I, 316. "Mr. Herkomer" was Sir Hubert von Herkomer (1849–1914) who began exhibiting at the Royal Academy in 1869 and was made an Academician in 1879. Charles Fairchild was an American painter and Howells' neighbor at Belmont. Howells remarked that Herkomer's portraits "do not sit in their frames, but walk all about the room and would shake hands with you as if they were not lords and ladies."

17. Lawrence Alma-Tadema, R. A. Townshend House, North Gate, Regent's Park. A Dutch painter, residing in London, who specialized in paintings of scenes from Egyptian, Greek and Roman history. See Cosmo Monkhouse, "Some English Artists and Their Studios," *Century,* XXIV (August, 1882), pp. 566–568. See also Ellen Goode, "Lawrence Alma-Tadema," *Century,* XLVII (February, 1893), 483–497.

18. Edmund Gosse, "The Passing of William Dean Howells," London *Sunday Times* (1922).

19. *Life in Letters,* I, 317. George Henry Boughton (1833–1905), painter and illustrator.

20. From Laurence Hutton (1905), *Hours in a Library,* facing page 334. See also Carl Weber, *The Rise and Fall of James R. Osgood* (1959), pp. 198–201.

21. Letter, Houghton Library, Harvard. This notable dinner was also referred to by Howells in "Meetings with King (1958)," in *Memoirs of Clarence King* (1904), pp. 144–145. See also Thurman Wilkins, *Clarence King, A Biography* (1958), pp. 288–289.

22. *Life in Letters*, I, 320.

23. *Life in Letters*, I, 348–349.

24. P. 287.

25. Pp. 287–288.

26. See "Meetings of 'The Kinsmen,' with List of Members Present." Houghton Library, Harvard.

27. Brander Matthews gives the date of this meeting as Apr. 3, 1882. *These Many Years*, p. 232.

· 2 ·

Italy Revisited

Hardly had Gilder become editor of the *Century* in 1881 before he was in communication with Howells concerning a series of articles on the Tuscan cities of Italy to be illustrated by Joseph Pennell, one of the many artists employed by the reorganized magazine.[1] Howells, who had recently resigned from the *Atlantic,* was with his family in Florence when Gilder proposed, the following December, to send Pennell to Italy to travel with the writer and sketch the market places, the cornices of palaces, and the church belfries on which Howells' eye fell. The new editor thus hoped, not only to duplicate the success of *Italian Journeys,* but to surpass it with the aid of Pennell's etchings.[2]

Roswell Smith, the owner-publisher of the *Century,* had made the proposal definite while Howells was still in Switzerland in the autumn of 1882. Howells wrote at once, "I shall have plenty of work cut out for Mr. Pennell when he comes." Howells enjoyed just such friendly and sympathetic relations with artists, especially if he thought his own ideas would predominate. "I am expecting Pennell the artist every day, but he hasn't come yet," Howells wrote to Osgood, on January 28, 1883.[3]

Pennell arrived in Florence on the 9th of February, 1883. "Got here," he wrote home to his wife. "Howells is a *howling swell*— very impressive and also very jolly when you can get him alone which isn't very often." [4] Soon Pennell was writing his wife that he had finished his work in Florence, and was about to go with Howells to Siena.[5] "*We shall run down to Rome* for Sunday," [6] he added, emphasizing his pleasure in the prospect by underscoring his words. Several weeks later, he wrote to his wife from Pisa, "am off here with the 'most finished American novelist'—he'll finish me financially before long." [7]

Not only did artist and writer discover that they had to adjust to one another in the practical problems of travel, but in their literary and artistic views and opinions as well. Pennell's hasty note to his wife continued with the reassuring comment, "I'm getting along much better with him, but when a man incidentally mentions that Dickens' work 'is trash' [8] I feel like stopping the production of Am. novels." The following day Pennell wrote to his wife again of his excursions with Howells in and around Pisa:

> This week I have been running around with Howells—yesterday we started from here—drove across the country to Lucca. I am getting along very much better with him than I did at first—and if he wasn't going to Venice next week—I would probably fall desperately in love with him.[9]

A letter from Howells to Osgood, written in Venice on April 20, 1883, suggests a discussion between the travelers that might have been responsible for Pennell's mixed feelings about Howells, who knew all too clearly what he expected of his illustrator:

> Pennell got a letter the other day from the Art Editor of the C. telling him to get fotografs of old masterpieces, to be introduced as illustrations. *I don't want them.* I want life and character, past and present. I don't want anything about old art, and shall not avoidably speak of it. Do make them under-

stand this, please. Mr. Gilder seems to get my idea; but the Art Editors are all off the track.[10]

Though Howells frequently spoke of "old art" in his essays for the *Century,* he did so in a fresh and independent manner, quite new to the readers of travel books from Italy.

His contemplation of the "poor, splendid, stupid, glorious past," left Howells as thankful that he was a "modern" in 1883 as he had been twenty years earlier when he had visited "A Little German Capital" and filled his notebook with comments on the daily life of the simple folk living under the rule of fat and strutting, tyrannical, little kings. Looking out of one of the long windows of the Signory of Siena, similar ideas accosted him, for thoughts on how people actually lived were never far from his imagination as he contemplated "old art":

> It is well enough for the tourist to give a thought to these facts and conditions of the times that produced the beautiful architecture of the Palazzo Communale and the wonderful frescoes which illumine its dim-vaulted halls and chambers. The masters who wrought either might have mixed the mortar for their bricks, and the colors for their saints and angels, and allegories and warriors, with human blood, it flowed so freely and abundantly in Siena. Poor, splendid, stupid, glorious past! I stood at the windows of the people's palace and looked out on the space in the rear where those culprits used to disturb the signory at their meals, and thanked Heaven that I was of the nineteenth century. The place is flanked now by an immense modern prison, whose ample casements were crowded with captives pressing to them for the sun; and in the distance there is a beautiful view of an insane asylum, the largest and most populous in Italy.[11]

In spite of an oppressive sense of the wicked abuses that were an accompaniment to all the beauties of Italy, Howells was soon lost in a revery as he studied the faces that looked down on him from the frescoes. Though he realized that his comments could mean little to his readers, he attempted, nevertheless, to renew for himself "the curious realist's interest" of the innumerable faces that peered at him in the "hovering twilight" of the gloomy gallery and remained with him long afterwards.

> I suppose the reader will not apprehend a great deal of comment from me upon the frescoes, inexpressibly quaint and rich, from which certain faces and certain looks remain with me yet. The pictures figure the great scenes of Sienese history and fable. . . . In one of these . . . there is a procession of Sienese figures and faces of the most curious realistic interest, and above their heads some divine and august ideal shapes,— a Wisdom, from whose strange eyes all mystery looks, and a Peace and a Fortitude, which for an unearthly dignity and beauty, I cannot remember the like of. There is also, somewhere in those dusky halls, a most noble St. Victor by Sodoma; and I would not have my readers miss that sly rogue of a saint . . . For the rest, there is an impression of cavernous gloom left from many of the rooms of the palace which characterizes the whole to my memory; and as I look back into it, beautiful, mystical, living eyes glance out if it; noble presences, solemn attitudes, forms of grandeur faintly appear; and then all is again a hovering twilight, out of which I am glad to emerge into the laughing sunshine of the piazza.[12]

Clearly what interested Howells in this tour of the little towns of Italy, was, not merely the churches, the paintings, the statues, but the people in the sunny piazzas, who still moved about among the relics of other days, forming for both Howells and Pennell fresh pictures against columns and archways. This humanizing of the travel book, so successful in *Venetian Life* and *Italian Journeys,* marks every page of *Tuscan Cities.* Howells could not pass a church door without wishing to go in, not merely for the pictures or statues, but for the delightful human beings one could be sure of encountering. No art editor could divert him from the insight he had gained when, as a young consul in Venice, he had learned to observe people as well as paintings. Impressive as the past glories of history and art might be, they were secondary in his mind to the figure of a miller lounging on his doorstep or of a "poor mountebank" strolling by the river Arno at night. But Howells' pictures of characters are themselves related to the artist's vision; not only did Howells teach Pennell something of the modern writer's aims, but he was no doubt encouraged by Pennell to look for the picture quality of his surroundings.

One spring day the two travelers engaged a carriage and drove out of the town of Pisa to observe the countryside; Howells, too, saw the scenes about him with the eyes of a painter. "It was a plain country," he wrote, in his essay for *Century*,

> and at this point a line of aqueduct stretched across the smiling fields to the feet of the arid, purple hills, that propped the blue horizon. There was something richly simple in the elements of the picture, which was of as few tones as a landscape of Titian or Raphael, and as strictly subordinated in its natural features to the human interest, which we did our best to represent. . . . Now, in the advancing spring, the grass and the wheat were long enough to flow in the wind, and they flowed like the ripples of a wide green sea to the feet of those purple hills, away from our feet where we stood beside our carriage on its hither shore. The warmth of the season had liberated the fine haze that dances above the summer fields, and this quivered before us like the confluent phantoms of multitudes . . . we could not help loitering along by the clear stream that followed the road, till it brought us to a flour-whitened mill, near the city wall, slowly and thoughtfully turning its huge undershot wheel. . . . [T]he miller, leaning upon a sack of wheat, . . . dimly loomed through the powdered air.[13]

Pennell and Howells, standing beside their carriage on an April day and gazing across the summer fields of waving wheat to the purple hill on the horizon, remembered the landscapes in the paintings of Titian and Raphael. Howells, at least, in his use of purple, blue, and green, as seen through the quivering light, himself seemed to paint a picture in terms of the early Impressionists that he had recently studied in the 1876 exhibition in Boston. The "human interest" he sought by reference to the miller as glimpsed through the "powdered air" of the "flour-whitened mill" was merely an anticipation of the peasant figure of a Von Gogh. If he himself had been "less modern, less recent, less raw," Howells mused, he would have been "by just so much, indifferent to the antique charm of the place." Accepting his modernity, Howells caught the "atmospheric quality" of old towns drowsing through warm afternoons. When he and Pennell returned to Pisa after their day in the country, they renewed their "impression of a quiet that was only equalled by its cleanliness, of a cleanliness that was only surpassed by its quiet." Recalling the scene later, Howells wrote, in terms suggestive of Cézanne's painting of the little park of Arles a generation later, "I think of certain genial, lonely, irregular squares, more or less planted with pollarded sycamores, just then woolily tufted with their leaf-buds; and I will ask the reader to think of such white light over all as comes in our own first real spring days."

After an unsatisfactory dinner at the inn of Pisa, Pennell and Howells repaired to a café for their after-dinner coffee and then walked by the side of the Arno "under the pale moon."

> We found the river roughed by the chill wind that flared the line of lamps defining the curve of the quay before the shadowy palaces, and swept through the quiet streets, and while we lounged upon the parapet, a poor mountebank—of those that tumble for *centisimi* before the cafés—came by, shivering and shrinking in his shabby tights. His spangled breechcloth emitted some forlorn gleams; he was smoking a cigarette, and trying to keep on by a succession of shrugs the jacket that hung from one of his shoulders. I give him to the reader for whatever he can do with him in an impression of Pisa.[14]

Cézanne would undoubtedly have known what to do with Howells' shivering mountebank smoking his cigarette by the side of the Arno. These waters, wrote Howells, "are turbid, almost black, but smooth, and they slip oilily away with many a wreathing eddy around the curve of the magnificent quay." [15] Thus Howells transmuted what he saw, as he sauntered by moonlight with Pennell "into the glory and charm of art," curiously suggestive of the French Impressionists, then coming into vogue.

Before quitting Pisa, Howells renewed his acquaintance with the Orcagna frescoes that he had contemplated many years earlier as an earnest young student of art. He perceived, by reference to his notebook of 1865, that in 1883 he had found the group less impressive. As a young man, Howells had said to himself, when studying these same frescoes, "in obedience to whatever art-critic" he had in his pocket, that here, certainly, was to be found "the highest evidence of the perfect sincerity in which the early masters wrought"; no one who did not believe in them, he thought, could possibly depict "those horrors of death and torments of hell." In the sober skepticism of middle age, he smiled at the seriousness of his youth and ventured to philosophize on "the modern quality in the great minds, the quickest wits, of all ages."

> But this time I had my doubts, and I questioned if the painters of the Campo Santo might not have worked with almost as little faith and reverence as so many American humorists. Why should we suppose that the men who painted the Vergognosa peeping through her fingers at the debauch of Noah should not be capable of making ferocious fun of the scenes which they seemed to depict seriously? There is, as we all know, a modern quality in the great minds, the quickest wits, of all ages, and I do not feel sure these old painters are always to be taken at their word. Were they not sometimes making a mock of the devout clerics and laics who employed them? It is bitter fun, I allow.[16]

But "it is worse than useless to be specific about pictures," Howells realized as he gazed at the paintings in churches, libraries and town halls in quest of the very qualities of realism, actuality, and liveliness that he, as an artist in words, had learned to appreciate. Pinturicchio's paintings in the library of the Cathedral of Siena are "surpassingly delightful in their quaint realism." [17] The della Robbias in Pistoia, "represent with the simplest reality, and in the proportions of life, the seven works of mercy of St. Andrea Franchi, bishop of Pistoja in 1399." The observer feels the sincerity of the artist in the primary colors he used; "in the broad, unmingled blues, reds, yellows, and greens, primary, sincere, you have satisfying actuality of effect." Though the critics had not decided that these were the artist's best works, Howells wrote that they gave him more pleasure than any other work of della Robbia. "I remember them," he said in retrospect, "with a vivid joy still. It is hardly less than startling to see them first, and then for every succeeding moment it is delightful." [18]

Of all the Tuscan cities visited by Howells and Pennell, Florence, where they first met, was the one in which they lingered longest and to which they devoted the most time and thought.[19] Larkin Mead, who still maintained a studio in Florence, and his Italian wife no doubt made life altogether too pleasant in the old familiar city, which the Howellses had last visited soon after their marriage. "It was quite three weeks before I began to keep any record of my impressions," he admitted.[20] After "a foolish round of 'pleasure' in Florence which almost spoiled [his] business there," Howells fled to Siena to "catch up" on his work.

A hard-working month in Siena enabled Howells to write up his notes on Florence, to which, he wrote to Charles Dudley Warner, the family would return for three weeks and thence to Venice for more work. "I hope to be writing there on my Tuscan cities, and to finish up the job by the time I get home at the end of the summer." [21] Having "done a great deal of society in Florence" in December and January, Howells was determined to stick to his "proper business of sightseeing" [22] on his second stay in April, before returning to England for a final month of writing.

Perhaps Howells partially carried out his plans, in spite of the lures of "society." As he remarked to Warner, "If I were at leisure I should like extremely to see something of English society; but there is little hope of that, now. I shall go to some quiet place in England, and work hard on the Italian papers. How would Oxford do? At Cambridge I know people." [23] As a matter of fact, Howells returned to London in June, saw many friends, and left for the United States early in July, glad to escape from so much social activity. Howells finished his Italian papers after his return to Boston,[24] in his ample study in his home on Beacon Street, which looked out upon the Charles River.

During these same months he was, in another sense, reliving the same experiences in his novel, *Indian Summer,* the opening chapters of which appeared in the July, 1885, issue of *Harper's,* one month after his series on Florence had ended in *Century* and a month before his study of Siena began to come out in the August and September issues of Gilder's magazine.

In Theodore Colville, the middle-aged hero of *Indian Summer* who returned to Florence twenty years after his first visit, the reader recognizes the ghost of Howells himself. Both Colville and Howells earned their daily bread by their work on newspapers; both men, weary of journalism, leaned on the parapet of the Ponte Vecchio and mused again on the unpublished books on Florence that they still dreamed of writing. Colville, indeed, had sold his newspaper in Prairie Des Vaches, Indiana, and

> had taken up, with as much earnestness as he could reasonably expect of himself, that notion of studying the architectural expression of Florentine character at the different periods. He had spent a good deal of money in books, he had revived his youthful familiarity with the city, and he had made what acquaintance he could with people interested in such matters. He met some of these in the limited but very active society in which he mingled daily and nightly.[25]

Howells, a more successful journalist, had by no means severed his connections with American magazines and newspapers; in his journeying through Tuscany with Pennell, he had merely enlarged his power of observation to include a closer view of art and architecture. Italy, he wrote, "is anywhere a study for a painter—preferably a water-colorist, I should say—and I do not see how an architect could better use his eyes in Italy than in perusing the excellent brickwork of certain of the smaller houses, as well as certain palaces and churches." [26]

As a young consul in Venice in 1863, Howells had become possessed with a desire to write a history of Venice—a desire that never left him [27] and that he bestowed upon the elderly Professor Elmore in *A Fearful Responsibility*. It is not difficult to feel Howells himself in the somewhat saddened person of Colville as he strolled through the Florentine garden, which "seemed to know him" after an absence of twenty years.

> . . . the great, foolish grotto before the gate, with its statues of Bandinelli, and the fantastic effects of drapery and flesh in party-colored statues lifted high on either side of the avenue; the vast shoulder of wall, covered thick with ivy and myrtle,

which he passed on his way to the amphitheater behind the palace; the alternate figures and urns on their pedestals in the hemicycle, as if the urns were placed there to receive the ashes of the figures when they became extinct; the white statues or the colossal busts set at the ends of the long alleys against black curtains of foliage; the big fountain, with its group in the center of the little lake, and the meadow, quiet and sad, that stretched away on one side from this; the keen light under the levels of the dense pines and ilexes; the paths striking straight on either hand from the avenue through which he sauntered, and the walk that coiled itself through the depths of the plantations; all knew him, and from them and from the winter neglect which was upon the place distilled a subtle influence, a charm, an appeal belonging to that combination of artifice and nature which is perfect only in an Italian garden under an Italian sky.[28]

In this long, sustained single sentence Howells united his observation of grotto and statue, tall pine and winding alley, with the mood —his own—of the American pilgrim, who, faced with the decaying beauty of Europe, became poignantly aware of "shadowy regrets" for the wasted effort of a busy life.[29] Colville wondered, as did Howells, how to define the mood, and finally decided that one might well call it a "debauch" and have done with it. "He was right in the name which he mockingly gave the effect before he felt it," Howells commented; "it was a debauch, delicate, refined, of unserious pensiveness, a smiling melancholy, in which he walked emancipated from his harassing hopes, and keeping only his shadowy regrets." Neither Colville nor Howells cared "to scale the easy heights from which you have the magnificent view . . . of Florence"; "seeing himself unseen," Colville wandered about the edge of "that silent meadow" where "those large scarlet anemones" used to grow, and stooped to pluck one when he was sure he was unobserved. In a sense, Howells, in this last nostalgic novel based on his Italian experience, was plucking the late-blooming flowers of an earlier period. Though Howells took a special pleasure in writing it, J. W. Harper regretted that Howells had not written a "Boston novel" as an opening bow to *Harper's* readers. The critics, indeed, have never done justice to this, one of Howells' most beautiful novels, perhaps because they have failed to appreciate the fact that, in his hero, Colville, Howells was defining his own vision of Europe through the double exposure of youth and age. Colville, with Howells by his side,

haunted the studios a good deal, and through a retrospective affinity with art, and a human sympathy with the sacrifice which it always involves, he was on friendly terms with sculptors and painters who were not in every case so friendly with one another. More than once he saw the scars of old rivalries, and he might easily have been an adherent of two or three parties. But he tried to keep the freedom of the different camps without taking sides; and he felt the pathos of the case when they all told the same story of the disaster which the taste for bric-a-brac had wrought to the cause of art; how people who came abroad no longer gave orders for statues and pictures, but spent their money on curtains and carpets, old chests and chairs, and pots and pans. There were some among these artists whom he had known twenty years before in Florence, ardent and hopeful beginners; and now the backs of their gray or bald heads, as they talked to him with their faces toward their work, and a pencil or a pinch of clay held thoughtfully between their fingers, appealed to him as if he had remained young and prosperous, and they had gone forward to age and hard work. They were very quaint at times. They talked the American slang of the war days and of the days before the war; without a mastery of Italian, they often used the idioms of that tongue in their English speech. They were dim and vague about the country, with whose affairs they had kept up through the newspapers. Here and there one thought he was going home very soon; others had finally relinquished all thoughts of return. These had, perhaps without knowing it, lost the desire to come back; they cowered before the expensiveness of life in America, and doubted of a future with which, indeed, only the young can hopefully grapple. But in spite of their accumulated years, and the evil times on which they had fallen, Colville thought them mostly very happy men, leading simple and innocent lives in a world of the ideal, and rich in the inexhaustible beauty of the city, the sky, the air. They all, whether they were ever going back or not, were fervent Americans, and their ineffaceable nationality marked them, perhaps, all the more strongly for the patches of something alien that overlaid it in places. They knew that he was or had been a newspaper man; but if they secretly cherished the hope that he would bring them to the *dolce lume* of print, they never betrayed it; and the authorship of his letter about the American artists in Florence, which he printed in the *American Register* at Paris, was not traced to him for a whole week.[30]

Howells had, in fact, written in 1863–65 in the Boston *Advertiser,* of the work of Larkin Mead and of other artists; now, however, like Colville, he viewed the young artists of Florence with a benign but critical eye. When Howells wrote that Colville "was not in the frame of mind for the hotel table, and he went to lunch at a restaurant," Howells was thinking, no doubt, of the many occasions when he and Pennell, and other friends, had dined at a "simple *trattoria*" in the Via Guelphe to which Larkin Mead had introduced them. Here one met the artists who had studied under the American artist Frank Duveneck,[31] and had become known, according to Pennell, as "the Duveneck boys." The restaurant was not frequented by artists only, however; "In the end," Pennell wrote, "all Florence got to know that *trattoria,* and all sorts and conditions of men came: Howells, William Sharp, Stillman, I think James Bryce, and all the artists save Arthur Lemon, who said he would not go in once he had seen the outside." [32] Pennell spent several nights with Howells, but "one or two days and nights of the respectability of the Minerva Hotel, where the Howellses were staying was enough for me. I did not like and could not afford the Minerva, so Howells found me a lodging with a respectable Swiss lady." [33] We are not surprised, then, to read in *Indian Summer* that Colville was familiar with the same little restaurant. Like Pennell,

[Colville] was not in the frame of mind for the hotel table, and he went to lunch at a restaurant. He chose a simple trattoria, the first he came to, and he took his seat at one of the bare, rude tables, where the joint saucers for pepper and salt, and a small glass for toothpicks, with a much-scraped porcelain box for matches, expressed an uncorrupted Florentinity of custom. But when he gave his order in off-hand Italian, the waiter answered in the French which waiters get together for the

traveller's confusion in Italy, and he resigned himself to whatever chance of acquaintance might befall him. The place had
a companionable smell of stale tobacco, and the dim light
showed him on the walls of a space dropped a step or two
lower, at the end of the room, a variety of sketches and carica-
tures. A waiter was laying a large table in this space, and when
Colville came up to examine the drawings he jostled him, with
due apologies, in the haste of a man working against time for
masters who will brook no delay. He was hurrying still when
a party of young men came in and took their places at the
table, and began to rough him for his delay. Colville could
recognize several of them in the vigorous burlesques on the
walls, and as others dropped in the grotesque portraitures
made him feel as if he had seen them before. They all talked
at once, each man of his own interests, except when they joined
in a shout of mockery and welcome for some newcomer. Colville, at his *risotto,* almost the room's length away, could hear
what they thought, one and another, of Botticelli and Michelangelo; of old Piloty's things at Munich; of the dishes they had
served to them . . . of the overrated coloring of some of those
Venetian fellows . . . Then Colville heard one of them saying
that he would like a chance to paint some lady whose name
he did not catch, and "She looks awfully sarcastic," one of the
young fellows said.

"They say she *is,*" said another. "They say she's awfully intellectual."

"Boston?" queried a third.

"No, Kalamazoo. The center of culture is out there now."

"She knows how to dress, anyhow," said the first commen-
tator. "I wonder what Parker would talk to her about when
he was painting her. He's never read anything but Poe's 'Ullalume.' "

"Well, that's a good subject—'Ullalume.' "

"I suppose she's read it?"

"She's read 'most everything, they say."

"What's an Ullalume, anyway, Parker?"

One of the group sprang up from the table and drew on the
wall what he labelled "An Ullalume." Another rapidly depicted
Parker in the moment of sketching a young lady; her portrait
had got as far as the eyes and nose when some one protested:
"Oh, hello! No personalities."

The draughtsman said, "Well, all right!" and sat down again.[34]

Among the artists in the *trattoria* were "the Inglehart boys" (Pennell's "Duveneck boys"), those desperately modern young blades of 1883, and the young lady in question was Imogene Graham, the beautiful American girl with whom Colville found himself involved. But Colville's interest in the past, like Howells' own, saved him finally from false romance by making him appear to Imogene something of a bore:

> "How you always like to burrow into the past!" interrupted Imogene when Colville began to discant on the Etruscan remains in Fiesole, which they were about to visit. "Well, it's rather difficult to burrow into the future," returned Colville defensively. Accepting the challenge, he added: "Yes, I should really like to meet a few Etruscans in Fiesole this morning. I should feel as if I'd got amongst my contemporaries at last; they would understand me." The girl's face flushed, "Then no one else can understand you?" "Apparently not. I am the great American *incompris*."

Unless one realizes that Howells himself visited Fiesole with Pennell, walked around the Roman theater with him, and watched him sketch the Etruscan wall beyond, one is apt to wonder how Colville became so learned in antiquities as to escort the whole party (which included the Inglehart boys, who were found sketching on the piazza) around the Cathedral, the Museum, and, finally, to that point in the wall called the Belvedere, from which one could command the best view of the valley below. An essay by Howells on Fiesole had appeared in *Century* in October, 1885, three months before his chapter on the jaunt to the little Etruscan town, which is a sufficient explanation of Colville's knowledge. Howells' fine appreciation of art, architecture, and their relationship to both the past and the present, his own meditative contemplation of the picture-quality of the passing scene, entered into the spirit of Theodore Colville and effactually prevented him from succumbing to the false romantic in the form of the beautiful but ignorant Imogene. What Howells had himself come to understand he immediately transferred to the mind of his hero.

Howells' often lightly expressed but certainly profoundly felt belief in "civilization," in terms of people and the history of their creative expression, is the very basis of his belief in realism and his mistrust of the romantic. Howells himself is "the great American *incompris,*" unless the reader understands his sense of the relationship of the arts. Like Colville, Howells always remained essentially the well-informed amateur, who sought in his study of art a deeper understanding of human nature. Howells' analysis of Colville's ill-fated affair with Imogene Graham is an amusing example of Howells' sense of these subtle interrelations. Indeed, the beautiful girl's inability to summon up any interest in Etruscan art and archeology on a day's jaunt to Fiesole—as well as her total lack of humor—caused Colville to question the wisdom of his engagement. A "cold perspiration of question broke on Colville's forehead" when he perceived, for example, that Imogene did not smile with the others at the sight of the pair of lovers who wandered through the Museum so wrapped in their dream that they had no interest in the paintings around them. "Was that her ideal of what her own engagement should be?" he wondered. This disturbing question led eventually to Colville's realization that he could not love such an insensitive woman as Imogene. Howells' journey through Italy with "my friend the artist" had awakened him to a realization of the part played by art in the many-sided battle for realism. Like Colville, Howells was a student of the eternal present of past civilizations and thus a searcher for the real as opposed to the romantic.

In his opening pages of his essay on Florence for the *Century,* Howells confessed to the reader at once that he had gone to Florence with the express intention of writing about it and not as a totally innocent tourist. He confessed, further, that in the languor of the first cold December days in Florence, he was loath to enter the chilly churches and museums. At last he "crept" into Santa Maria Novella across the square from his hotel, "for a look at the Ghirlandajo frescoes behind the high altar, the Virgin of Cimabue, and the other objects which one is advised to see there, and had such modest satisfaction in them as may come to one who long ago, once for all, owned to himself that emotions to which others testified in the presence of such things were beyond him." [35] As a middle-aged traveler, Howells addressed himself, half-humorously, to the old masters whom he had come to know as a younger man. "The old masters and their humble acquaintance met shyly after so many years," he wrote in 1883, for "these were the only terms on which I, at least, could preserve my self-respect; and it was not till we had given ourselves time to overcome our mutual diffidence that the spirit in which their work was imagined stole into my heart and made me thoroughly glad of it again." After a few weeks of perfunctory visits to the churches and galleries he had known before, Pennell, armed with easel and drawing pad, joined Howells in the early spring, and the novelist's heart warmed to a sense of how the artist "sees" the picture, both in and out of museums.

As his approach to an understanding of Venice had been in the sixties, so Howells' approach to Florence in the eighties was, first of all, through history. But as soon as he "began to be serious about [his] material," whether it dealt with history or art, he "found it everywhere in the streets and the books, and located it from one to the other." For, "even if one has no literary design upon the fact" —and Howells always had such a design—"that is incomparably the best way of dealing with the past. At home, in the closet, one may read history, but one can realize it, as if it were something personally experienced, only on the spot where it was lived." Moreover, "in this pursuit of the past, the inquirer will often surprise himself in the possession of a genuine emotion," which makes one wonder whether one has not caught a "vanishing glimpse" of a fifteenth-century personage just turning the corner of the square, or passing one on the bridge. An advantage in making full use of this "imaginative faculty," Howells observed, was "that you have your historical personages in a sort of picturesque contemporaneity with one another and with yourself, and you imbue them all with the sensibilities of our own time." [36] History and art, thus viewed through the "imaginative faculty" of a novelist, became curiously "modern." Colville, like Howells, saw people, as well as places, through the double lens of the past.

"I have been turning over a good many books, and putting myself in rapport with Italy again," Howells wrote T. S. Perry, on March 13, 1883.[37] After studying the history of Florence in the comfort of his hotel, Howells "resolved to visit the Ponte Vecchio with no more delay, lest they should be going to tear it down that afternoon"—as the English visitors at his *table d'hôte* assured him they might! It was not that he "cared a great deal for the bridge itself, but [his] accumulating impressions of Florentine history had centered about it as the point where that history really began to be historic." Howells added, "I had formed the idea of a little dramatic opening for my sketches there." So firm a hold had the scene made on Howells' imagination that the bridge, with its horse-drawn omnibuses, its carriages, carts and foot-passengers, became the setting for the opening scene in *Indian Summer* that was shaping itself in Howells' mind during these months when he was turning his notes into essays for *Century*.

Mrs. Bowen's complaint in *Indian Summer* that she could find no "brief, historical sketch of Florence" that would save her the trouble of reading ten or twelve heavy volumes was an echo of Howells' own search for a "compendious" history of Florence before he began "A Florentine Mosaic." In 1901 Howells was asked to prepare a reading list on the art, literature, and history of Florence for the Booklovers' Reading Club. In the preface to *Florence in Art and Literature,* in which an outline of the course appeared, Howells was quoted as saying that, "there is nowhere, to my knowledge, so compendious a sketch of all Florentine history as in my book, *Tuscan Cities.* I tried in vain for such a sketch before I wrote it." [38] Apparently the Director of the course agreed that Howells' sketch was still the best book on the subject, for it was recommended as one of the essential textbooks. Colville, on his second visit to Florence, was able to supply Mrs. Bowen and other Americans with that "sense of its past" that actually served to clarify Colville's own attitude toward his romance with Imogene Graham. Howells, too, on his second visit to Florence, deepened his concept of these interrelationships as he reconsidered his views in the company of Joseph Pennell.

NOTES

1. Gilder first approached Howells on the subject of illustrated articles in a letter of Mar. 12, 1881, when he wrote, "Isn't there some ideal illustrated article you would like to write some time?" Houghton Library, Harvard. Five illustrated essays, "Tuscan Cities," appeared in *Century* between February and October, 1885. "Tuscan Cities" was first issued

in the October number of *Century,* as the general title of the last three essays. In a letter to Charles Dudley Warner, written from Siena on March 4, 1883, Howells spoke of writing on his "Tuscan Cities." *Life in Letters,* I, 337. The title was perhaps suggested by a chapter heading of James's *Transatlantic Sketches,* 1875.

2. *Italian Journeys* (1867) was reissued in 1901 with 94 illustrations by Joseph Pennell.

3. Letter, Houghton Library, Harvard.

4. Elizabeth Robins Pennell, *Life and Letters of Joseph Pennell* (1929), II, 82.

5. Howells called Siena "a most fascinating old town, and medieval to the marrow of its bones." Letter to Thomas S. Perry, Mar. 13, 1883. *Life in Letters,* I, 338.

6. It is probable that Howells did not go to Rome with Pennell. In a letter to Charles Dudley Warner, March 4, 1883, he wrote, "John is going to Rome with Pennell (who is to illustrate me) but the rest of us joyfully refrain." *Life in Letters,* I, 337.

7. *Life and Letters of Joseph Pennell,* II, 84–85.

8. In his essay, "Henry James, Jr." (*Century,* November, 1882), Howells contrasted the old-fashioned technique of Dickens and Thackeray with the modernity of James. For Howells' comment on the argument stirred by this essay among English critics, see *Life in Letters,* I, 336–338. Gilder, undismayed, wrote to Howells, June 8, 1883, "Have you still in mind the Dickens and Thackeray papers—and if so, when so?" Letter, Houghton Library, Harvard.

9. *Life and Letters of Joseph Pennell,* II, 85.

10. Howells drew a sketch of a hand with a pointed forefinger to accompany the last sentence. This letter is owned by C. Waller Barrett and has been quoted here with his permission. Howells' irritation is explained by the fact that Gilder wrote to him, on Feb. 24, 1883, "The Tuscan Cities idea is excellent; but I wish to explain about the *Art* side." At some length Gilder tried to persuade Howells that photographs of the "old masters" were to be used for illustrations. Letter, Houghton Library, Harvard.

11. "Panforte Di Siena," *Tuscan Cities* (1886), pp. 155–156.

12. *Ibid.*

13. "Pitiless Pisa," *Tuscan Cities,* pp. 203–204.

14. *Ibid.,* p. 208.

15. *Ibid.,* p. 216.

16. *Ibid.,* pp. 208–209.

17. "Panforte Di Siena," *Tuscan Cities,* p. 184.

18. "Pistoja, Prato, and Fiesole," *Tuscan Cities,* p. 241.

19. "A Florentine Mosaic," illustrated by over thirty sketches by Pennell, *Century,* February, April, and June, 1885.

20. "A Florentine Mosaic," *Tuscan Cities,* p. 4.

21. Howells to Charles Dudley Warner, Mar. 4, 1883. *Life in Letters,* I, 337.

22. Letter to Thomas S. Perry, March 13, 1883. *Life in Letters,* I, 338.

23. Letter to Charles Dudley Warner, Mar. 4, 1883. *Life in Letters,* I, 337. For a discussion of the time when Howells actually wrote *Tuscan Cities,* see Woodress, p. 179.

24. "Industrious Lucca," *Tuscan Cities,* p. 231.

25. William M. Gibson (ed.), *Indian Summer* (1951), p. 92.

26. "Panforte Di Siena," *Tuscan Cities,* p. 153.

27. See Howells' proposal for such a history in letter to Henry Mill Alden, editor of *Harper's,* Jan. 6, 1900. *Life in Letters,* II, 122–125. See Woodress, pp. 191–192.

28. *Indian Summer,* p. 185–186.

29. Colville's character foreshadows that of Strether in Henry James, *The Ambassadors* (1902). For an account of how a remark of Howells' became the "germ" of *The Ambassadors,* see F. O. Matthiessen and Kenneth B. Murdock (eds.), *The Notebooks of Henry James* (1961), pp. 372–374. See also James's letters to Howells, Aug. 10, 1901. Percy Lubbock (ed.), *The Letters of Henry James* (1920), I, 375–377.

30. *Indian Summer,* pp. 95–97.

31. Frank Duveneck (1848–1919), American painter, etcher, sculptor, and art teacher. He established an art school, first in Munich and later in Florence, returning permanently to this country in 1888. Among his pupils in Europe were John M. Alexander, William M. Chase, and John Twachtman.

32. Joseph Pennell, "Adventures of an Illustrator—with Howells in Italy," *Century,* CIX (May, 1922) 135–141. Cited by Woodress, footnote 44, p. 185. In footnotes 45–49, Woodress indicates other points of comparison between *Indian Summer* and *Tuscan Cities.*

33. *Ibid.,* p. 135.

34. *Indian Summer,* pp. 83–85.

35. "A Florentine Mosaic," *Tuscan Cities,* pp. 12–13.

36. *Ibid.,* pp. 17–18.

37. *Life in Letters,* I, 338.

38. Woodress, p. 181.

· 3 ·

Taste and Class
in Boston

When Howells returned from Europe in July, 1883, he found himself, like many another homecoming wanderer, "in a frenzy of house-hunting." [1] Before many weeks had passed, he wrote to Mark Twain, from 4 Louisburg Square, "We have taken this house for a year, and you can't come to see us in it any too soon." [2] The Howellses were already familiar with the sedate, tree-lined old square to which they had retreated from the remoteness of Belmont in January, 1882. Here at 16 Louisburg Square they had lived for a few months while Howells finished *A Modern Instance* [3] before their prolonged stay in Europe. In Boston once more Howells brooded—as he had when he first journeyed to Boston in 1860—on the relation between the houses in which people live and the kind of civilization they represent.

Two novels written at this time, *The Rise of Silas Lapham* (1885) and *The Minister's Charge* (1887), which reflect Howells' serious thought on the meaning of classes in America, also show his meditations on architecture, neighborhoods, city parks, factories, tenements, and offices—as well as taste in wallpaper, woodwork, paintings, and dress. Howells' recent sojourn in England and Italy had sensitized him to the language of art, architecture, and taste, down to the smallest item of domestic decoration, and had provided him with a means of measuring the culture of Boston itself.

The Minister's Charge, the story of a country boy adrift in the parks and streets of Boston, was conceived and written at 4 Louisburg Square. *The Rise of Silas Lapham,* also concerned with the impact of the city on a man of simpler culture from the country, was written after Howells moved, in the summer of 1884, to his new home at 302 Beacon Street. Though the story of young Lemuel Barker appeared two years after that of Silas Lapham, these novels were in Howells' mind simultaneously, and both were closely bound up with his move from the rented house on Louisburg Square to the home he purchased on Beacon Street.[4]

Howells' letter to his father written from the new home on August 10, 1884,[5] suggests that Lemuel Barker was not far from his thoughts as Howells wrote of his efforts "to put the house in order" during a hot, lonely summer in Boston. "There is not only nobody else in the house," he complained, "but nobody else I know sleeps in town. Altogether the effect is queer. There are miles of empty houses all round me. And how unequally things are divided in this world. While these beautiful, airy, wholesome houses are uninhabited, thousands upon thousands of poor creatures are stifling in wretched barracks in the city here, whole families in one room. I wonder that men are so patient with society as they are."

The conversation between the elder Corey and Miss Kingsbury at the famous dinner party in *The Rise of Silas Lapham* repeated Howells' thoughts in almost the same words, thoughts this time expressed by a guest at the dinner, concerning "the beautiful, airy, wholesome houses that stand empty the whole summer long, while their owners are away in their lowly cots beside the sea!" Miss Kingsbury replied to the implied criticism of homeowners "with quick earnestness, while her eyes grew moist"; Bromfield Corey, however, like Howells himself, was "serious about this matter." His rather bitter speech, ending with a whimsical lightness, reflected the feeling of his author: "I spend summers in town, and I occupy my own house, so that I can speak impartially and intelligently; and I tell you that in some of my walks on the Hill and down on the Back Bay, nothing but the surveillance of the local policeman prevents my offering personal violence to those long rows of close-shuttered, handsome, brutally insensible houses. If I were a poor man, with a sick child pining in some garret or cellar at the North End, I should break into one of them, and camp out on the grand piano."

Like Corey, Howells was saddened by the sight of poverty and deprivation that he could not but observe in his solitary walks on Boston Common and in the sloping streets behind the State House; again, like Corey, Howells enjoyed the satisfaction of associating with the cultivated men and women of Boston, who lived in just such houses and did not throw them open to the poor during the sweltering summer months. Through the elder Corey, Howells expressed the feelings of a generous-minded man, aware of the plight of the poor, who nevertheless consciously enjoyed the ripe fruits of civilization.

Like Silas Lapham, however, Howells was an outsider who himself had faced the problem of winning his way into an established society. As George Parsons Lathrop had observed in "Literary and Social Boston," [6] "The social world [of Boston] divides itself into a number of air-tight compartments." Merit, birth—and wealth—all counted; but in what proportion? Nobody could say, for few outsiders, even the more gifted, were ever invited to the dinner parties of the old Bostonians. However, Lathrop remarked cheerfully, "What Boston, pure and simple, lacks socially, it makes up in clubs."

Apparently Howells had come to the same conclusion concerning Boston society. If one joined a club, and if one were willing to spend lavishly, then—at least that is what the elder Corey concluded after a sympathetic conversation with his son Tom on the subject of the Laphams' social ineptitude. Tom laughingly remarked, "To tell you the truth, sir, I don't think they have the most elemental ideas of society, as we understand it. I don't believe Mrs. Lapham ever gave a dinner." Bromfield Corey, with disarming kindness, replied: "Well, then, they must spend. There is no other way for them to win their way to general regard. We must have the Colonel elected to the Ten O'clock Club, and he must put himself down in the list of those willing to entertain. Anyone can manage a large supper. Yes, I see a gleam of hope for him in that direction."

Something of the atmosphere of the sophisticated groups in which Howells—and the Coreys—moved may be caught by a glance at the clubs to which Howells belonged after his return from Europe. Club life was by no means new to Howells. Very soon after Howells' first appearance in Boston, in 1866, as James T. Field's assistant on the *Atlantic,* fourteen congenial friends had formed a dining and conversing group, known merely as "The Club." [7] Many of the members of this group also belonged to the Saturday Club, founded in 1856, which Howells was invited to join in 1874.[8] It is interesting that, in the early eighties, Howells was active in a number of clubs and that he was critically considering their value at the moment when he was participating in their sociability. The two novels on which he was working at this time, *The Rise of Silas Lapham* (1885) and *The Minister's Charge* (1887), were peopled with the men and women with whom Howells was associating; they also carried serious indictments of Boston snobbery, which sometimes lapsed into social injustice. Both novels, though written in Boston, were first serialized in New York magazines.[9]

In an article entitled "Literary Life in Boston," written for the May, 1887, issue of the *Brooklyn Magazine,*[10] William H. Rideing described the clubs of Boston, supplying information on the Tavern Club, with which Howells' name was particularly associated. Rideing described himself as "a working literary man," long a resident of New York, who had arrived in Boston to continue his profession. The social and intellectual life of his adopted city, he confessed, at first appeared to him "narrow and stagnant," but after a year's study of clubs of the old city, he concluded that they, like the twisted streets and alleys of the town, opened up new vistas to a "foreigner" from New York, who was without "condescension."

After describing in some detail the Saturday Club, the Thursday Evening Club, and the Round Table [11]—all from the point of view of "a New York Bohemian of the better sort engaged in something more serious and less ephemeral than journalism"—our guide turned to the Tavern Club.[12] This flourishing club, which had recently moved into new quarters, had begun five or six years earlier in

"a questionable little restaurant in the shadow of the Providence depot" when an Italian cook changed "the old regime of cracked
crockery and soggy cookery" to "a table d'hôte dinner at six, at
which gathered artists, musicians, and a few authors, to the exclusion
of the old customers, with their carpet-bags and railway appetites."
Here, where the company was as good as the food, Howells frequently dined. Members were glad to bring with them notables in
art and literature, for the long, low, candle-lit dining room was
cheerful and the talk varied and gay. Though the Tavern Club had
among its members more painters and musicians than authors,
Rideing classed it among the "literary clubs" of Boston "since its
president is Mr. Howells and one of its distinguished features is its
hospitality to literary men." But Antonio, the cook, began to quarrel with his customers, distinguished though they were. The Club
was forced to seek a new domicile, over a grocer's shop and under
a painter's studio, on Park Square. "This is the true history of the
Tavern Club," Rideing concluded; it had "prospered much under
the presidency of Mr. Howells, and taken its place as an active agent
among the literary agents of the city."

The "little restaurant" to which Rideing referred was the Carrolton Hotel, and the "painter's studio" was that of Frederic P. Vinton, 1 Park Square, formerly the studio of William Morris Hunt,
who had moved into Boston from Newport.[13] Mrs. Vinton had urged
the members of the club to give up the small, bare rooms of the
Carrolton Hotel and to make use of her husband's studio, and here
the club prospered and grew until, in April, 1887, the members were
able to buy a house of their own on Boylston Place.[14] "In behalf
of the gentlemen of the Club," Howells wrote to Mrs. Vinton to
thank her for her "graceful hospitality" and to beg her to accept
"the accompanying pieces of silver" as a token of their gratitude.
With manners worthy of Boston's best, this "Bohemian of the better
sort" wrote his hostess that "without the generous and unfailing
welcome which [the members] have found in the Vinton Studio,
and which they gratefully ascribe to your inexhaustible patience, no
festivity of the Club could have been complete, and with it each has
been an increasing success."

A group of wider social pretension with which Rideing associated
Howells' name, was St. Botolph, "the leading intellectual club" of

Boston. Here "art and music go hand in hand" and here, amid clouds of smoke intermingled with "the strains of classical music, one can loll in an arm-chair before one of the big open fireplaces and watch the tangled flames of the soft coal fire flickering over the glazed surface of the frame of tiles." If conversation was desired, in this un-Bohemian Boston Paradise, one could join a group of men "whose opinions have the authority of special research and extensive knowledge," said Rideing, who had perhaps himself strolled among these Augustan clubmen.

> Perhaps the subject of the conversation is the propriety of the use of *rétroussage* in etching; perhaps a difficult operation in surgery; perhaps thought-transference; perhaps realism in the art of fiction, or it may be a new symphony by Brahms.

Whatever the members were discussing, whether literature, science, music, the lost Atlantis, or industrial education, the writer assured readers that the conversation "flows along with scholarly fluency." Once a month these distinguished gentlemen unbent to the extent of serving dinner in the spacious art gallery of the club, down the center of which ran "a long table loaded with supper and pitchers of beer and bowls of punch." Rideing undoubtedly attended one of these dinners, for even the paintings on the wall returned to his mind through a blue haze as he wrote: "Pictures with their messages from nature make the barest room luxurious, but they are never seen to greater advantage than through the soft blue incense that breathes upward at the suppers of St. Botolph."

The Papyrus Club, to which Howells also belonged, considered its object, like that of the Tavern Club and St. Botolph, to be "to promote good fellowship and literary and artistic taste among its members." A "unique feature of the club," the passing of a silver "loving cup" between the end of dinner and the opening of the "literary exercises," gave special "individuality" to the club in Rideing's eyes. So much emphasis, indeed, was placed on the after-dinner punch that the reporter from New York was forced to "withdraw the statement that there is no Bohemia in Boston." But the Papyrus Club was not to be considered "really Bacchanalian, though it likes to think of itself as being 'most potent in potting.'" The list of members, which included the names of W. D. Howells, G. P. Lathrop, T. W. Higginson, Barrett Wendell, George Ticknor, and many others known to *Atlantic* readers of the day, was a guarantee of sobriety and respectability; if any lingering doubts remained, a description of "ladies' night" at the club should have dispelled them:

> Once a year ladies are invited to the dinner, and all other guests are excluded. Then instead of cigarettes after the sherbet, there are flowers and music, and before each plate there is a souvenir of the club—perhaps a little etching, a tile, a picture of the loving cup, or a mummy case covered with hieroglyphics, and holding within it not the sear relic of ancient Egypt, but a rose or a violet, fresh and moist from an American garden.

Mention of the ladies reminded Rideing of the "Old Corner Book Store," where one met "authoresses" as well as authors strolling in and out. Rideing listed Mrs. James T. Fields, Sara Orne Jewett, Nora Perry, and many more in this literary center where bluestockings were appreciated. If one questioned the "literary supremacy" of Boston, one had only to spend an afternoon at the Athenaeum, or step out on the Common, where "almost any fine day 'the autocrat' himself may be met," or James Russell Lowell "daring the east wind" in a thin overcoat. On the same day one might encounter Thomas Bailey Aldrich "coming down from the office of *The Atlantic Monthly*" or "Mr. Howells as likely as not in Beacon Street, where he has a little house, or in the Public Gardens."

The "little house" at 302 Beacon Street to which Howells moved soon after his return from Europe had already been described by various writers in special articles for both the Boston and the New York papers. Those who were following the experiences of Silas Lapham as they were unfolded in the *Century* between November, 1884, and August, 1885, were quite aware of the fact that Silas' move from Nankeen Square to Beacon Street paralleled that of Howells from Louisburg Square to the more fashionable "New Lands" overlooking the Charles River. What sort of home did Howells live in? Was it the same as the mansion built by Colonel Lap-

Conventional home or back boy vs. elaborate ornate, of littlehouse purpose

ham? How was it furnished? And what did the architecture of the house and the interior decoration reveal about taste and class in relation to Howells as well as to his well-known character, Silas Lapham?

In his article, "W. D. Howells, His Career and His Home," [15] George Parsons Lathrop presented to readers of the New York *Tribune* a description of the various homes in which he had visited Howells since the assistant editor of the *Atlantic* had first appeared in Boston. Lathrop perceived at once that the Beacon Street house was not, in fact, the mansion described in *Silas Lapham*. It was, he wrote, "entirely a conventional residence; what might be called 'a carpenter's box,' adorned with woodwork moulded in forms adapted to ordinary display." Since Lathrop had known Howells ten years earlier when he had built his second home in Cambridge (at 37 Concord Avenue), he suggested that "the interest which Silas Lapham . . . devoted to his unfinished dwelling may have been a reminiscence of that time." Lathrop remembered, too, that in the early seventies, Howells was "wont to speak of the social and intellectual atmosphere about Boston, with a sort of shiver, as 'cold, cold.' "

Perhaps to avoid the chill of Boston society, both for himself and his growing family, Howells moved, in 1878, wrote Lathrop, to his hilltop home in Belmont, only to find it too remote from the office of the *Atlantic Monthly* on Tremont Street and to the pleasant interchange of sociability of the Saturday Club meetings in the Parker House on the next corner. Whatever his motive, on his return from Europe in 1883, Howells "laid his course straight for the heart of Boston," settling for a year on Louisburg Square before moving to his comfortable, three-story, red-brick home on Beacon Street, a few doors from the similar dwelling of Oliver Wendell Holmes.

Howells continued to live in this modest, vine-covered home after he became a member of the staff of *Harper's* in March, 1886. On a "warm day before noon" in August of that year, a reporter from the Boston *Globe* arrived to discover, if he could, whether Howells' home was similar to that of Lapham's.[16] He found Howells wearing "a sack suit and waistcoat of Japanese silk a little darker than the usual pongee shade, a dark blue silk tie and dark trousers." After a "cordial" greeting, the reporter began:

"You must have rebuilt Silas Lapham's house and moved in."

"Ah, you see if I hadn't already lived here I couldn't have built Lapham's house in the first place," he replied. "Yes, on this spot before it burned down was the home of a happy family, who suffered none of the blights that fell upon poor Silas."

"Oh," I said, looking about, "how could you burn up such a home as this, even on paper?"

"I didn't," said Mr. Howells with a laugh. "I only burned an unfinished house before the family had moved in or any home been really formed."

These somewhat teasing remarks to the reporter from the *Globe* suggest that, as usual, Howells had, in writing *The Rise of Silas Lapham,* fused his earlier experience in house-building in Cambridge with his later search for a home on the water-side of Beacon Street. Further, he had constructed, in his mind, the former unfinished mansion, which had burned before the row of brick dwellings had been erected, and made it Silas Lapham's dream, as he explained to the representative of the *Globe.*

The reporter's simple description of the interior of the actual house caught the very atmosphere of the free, pleasant, and "modern" taste of the Howells family, which was in marked contrast to the taste of his imagined family:

The front door opens into a large, square hall, with wide oaken staircase extending above. Here everything looks inviting. Rugs are upon the floor, a hall table, on which is a small tray filled with visitors' cards, stands near the door, and a mirror hangs above. In front is a reception-room, prettily and comfortably furnished, the prevailing color red, which harmonized well with the oak furnishings and woodwork. Beyond and across the hall is the dining-room, which looks out on Mr. Howells' flower garden. The woodwork of this room is also of oak. Engravings hang upon the walls, and, altogether, it presented a cheerful picture, heightened by the shining light on decanters, wine glasses and silver on a massive oak sideboard. Mr. Howells is quite as hospitable as his surroundings indicate. There is very little of a bookish appearance about the house. Its appointments suggest the home of a wealthy banker or merchant, rather than that of a literary man.

Over the reception room is a parlor the full width of the house; no antique furniture or attempt to carry out a distinctive period in furnishing, only a comfortable, perhaps more, a luxurious home; carpets of a light color, with bright figures, and handsome upholstered furniture.

The staircase winds through the centre of the house, leaving much hall space. At the back of the house on the second floor is Mr. Howells' study. Here Mr. Howells does his writing. It is the room in which "The Lady of the Aroostook," "Penelope" [*sic*], "Silas Lapham" and other delightful creations were brought into being. The room is large and square, filled with light from a large window; all around are books and papers, several engravings and etchings hang upon the walls, but no paintings. Authors seldom care for color pictures. In the centre of the room is a large writing-table with green baize top, littered with pens, papers, pen wipers, stationery, and all the odds and ends of a real work-table. A leather-cushioned arm-chair is before the table.

The window looks out upon the bright shining waters of Charles River, while beyond, Charlestown, Cambridge and the tops of many of the Harvard College buildings, church spires and smoking chimneys of factories fill in the background. It is, in fact, the view from Silas Lapham's new house "on the water side of Beacon Street" as Howells described it. There is a large garden in the rear of the house, with a gate opening on the water's edge. It is filled with many old-fashioned flowers, sweet peas, hollyhocks, gilly flowers, four o'clocks, a sunflower and "marigolds all in a row." Here I found the novelist.

After they had returned to the house and mounted to his study on the second floor back, Howells observed to the reporter:

"I like best to sit here by myself and write in my own way. I enjoy writing, here especially," he said, after a pause; "it seems just the place. I like the water; it is restful. I was very fond of Venice; perhaps my life there made me so fond of a watery view. At night, when the lights twinkle all along the river front, one can quite imagine one's self in Venice, except for the massive buildings and palaces at the water's edge. The boats splash

along, and sometimes parties of Harvard students row by singing to the accompaniment of a guitar or mandolin played by
one of their number. The river gives much that is varied. In the
winter there is skating, and in front of the house sleighs fly by
at a furious speed sometimes. One has plenty of amusement
watching them."

Mr. Howells took me back to the window and pointed out
many places of interest to be seen on the other side of the river
—the towns of Somerville, Belmont, Arlington, and even as far
as Lexington. Bunker Hill Monument stood out boldly against
the sky, forming part of the picture. "I am fond of those tall,
smoking chimneys of the factories," he said, "they look like
bustle, civilization and life. They are not near enough to be in
any way objectionable. At night they are like so many giant
torches."

Though the unidentified reporter for the *Globe* considered "the
Howells residence" merely as "one of a block," William Henry
Bishop, writing for the New York *Critic* the following November,[17]
described the house and the street in more elegant terms. One could
not help wondering, he wrote, "how it is that all about you is in so
much better taste than in New York, so much handsomer, neater,
more home-like and engaging than our fast-becoming-shabby Fifth
Avenue." Bishop, a friend of Howells' and a contributor to the *Atlantic Monthly,* no doubt expressed Howells' own view when he
said, "Beacon Street is a stately street . . . The eye traverses a
long fret-work of good architectural design, and there is no feature
to jar upon the feeling of quiet elegance and respectability. The
houses seem like those of people in some prosperous foreign towns,
like newer Liverpool, Düsseldorf or Louvain. The comfortable hori-
zontal line prevails. There are green front doors, and red; and brass
knockers." The "fictitious Lapham" built his mansion in this same
quarter, Bishop pointed out, and some might have thought it identical with Howells' so feelingly did the author describe the building
of Lapham's new home. "But Howells' abode does not savor of the
architect, nor the mansion. It is a builder's house, though even the
builder, in Boston, does not rid himself of the general tradition of
comfort and solidity." Howells' study "is almost as modern in effect
as Silas Lapham's famous warehouse of mineral paints. . . . [H]e

is intensely concerned with the present and the future," as the "strong light from the windows" suggests.

Bishop, himself a New York art critic, did not hesitate to link Howells' taste in furniture and pictures to his "new" method of writing. Casting an observant eye about the rooms, Bishop reported to his New York readers:

> We find in his house no amount of blue china or Chippendale, no trace of the bric-a-brac collector's enthusiasm . . . In his parlor we find tables and chairs, perfectly proper and comfortable, and drawing no attention to themselves. On the wall there are some few specimens of old paintings, from Florence, a pleasing photograph or two, an original water-color by Fortuny,[18] which has a little history, and an engraving after Alma Tadema, presented by the painter to the author. These are a concession to the fine arts, and not an overmastering by them; and it seems proper to connect this indication with the strong moral purpose of his books, his resolute refusal to postpone the essential and earnest in conduct to the soft and decorative, and his proposing, at times, as the overworldly will have it, of ideals that seem impracticable and almost fantastic.

The stages by which Lapham [19] was persuaded by the architect—whom he unwillingly engaged—to alter his idea of a comfortable home was closely connected with his moral confusion. The architect told Lapham that he did not want a house with a brownstone front, four stories high, and finished within in black walnut but that he surely preferred something more akin to "those pretty old-fashioned country houses" of the early nineteenth century, with white woodwork throughout and trimmed "with a little gold here and there." Of course, he should have white marble chimney pieces, "treated in the Empire style." Understanding nothing of the architect's concept but dimly apprehending that there was a connection between architecture and social status, Lapham agreed to all that was proposed. His total lack of taste, apparent to all with whom he dealt, involved him in a house costing, not $26,000, but $100,000 —an involvement that finally led him beyond his depth, morally and psychologically. With an expenditure of suffering, not only by Silas himself, but also on the part of his wife and daughters, Lapham at last "rose" to his better self, shook off his tormentors, and retired to the comfortable Vermont farmhouse where he was born and where he should have remained.

The "strong moral purpose" of Howells' novel was apparent, especially to Bostonians of the eighties, who were sensitively responsive to the message of architecture and art. While Silas sipped his wines in a haze at the Bromfield Corey's dinner table, the other guests followed with understanding the discussion carried on between the host and the architect of the Lapham mansion. "With all your modern fuss about it," the elder Corey challenged the architect to prove to the company that the house he was building for Colonel Lapham was superior in any way to the one in which they were then dining.

"Ah," said the architect, "nobody can do better than well. Your house is in perfect taste; you know I've always admired it; and I don't think it is at all the worse for being old-fashioned. What we've done is largely to go back of the hideous style that raged after they forgot how to make this sort of house. But I think we may claim a better feeling for structure. We use better material, and more wisely; and by and by we shall work out something more characteristic and original."

"With your chocolates and olives, and your clutter of bric-a-brac?"

"All that's bad, of course, but I don't mean that . . ."

And so the conversation progressed—to family portraits, to the poor of Boston, to the latest novel—leaving Lapham in deeper and deeper darkness through which he broke at last only by means of drunken assertiveness. Penelope, the clever daughter, would have been able to converse with these Boston aristocrats, for Penelope had been reading the books from the public library near Nankeen Square. But Penelope had refused to come to the dinner party, knowing too well that her poor family could not cope with aristocratic Bostonians.[20] Penelope preferred to receive her lover, the young Tom Corey, in the Lapham drawing room in Nankeen Square, for she wished him to know her family as they really were. The colors of the room first struck the gazes—the colors that Lapham so admired that he had hoped to have them repeated in the new mansion on Beacon Street:

> The trim of the doors and windows was in light green and the panels in salmon; the walls were a plain tint of French grey paper, divided by gilt mouldings into broad panels with a wide strip of red velvet paper running up the corners; the chandelier was of massive imitation bronze; the mirror over the mantel rested on a fringed mantel-cover of green reps, and heavy curtains of that stuff hung from gilt lambrequin frames at the window; the carpet was of a small pattern in crude green, which, at the time Mrs. Lapham bought it, covered half the new floors in Boston.[21]

Though *The Rise of Silas Lapham* appeared as a book in 1885, the story was set in the year 1875. Howells was conscious of the bright and clashing colors of American "parlors" of that decade— even those of Boston—and, as editor of the *Atlantic,* had attempted to improve the level of "art in the home." [22] Paintings— really good ones—should be hung, he felt, against the subdued colors stressed by the Pre-Raphaelites and the early Impressionists. These tones were to be preferred to salmon and green interiors and anomalous bric-a-brac. "Never were our houses better arranged for pictures," the anonymous writer of the August, 1878, "Contributors' Club" reminded the reader, "and never have people been less inclined to purchase them."

> The subdued colors of the Morris paper-hangings, the rich, dark tints of curtains and upholstered furniture, are admirably fitted to set off the colors of oil-paintings, provided there is any light in which to show them; and our somber parlors and libraries actually demand the relief of the gold frame as well as the brass sconce.

"Fine heads" and "figure-painting" are all very well, but Howells felt one should not overlook "the good landscape," which "is like an open window, giving upon a beautiful country scene." Such a painting has "atmosphere and distance" and actually gives length and breadth to a room. "When the *bric-à-brac* fever has spent itself, it will be succeeded by a return to the purchase of good painting, and we know better how to buy them than we did ten years ago." [23]

The *Atlantic Monthly* was certainly not read by any member of the Lapham family. Howells' enumeration of the objects of "art" in their drawing room was an eloquent comment on the total confusion in the minds of the elder Laphams, a confusion that extended beyond a mere question of "art" to include religion and politics as well.

In the paneled spaces on the walls were some stone-colored landscapes representing the mountains and cañons of the West that the Colonel and his wife had visited on one of the early official railroad excursions. In front of the long windows looking into the Square were statues, kneeling figures that turned their backs upon the company withindoors and represented allegories of Faith and Prayer to people without. A white marble group of several figures, expressing an Italian conception of Lincoln freeing the Slaves—a Latin Negro and his wife, with the American Eagle flapping his wings in approval at Lincoln's feet—occupied one corner and balanced the whatnot of an earlier period in another corner.

Neither Penelope nor Tom remarked on the room in which they found themselves after the disastrous dinner party. Instead, they sat stiffly before the soft glow of the coal fire and wordlessly declared their mutual affection. The taste of the absent parents, however, played a paramount part in their relationship, for "taste," in this subtle novel of social distinctions, meant "civilization" with both the good and bad implications of that word.

When, at last, some adjustment in values had been made between the Laphams (new America) and the Coreys (old Boston), and the young people were safely married, it became clear that Tom and Penelope must find their happiness far from Boston. Fortunately, the paint business decided the matter, and they set out for Mexico to begin their married life. As the carriage door closed on the couple, Penelope sighed and observed, "I don't think I shall feel strange amongst the Mexicans now." Tom looked at her with a puzzled smile as she hastily explained, "I only meant that I should have you all to myself." Here Howells paused to make one of his rare direct comments as an author. "There is no proof that she meant more," he mused, "but it is certain that our manners and customs go for more in life than our qualities. The price that we pay for civilization is the fine yet impassable differentiation of these. Perhaps we pay too much; but it will not be possible to persuade those who have the difference in their favor that this is so."

That Howells should have returned to Boston in 1883, purchased a red-brick, vine-covered home on Beacon Street, renewed his contacts with the rich and varied club life of the old city, of which he had been a part for many years before his stay in Europe, and then that in 1888 he should have turned his back on the world of the Coreys and the Bellinghams and transferred his home to New York, does, indeed, invite consideration. The reporters who questioned him—and with whom he freely talked—might have found the answers in his two novels, *The Rise of Silas Lapham* and *The Minister's Charge*. The story of Lemuel Barker of Willouby Pastures and of his effort to find a place in the intricacies, not only of Boston streets, but also of Boston society, is essentially concerned with a similar intermingling of old and new values in American civilization. How Howells gathered his materials for this less amusing, more naturalistic novel, the reporters could not understand. As William H. Rideing said of Howells in *The Brooklyn Magazine* in referring to *The Minister's Charge,*

> he has always been so shy and reticent a person in this city, which he has localized in his stories by a process of permanent photography, that it would be interesting to learn how he ever reached the intimate knowledge of police stations and common lodging-houses shown in the adventures of Lemuel Barker.

Like all writers, Howells took hints and suggestions from a glance out of his front window, from a walk in the Public Gardens, from a conversation at the Tavern Club. Especially through contemplation of Boston taste in buildings and drawing-rooms, he read the secret of Boston culture and of those who formed it.

NOTES

1. Letter to John Hay, July 30, 1883. *Life in Letters,* I, 350.
2. Letter to S. L. Clemens, Aug. 12, 1883. *Life in Letters,* I, 352.
3. "I am working away all the time at the story now running in the Century." Howells to Clemens, Jan. 31, 1882. *Life in Letters,* I, 307.

4. See Mildred Howells, Foreword to *The Rise of Silas Lapham* (1937). George Santayana lived here as a boy, between the age of eight and seventeen (1872–1881). The house is described by him in *Persons and Places* (1944), Chap. IX, "No. 302 Beacon Street," pp. 140–147.

5. *Life in Letters,* I, 363–364.

6. George Parsons Lathrop, "Literary and Social Boston," *Harper's,* LXII (February, 1881), 380–398.

7. "Presently Perry and a group of congenial friends formed a dinner and conversation club, which through the nearly sixty years of its existence was known merely as The Club. It started with fourteen members—Henry and William James, William Dean Howells, Arthur G. Sedgwick (who held a position on the editorial staff of the New York *Evening Post* and of the *Nation* in later years); two law partners, John Codman Ropes and John Chipman Gray; Charles Grinnell and William E. Perkins, also Boston lawyers; Henry Adams, Oliver Wendell Holmes, Jr., John Fiske, John T. Morse, Jr., John R. Dennett, and Thomas S. Perry. Very soon others were invited to join—Wendell Phillips Walley, Charles Hale (a nephew of Edward Everett Hale's, and himself a Massachusetts state senator), Moorfield Storey, and two members of the medical profession, Dr. John Collins Warren and Dr. John Homans, Jr. During its later years The Club included Henry Lee Higginson, Alexander Agassiz, Edward Hooper, James Ford Rhodes, George A. P. Duncan (later Lord Camperdown), William Sturgis Bigelow, Raphael Pumpelly, and Bliss Perry. At first the meetings were held on the second Tuesday of each month, but the date was later changed to the first Friday, and Perry, among other members, seldom missed a meeting unless he was out of Boston." Virginia Harlow, *Thomas Sergeant Perry* (1950), p. 46. See also Robert Grant, "William Dean Howells." In M. A. De Wolfe Howe (ed.), *Later Years of the Saturday Club,* 1870–1920 (1927), pp. 69–77.

8. Edward W. Forbes and John H. Finley, Jr. (eds.), *The Saturday Club: A Century Completed* (1958). See the chart of members pasted inside the back cover. See Edward Waldo Emerson, *The Early Years of the Saturday Club* (1918), p. 406, for a description of the visit of Holmes and Howells to the Saturday Club in 1860.

9. *The Rise of Silas Lapham, Century,* XXIX–XXX (November to August, 1884–1885). *The Minister's Charge, Century,* XXXI–XXXIII (February to December, 1886).

10. Vol. IV. The magazine later changed its name to *The American Magazine.*

11. See also Lathrop, "Literary and Social Boston," *op. cit.*

12. See also Justine McCarthy, *Reminiscences* (1899), two volumes, I, 208–209. Appendix III of this book. Here the author describes a dinner at the Tavern Club to which Howells invited him on September 21, 1886. Howells wrote, in his invitation, "The Tavern Club is made up of all the best and nicest young lawyers, doctors, artists, and *litterateurs* here, and we have entertained Lowell, Salvini, Irving, and others, at the simple dinners which our Italian artist makes for us."

13. Apr. 21, 1887. *Life in Letters,* I, 391.

14. In 1906 Howells responded to a request for his picture to be hung in The Tavern Club. He enclosed the following verse:

> Tavern! where long ago I once was host,
> Let me come back again and be your Guest.
> And while I share the joy of Song and Toast,
> Still keep the silence that I shine in best.

Life in Letters, II, 220.

15. New York *Tribune,* Nov. 8, 1885.

16. Aug. 23, 1886.

17. *Critic,* Nov. 27, 1886, pp. 259–261. The *Critic* was a weekly, edited by J. L. and J. B. Gilder. The article, "Mr. Howells in Beacon Street, Boston," was No. XXII of a series entitled "Authors at Home."

18. Presented to Howells by Clarence King in London in 1883. *Memoirs of Clarence King,* pp. 144–145.

19. Chapter III, *The Rise of Silas Lapham* (1885).

20. *Ibid.,* Chapter XIV.

21. *Ibid.,* p. 223.

22. For a sense of "Popular Art," see the article by Mary E. Neally in *The Ladies' Repository,* XXXV (December, 1876) 549–552.

23. *Atlantic Monthly,* XLII (August, 1878), 248.

· 4 ·

The Artist and the
Novelist in New York

In February, 1888, Howells finally decided to give up his Boston home and, like Basil March, to risk "A Hazard of New Fortunes" [1] in "the huge, noisy, ugly, kindly" metropolis, New York.

Two months after establishing his family in a "flat" at 46 West Ninth Street, Howells wrote to Thomas S. Perry, his friend and colleague on the *Atlantic,* that he was still "trying to catch on to the bigger life of the place." He added, "It's immensely interesting, but I don't know whether I shall manage it; I'm now fifty-one, you know. There are lots of interesting young painting and writing fellows, and the place is lordly free, with foreign touches of all kinds all thro' its abounding Americanism: Boston seems of another planet." [2]

Howells' hero, Basil March, was also lured from the quiet security of the South End of Boston [3] to the wider opportunities offered by the new illustrated magazines of New York. Like Howells, Basil mistrusted his ability to "catch on" to the interesting new world of "painting and writing fellows." When Fulkerson, the agent for *Every Other Week,* first casually mentioned to Basil that the maga- zine was to be enhanced by illustrations, Basil exclaimed, "Going to have illustrations?" Fulkerson replied with the knowing air of a New York journalist, "My dear boy! What are you giving me? Do I look like the sort of lunatic who would start a thing in the twilight of the nineteenth century *without* illustrations? *Come* off!" Basil's reply—"Ah, that complicates it! I don't know anything about art" [4] —by no means discouraged Fulkerson, for he saw that Basil, though hesitant, was eager to try the "bigger life" of New York.

Basil March was only a faint shadow of Howells himself; the very next paragraph in Howells' letter to Perry reminds the reader of the deeper concerns of Howells who, a few months earlier, had written his famous letter to the New York *Tribune* [5] in defense of the Chicago anarchists. "I am enclosing my letter about the An- archists," he wrote Perry, "which I wrote just before their civic murder. I came to that mind about it through reading their trial, in which they proved themselves absolutely guiltless of the murder charged against them . . . They died with unsurpassable cour- age." In publicly defending the anarchists, Howells had, for the time at least, impaired his own literary standing. As he remarked to Perry, "some of the papers abused me as heartily as if I had been a dynamiter."

But Howells' sense of social injustice extended far beyond the particular case of the Chicago anarchists and caused him, for the first time in his life, seriously to question the entire political struc- ture of his former beliefs. "I care little for either party," he con- fessed to Perry. "Sometimes I think that if there were a labor party, embodying any practical ideas I would vote with it; but there's none." Basil, on the other hand, was troubled with no social or political ideas; they were forced upon him, however, during his first year in New York.

Several months after writing to Perry, Howells took two floors in an old house at 330 East Seventeenth Street, overlooking Stuy- vesant Square—the very apartment to which Basil transported his family when he moved them to New York. Howells wrote to Henry James,[6] then in London, of his change of address and remarked that his daughter had joined a "life class in New York." He added that "at the bottom of our wicked hearts we all like New York," and, further, that he hoped to "get some of its vast, gay, shapeless life into [his] fiction."

New York certainly seemed "vast, gay, shapeless" to Howells at that time; it also seemed to him profoundly unjust and dishearteningly illogical, as he observed in this same letter to James:

> I'm not in a very good humor with "America" myself. It seems to be the most grotesquely illogical thing under the sun; and I suppose I love it less because it won't let me love it more. I should hardly like to trust pen and ink with all the audacity of my social ideas; but after fifty years of optimistic content with "civilization" and its ability to come out all right in the end, I now abhor it, and feel that it is coming out all wrong in the end, unless it bases itself anew on a real equality. Meantime [added Howells ruefully], I wear a fur-lined overcoat, and live in all the luxury my money can buy.

Just as Howells in *The Rise of Silas Lapham* expressed his sense of the inequalities in American society by reference to the details of personal taste in drawing rooms, public buildings, and city streets, so, in *A Hazard of New Fortunes,* Howells expressed his essential concept of "civilization." The scene of this most ambitious of Howells' novels, he reflected some years later, filled the "largest canvas I had yet allowed myself . . . It became, to my thinking, the most vital of my fictions, through my quickened interest in the life about me, at a moment of great psychological import." [7] This stirring social novel opened, however, with an amusing account of apartment-hunting in New York, for by his half-humorously conceived examination of the false fronts, the disreputable, the exorbitantly expensive, and the vulgarly ornate apartments available, Howells found his characteristic way of commenting upon the social chaos behind the inequalities of American society.

The Marches' endeavor to rent a furnished flat with steam heat and an elevator at eight hundred a year constitutes the first of the five parts of *A Hazard of New Fortunes.* The final decision to settle for the "Xenophon"—a decision made by Basil after Isabel's departure for Boston in despair—was forced upon Basil by the circumstances of life in New York, where all was pretentious, bustling, crowded, and makeshift. The very entrance to the Xenophon, with its "heavily spiked, aesthetic-hinged black door," its "large, fat Buttons," who kept the Marches waiting in "the dimly splendid, copper-colored interior," while he summoned the superintendent, filled these super-refined Bostonians with misgivings. When the superintendent lit the gas jet in the narrow hall of Mrs. Grosvenor Green's apartment, "they faltered abashed at the threshold" as they glanced into the drawing room and at "the succession of chambers stretching rearward to the kitchen." In this confined area, where everything had been done by the architect to economize on space and everything had been done by Mrs. Green to waste it, portières hung from large rings on brass rods at every door. As the bewildered Marches made their way from room to room they perceived that

> every shelf and dressing-case and mantel was littered with gimcracks, and the corners of the tiny rooms were curtained off, and behind these portières swarmed more gimcracks. The front of the upright piano had what March called a short-skirted portière on it, and the top was covered with vases, with dragon candlesticks and with Jap fans, which also expanded themselves bat-wise on the walls between the etchings and the watercolors. The floors were covered with filling, and then rugs and then skins; the easy-chairs all had tidies, Armenian and Turkish and Persian; the lounges and sofas had embroidered cushions hidden under tidies. The radiator was concealed by a Jap screen, and over the top of this some Arab scarfs were flung. There was a superabundance of clocks. China pugs guarded the hearth; a brass sunflower smiled from the top of either andiron, and a brass peacock spread its tail before them inside a high filigree fender; on one side was a coal-hod in *repoussé* brass, and on the other a wrought-iron wood-basket. Some red Japanese bird-kites were stuck about in the necks of spelter vases, a crimson Jap umbrella hung open beneath the chandelier, and each globe had a shade of yellow silk.[8]

Because of all this grandeur, Mrs. Green was asking two hundred and fifty *a month* for her apartment. After another weary day of seeking for a reasonably comfortable flat within their means, Basil

—against the explicit directions of his wife—accepted Mrs. Green's reduced rental and summoned the family from Boston. When callers began to show themselves in the Marches' drawing room, Mrs. March "disclaimed all responsibility for the upholstery and decoration," laughingly explaining that it was "Mr. March's fancy" that made them take such an apartment. She soon noticed, however, that "nobody really seemed to think it otherwise than pretty; and this again was a triumph for Mrs. March, because it showed how inferior the New York taste was to the Boston taste in such matters." [9] "Gimcrackery," to New Yorkers, was good taste; Boston knew better, because, indeed, Boston was morally and intellectually superior to sprawling and vulgar New York—at least according to the standards of the Marches.

The zigzag route of the coupé in which the Marches drove through the streets of New York in search of a home, took them past East-side tenements as well as by brownstone mansions; these they attempted at first to think of as "picturesque," with something of the atmosphere of Florence or Naples. They wondered why artists did not come to paint these crowded thoroughfares instead of going abroad in quest of the quaint. Suddenly, however, Isabel pulled up the window of the coupé to shut out the summer odors. "Why does he take us through such a disgusting street?" she demanded. Basil replied that perhaps the driver was "a philanthropist in disguise" and wished them to see where the poor were doomed to live, winter and summer, "with no hope of driving out of it, except in a hearse." [10]

Basil's ensuing monologue on the subject of the hazard of life for the poor moved Isabel to suggest that he save his remarks for an essay in *Every Other Week,* for, Isabel reminded him in her wifely way, "We've no time to waste" on unprofitable moralizing. When they returned to their hotel room in the evening, however, Basil reverted to the question of flats and tenements and their effect on the people who inhabited them. "I've been thinking about that home business ever since my sensibilities were dragged—in a coupé —through that tenement-house street," he remarked; and he launched forth on an analysis of "the pretense of social life" in New York as exemplified by the flat, which meant merely "society life."

"It's made," he said, "to give artificial people a society basis on a little money—too much money, of course, for what they get."

> So the cost of the building is put into marble halls and idiotic decoration of all kinds. I don't object to the conveniences, but none of these flats has a living room. They have drawing-rooms to foster social pretense, and they have dining-rooms and bedrooms; but they have no room where the family can all come together and feel the sweetness of being a family.[11]

The bedrooms were merely "black-holes," with a foolish waste of space at that. Marble halls, vulgar decorations, and expensive finish did not make a home. "Why, those tenements are better and humaner than those flats!" he exclaimed, for at least in a tenement the whole family lived in the kitchen. A flat was not a home "not because it's humble, but because it's false."

But for all the noise and squalor, for all the disparity between rich and poor, Basil wondered whether there was more misery in New York than in the rest of the country. New Yorkers were so gay that "the outward aspect of the place and the hilarity of the sky and the air must get into the people's blood." Moreover, "the weather is simply unapproachable." Though the city "shrieks and yells with ugliness . . . it never loses its spirit." After a year in the great city, one could no doubt be "as gay—as gay as an L road." "Yes, gay is the word," Isabel admitted with a sigh, "but frantic. I can't get used to it." Basil proposed a trip "on the Elevated road as far as it would carry them into the country" to shake off the burden of househunting.[12]

To Howells, as well as to Basil, such an excursion was "better than the theatre, of which it reminded him to see those people through their windows" [13]—a mother sewing by a lamp, a tired workman with his head in his hands, two lovers leaning over a window sill. Howells' delight in "those bends in the L that you get in the corner of Washington Square, or just below the Cooper Institute" [14] was a precursor to the paintings by John Sloan of elevated trains in downtown New York. Basil and Isabel paused a moment on the bridge over the railroad tracks at Forty-second Street and found themselves caught up in the romantic beauty of New

York at night. Much as a painter of the new school might have responded to the scene, Basil shared with his wife "a moment of rich silence" as he gazed in wonder at

> the track that found and lost itself a thousand times in the flare and tremor of the innumerable lights; the moony sheen of the electrics mixing with the reddish points and blots of gas far and near; the architectural shapes of houses and churches and towers, rescued by the obscurity from all that was ignoble in them, and the coming and going of the trains marking the stations with vivider or fainter plumes of flame-shot steam.

The scene formed for Basil "an incomparable perspective," a "superb spectacle, which in a city full of painters nightly works its unrecorded miracles." [15] Basil, who professed to know nothing about art, responded more vividly to the changing effects, both somber and gay, that played over the streets of New York night and day than did "the painting fellows" with whom he and Fulkerson had to deal in their efforts to produce a "chic" illustrated magazine, *Every Other Week*.

Angus Beaton, artist, sculptor, architect, writer, was prevailed upon by Fulkerson to support "the art leg" of the magazine—the only drawback to the arrangement, according to the manager, being that Beaton was "as many kinds of an ass as he was kinds of an artist." [16] Living upon the allowance sent him by his old tombstone-cutter father in Syracuse, Beaton nevertheless could not resist purchasing rugs, brocades and Japanese bric-a-brac, and strewing them about his studio. For Beaton, like Mrs. Grosvenor Green, belonged to the "gimcrack" civilization of "artistic" New York. A glance into his studio in Greenwich Village displayed

> a gray wall quandrangularly vaulted to a large north light; casts of feet, hands, faces hung to nails about; prints, sketches in oil and watercolor stuck here and there lower down; a rickety table, with paint and palettes and bottles of varnish and siccative tossed comfortably on it; an easel, with a strip of some faded mediæval silk trailing from it; a lay figure simpering in incomplete nakedness, with its head on one side, and a stocking on one leg, and a Japanese dress dropped before

it; dusty rugs and skins kicking over the varnished floor; canvases faced to the mop-board; an open trunk overflowing with costumes.[17]

Beaton's zeal for his canvas was temporarily forgotten when he was first introduced to the reader, for he was at the moment engaged in modeling the bust of Judas with nervous impatience, since he had not yet finished his "art-letter" for Fulkerson. Beaton, with his pointed black beard and his long curly bangs, was, in fact, superficially talented in many fields but serious in none—a product of the spurious concept of art that had no relation to the complex civilization sensed by Basil on his exploration of New York. Significantly, though Beaton was employing Berthold Lindau as his model for his sculptured head of Judas, he was completely unaware of the personality of the fine old German scholar who quietly posed for him. Through talking with Lindau, on the other hand, Basil came into closer contact with the real life of the cruel but beautiful city where "the fierce struggle for survival" was to be studied on every street corner.

When Basil finally decided to seek out his former German teacher whom he had known in Ohio, he made his way to Chatham Square and walked about the neighborhood "with a sense of the neglected opportunities of painters in that locality." Again he thought of street scenes in Europe:

He said to himself that if one of those fellows were to see in Naples that turmoil of cars, trucks, and teams of every sort, intershot with foot-passengers going and coming to and from the crowded pavements, under the web of the railroad tracks overhead, and amid the spectacular approach of the streets that open into the square, he would have it down in his sketch-book at once.[18]

Perhaps remembering his trip through Italy with illustrator Joseph Pennell, Howells, speaking through Basil, "decided simultaneously that his own local studies must be illustrated, and that he must come with the artist and show him just what bits to do, not knowing that the two arts can never approach the same material from the same point."

Beaton, the eternal poseur, was not the artist to illustrate Basil's sketches of New York for he was romantically charming only and had no insight into the kind of "realism" that Basil was beginning to grasp. However, when the first number of *Every Other Week* appeared, Basil was forced to confess that the artistic result achieved by Beaton's clever hand "was better than the literary result," by the test of popular appeal; he foresaw that "the number would be sold and praised chiefly for its pictures." [19] As Basil observed to Beaton about his illustrations, "You've got to doing them so prettily that you take our eyes off the literature, if you don't take our minds off." [20]

But if Beaton's form of art was distractingly decorative, so also was Basil's writing shadowed by "a prevailing literary quality" from which he struggled to escape. Too many of his social-artistic concepts he had borrowed from Ruskin, and these he regarded "with amusement as the chimeras of a rhetorician run away with by his phrases." [21] While Beaton was dabbling in all the arts—and at the same time falling in love with three different women, one of them Alma Leighton, herself an artist [22]—Basil was training himself to observe more directly by taking solitary walks through Greenwich Village to the waterfront. "He liked the streets of small brick houses, with here and there one painted red and the mortar lines picked out in white, and with now and then a fine wooden portal of fluted pillars and a bowed transom." Not infrequently the "rear of the tenement-houses showed him the picturesqueness of clotheslines fluttering far aloft," just as they appeared to John Sloan who came to live in the same neighborhood a few years later. Basil enjoyed catching glimpses of "the eyes and earrings of Italians" as they twinkled "in and out of the alleyways and basements" in the streets where "long ranks of trucks" were drawn up by the curbstones.

"March liked the swarthy, strange visages," as did the painter Robert Henri. Another member of the Ashcan school of painting, Henri was just then breaking away from the ranks of magazine illustrators and establishing himself as the founder of a new generation of artists attracted by the vivid life of New York streets. March himself, intent on making a similar "escape into reality," was an unconscious precursor of the naturalistic painters. For Basil did not linger in the tree-lined streets of the Village near Fifth Avenue, but "found his way among the ash-barrels and the groups of decently dressed church-goers, to the docks." "Some of the streets," he discovered,

> were filthier than others; there was at least a choice: there were boxes and barrels of kitchen offal on all the sidewalks, but not everywhere manure-heaps, and in some places the stench was mixed with the more savory smell of cooking. One Sunday morning, before the winter was quite gone, the sight of the frozen refuse melting in heaps, and particularly the loathsome edges of the rotting ice near the gutters, with the strata of waste-paper and straw litter, and egg-shells and orange-peel, potato-skins and cigar-stumps, made him unhappy.

Basil glanced at "the squalor of the neighboring houses" and observed whimsically to his son, who happened to be with him this Sunday morning, "It's curious, isn't it, how fond the poor people are of these unpleasant thoroughfares? You always find them living in the worst streets." Tom replied sententiously, "The burden of all the wrong in the world comes on the poor. Every sort of fraud and swindling hurts them the worst. The city wastes the money it's paid to clean the streets with, and the poor have to suffer, for they can't afford to pay twice, like the rich." His father paused and looked at his son, "Hallo, Tom! Is that your wisdom?" "It's what Mr. Lindau says," answered the boy stubbornly.[23]

Lindau—whom Beaton had used so casually as a model for the head of Judas, the betrayer—was the noble old Socialist, the prophet, indeed, who taught not only Basil March but also his son Tom to look with more understanding on the chaotic street scenes so near the quiet retirement of Stuyvesant Square. As the "literary leg" of *Every Other Week,* Basil learned to use his eyes with the honesty of a Stephen Crane or a Theodore Dreiser. Knowing nothing about art at the outset, he soon became aware of the limitations of the "artistic," as represented by Beaton. Shrieking elevated trains, swarming tenement children, towering office buildings, and filthy streets—all the confusion and grandeur of New York, Basil saw with the eyes of an artist as well as a writer, and understood the import of what he saw. Thus he was prepared to meet the crisis of the strike into which he and his whole staff were finally drawn. Beaton, on the other hand, never glanced beneath the surface; as a result, caught by his own selfishness and confusion, he failed to comprehend the issues of the struggle.

Though Basil had everything to learn about the relation of artists and writers when he left his insurance business in Boston and risked his fortune in New York, Howells himself had known and worked with artists, architects, and sculptors for many years and understood something of the meaning of the common quest of all creative people. At the time when he transferred his family to Stuyvesant Square, his old friends, the Gilders, had themselves moved to 13 East Eighth Street, a few blocks from the Howellses' new home. Here the talk with writers, architects, painters, editors was resumed for Howells—if, indeed, it had ever lapsed. To the men and women gathered in the Gilders' parlors, the civic as well as the artistic future of the burgeoning city seemed limitless. The new wing of the Metropolitan Art Gallery had just been opened in 1888; the Washington Memorial Arch in Washington Square was erected at the time of the Centennial in 1889; John La Farge, whose studio was at 51 West Tenth Street, was painting his immense altar piece [24] in the Church of the Ascension at the corner of Fifth Avenue and Tenth Street, and Augustus Saint-Gaudens [25] was working on the bust of Sherman, later to be used as the model for the statue of the general erected at the Fifth Avenue entrance to Central Park. Before his return to the city, Howells had known many of the men associated with the remarkable growth of New York and had shared in their discussions.

Saint-Gaudens, in fact, talked over his figure of Sherman with Howells, who frequently visited him in his New York Studio in Twentieth Street. On one occasion, Saint-Gaudens explained that the model for Victory, to be placed before the mounted general, was a young Southern girl; characteristically, Howells urged the sculptor to make the figure more like the actual girl and less like an allegorical cypher. "I own I did not like the introduction of the ideal in that group," Howells wrote Homer Saint-Gaudens, the sculptor's son, when in 1908 he was assembling reminiscences of his father.[26] Howells' memory of friendly meetings with Augustus Saint-Gaudens included a small dinner party in 1890:

> My first meeting with your father I do not remember, but I recall with great interest and distinct pleasure a dinner with him and two painters at Miss Lazarus' in 1890. Though he could talk so wisely and charmingly, he was willing to let the painters talk, for they talked mighty well, but he interceded with them for my share of the say, which I also could have been so willing to leave altogether to them. "Now you be still. I want to hear Mr. Howells." What more was needed to make me love him?

A reflection of at least a portion of Howells' "share of the say" is to be found in the "Editor's Study" of July, 1888,[27] in which Howells commented on Matthew Arnold's remarks on the lack of "distinction" in American civilization. Arnold's "censure" in his *American Discourses,* Howells pointed out, was not so much that Americans had no literature and no art, as that neither one reflected anything strictly American. But Arnold, said Howells, was speaking "without the documents," for the native American tone had been heard

> more and more in our fiction and no one can look at Mr. St. Gaudens's head of Sherman in the Academy and fail to see how possible the like achievement is in sculpture—at least to a St. Gaudens. It has no distinction, in Mr. Arnold's sense, no more distinction than he would have found in the great soldier's actual presence, but it seems to express the grandeur of a whole people, a free people, friendly, easy, frank, and very valiant.

In his *Reminiscences,* Saint-Gaudens connected Howells' sympathetic understanding of his bust of Sherman with his own desire to make the medallion of Howells and his daughter in 1897.

> At this time Mr. William Dean Howells had been kind enough to speak in pleasant terms of the bust of Sherman which I had adapted to the statue. So in appreciation of that, as well as the deep admiration I had for his achievement, his delightful per-

sonality, I begged that he allow me to make his portrait and that of his daughter, Miss Mildred Howells.

Howells, of course, consented, and the medallion, which Miss Howells considers the best portrait ever made of her father,[28] was completed during a "tropical summer" in the stifling heat of the studio of Saint-Gaudens at 148 West Thirty-sixth Street. "He was perpetually entertaining us with stories and reminiscences," Howells wrote to his son in 1908. Moreover, he added, to watch an artist at work was reward enough for the labor of posing—to notice that a sculptor, like a novelist, was searching for "the fact" and trying to keep his own likeness out of the portrait. The heat of the small studio did not prevent Howells from being thoroughly interested in the process:

> It was most interesting to watch the working of his mind as well as his hand. He changed the position of one of my arms, but changed it back, thoughtfully, almost ruefully. Like all artists he had a difficulty in keeping his own portrait out. He especially kept giving my daughter's profile his noble leonine nose. He could not see that he did this, but when he was convinced of it, he forced himself to the absolute fact, and the likeness remained perfect.[29]

Saint-Gaudens also remembered his indecision about this medallion, concerning which he and Howells must have exchanged sympathetic comment. Ten years later Saint-Gaudens studied "the low relief," which was bought by the French government and hung in the Luxembourg Museum in Paris, and remarked,

> To show how uncertain we are, or I am about our judgment of the work that is at hand, I will explain that when I made this medallion I felt very happy about his portrait and unhappy about that of Miss Mildred. Now, ten years later, I see that the reverse would be the proper state of mind.[30]

Though, as his son pointed out, Saint-Gaudens lacked theories of art, he was intensely interested in modern art and enjoyed conversing with fellow artists, such as Howells, who were experimenting in new forms.

Through the "literary hospitality" of editors such as Gilder, Howells grew into an understanding of the relationship of his own writing to that of artists who were often his illustrators. Convivial, sympathetic, intuitively understanding, Howells grasped what the artists had to offer him as a writer; in return, he freely contributed his comments to the evolving work of such artists as Augustus Saint-Gaudens, whom he knew and enjoyed as friends, as well as fellow artists. The "lordly free" atmosphere of New York swept Howells along in its current and finally played its part in his decision to move permanently, in 1891, to the new bustling center of writers, artists, and publishers.

Howells' plunge into the more complex social scene of New York, at the age of fifty-two, enabled him to produce the most impressive novel of his long career, *A Hazard of New Fortunes*. Essentially a social novel dealing with streetcar strikes and trade unions, it is, in a deeper sense, concerned with the meaning of civilization itself, especially that of America in the 1890's. Closely tied to questions of "the rich" and "the poor" and how they lived, were a wide range of questions having to do with taste that accosted Basil as soon as he undertook the editorship of *Every Other Week*. Living in a "gimcrackery flat," reflecting a "gimcrackery" culture, Basil found relief in wandering through the crowded streets of lower New York tenement districts. The "huge disorder," and, at the same time, the violent "play of energies" in these picturesque scenes, made Basil marvel at "the neglected opportunities of painters" who refused to open their eyes to the life about them. Facing the problems involved with finding the proper "artist fellows" to work with the "writing fellows" of an illustrated magazine, Basil was forced to become aware of the dangers of the merely decorative illustrator.

On one occasion, as Basil paused near Chatham Square to buy a ballad from a street vendor, he observed a woman, "pushed along by two policemen on a handcart, with a gelatinous tremor over the paving and a gelatinous jouncing at the curbstones. She lay with her face to the sky, sending up an inarticulate lamentation," while laughing children trooped after her as she was wheeled away by the indifferent officers. "Even the young fellow and young girl exchanging playful blows in a robust flirtation at the corner of a liquor store suspended their scuffle with a pleased interest as she passed." Such scenes suggest the naturalistic writers Hamlin Garland, Stephen Crane and Theodore Dreiser, as well as the painters of the Ashcan school, such as John Sloan and Robert Henri.

Small wonder that Howells wrote to T. S. Perry after several months in New York in 1888, "Boston seems of another planet."

NOTES

1. First printed in *Harper's Weekly,* Mar. 23 to Nov. 16, 1889. References are to the book edition, published Jan. 27, 1890.
2. Apr. 14, 1888. *Life in Letters,* I, 413.
3. Like Silas Lapham, Basil March lived on Nankeen Square, i.e., Louisburg Square.
4. Van Wyck Brooks (ed.), *A Hazard of New Fortunes* (1960), p. 7.
5. Nov. 6, 1887.
6. Oct. 10, 1888. *Life in Letters,* I, 417.
7. "Bibliographical," Library edition, 1911, pp. v–vi.
8. *A Hazard,* pp. 37–38. Compare Howells' comment on taste and fashion in *Criticism and Fiction and Other Essays by W. D. Howells* (1959), pp. 10, 53. See also *Harper's Weekly,* XXIX (July 6, 1895), "Life and Letters," p. 628. Here Howells lamented to a friend who called on him in his shrouded apartment the agonies of putting away the furniture for the summer. The friend recommended that "hired houses, such as we live in, shall all be furnished houses, and that the landlord shall own every stick in them, and every appliance down to the last spoon and ultimate towel." *Ibid.* (July 13, 1895), p. 653.

   The conversation continued. Howells' friend said, "At each remove we drag a lengthening chain of tables, chairs, sideboards, portraits, landscapes, bedstands, washstands, stoves, kitchen utensils, and bric-a-brac after us, because, as my wife says, we cannot bear to part with them. At several times in our own lives we have accumulated stuff enough to furnish two or three houses, and have paid a pretty stiff rent in the form of storage for the overflow. Why, I am doing that very thing now! Aren't you?"

   "I am—in a certain degree!" Howells assented. The friend took him up.

   "We all are, we well-to-do people, as we think ourselves." He recommended the Standard Household Effect Company.

   "But," Howells asked, "wouldn't our household belongings lose a good deal of character if they didn't belong to us? Wouldn't our domestic interiors become dreadfully impersonal?"

   The friend continued, "How many houses now have character, personality? Most people let the different dealers choose for them, as it is. Why not let the Standard Household Effect Company, and finally the State? . . . In most interiors the appointments are without fitness, taste, or sense; they are the mere accretions of accident in the greater number of cases; where they are the result of design they are worse. I see what you mean by character and personality in them. You mean the sort of madness that let itself loose a few years ago in what was called household art, and has since gone to make the junk-shops hideous . . . [every woman] was supposed suddenly to have acquired a talent for decoration and a gift for the selection and arrangement of furniture, and each began to stamp herself upon our interiors. One painted a high-shouldered stone bottle with a stork, and stood it at the right corner of the mantel, on a scarf; another gilded the bottle and stood it at the left corner, and tied the scarf through its handle. One knotted a ribbon around the arm of a chair; another knotted it around the leg. In a day, an hour, a moment, the chairs suddenly became angular, cushionless, springless; and the sofas were stood across corners, or parallel with the fireplace, in slants expressive of the personality of the presiding genius. The walls became all frieze and dado; and instead of the simple and dignified ugliness of the impersonal period, our interiors abandoned themselves to a hysterical chaos full of character. Some people had their doors painted black, and the daughter or mother of the house then decorated them with morning-glories. I saw such a door in a house I looked at the other day, thinking I might hire it. The sight of that black door and its morning-glories made me wish to turn aside and live with the cattle, as Walt Whitman says. No, the less we try to put personality and character into our household effects the more beautiful and interesting they will be. . . . The company's [Standard Household Effect Company] agents will begin by convincing her [the lady of the house] that she does not need half the things she has lumbered up her house with, and that every useless thing is an ugly thing, even in the region of pure aesthetics. I once asked an Italian painter if he did not think a certain nobly imagined drawing-room was fine, and he said, 'Si. Ma troppa roba.' There were too many rugs, tables, chairs, sofas, pictures, vases, statues, chandeliers . . ."

"That might be all very well, as far as furniture and carpets and curtains are concerned," Howells agreed, "but surely you wouldn't apply it to pictures and objects of art?"

"I would apply it to them first of all and above all," rejoined his friend. "Among all the people who buy and own such things there is not one in a thousand who has any real taste or feeling for them, and the objects they choose are generally such as can only deprave and degrade them further. The pictures, statues, and vases supplied by the Standard Household Effect Company would be selected by agents with a real sense of art, and a knowledge of it. When the house-letting and house-furnishing finally passed into the hands of the State, these things would be lent from the public galleries, or from immense municipal stores for the purpose."

"And I suppose you would have ancestral portraits supplied along with the other pictures?" Howells sneered.

"Ancestral portraits, of course," replied his friend, unruffled.

"So few people have ancestors of their own, that they will be very glad to have ancestral portraits chosen for them out of the collections of the Company or the State. . . ."

Howells lamely suggested that individuality might be lost in the process.

"My dear friend . . . do you mean to say there is any individuality in such things now?"

9. *A Hazard*, pp. 81–82.

10. *Ibid.*, p. 51.

11. *Ibid.*, p. 53.

12. *Ibid.*, p. 49.

13. *Ibid.*, p. 61.

14. *Ibid.*, p. 49.

15. *Ibid.*, p. 61.

16. *Ibid.*, p. 84.

17. *Ibid.*, p. 99.

18. *Ibid.*, p. 156.

19. *Ibid.*, p. 165.

20. *Ibid.*, p. 117.

21. *Ibid.*, p. 164.

22. Alma Leighton studied at the Art Students' League. See John C. van Dyke, "Art Student League of New York," *Harper's Monthly*, LXXXIII (October, 1891), 688–698.

23. *A Hazard*, pp. 255–256.

24. This painting was begun in 1886 and completed in 1888.

25. Augustus Saint-Gaudens wrote to Howells on Dec. 30, 1886, inviting him to join an informal club of professional men. Letter, Houghton Library, Harvard.

26. Homer Saint-Gaudens, *The Reminiscences of Saint-Gaudens* (1908), p. 13.

27. *Harper's Monthly*, LXXVII, 314–318.

28. *Life in Letters*, II, 78.

29. *Reminiscences of Saint-Gaudens*, I, 216.

30. *Ibid.*, pp. 77–78.

PART

THREE

· 1 ·

Criticism and Fiction—
and Art

Both critics and teachers tend to support "the vested interests of criticism," Howells declared from the "Editor's Study" of *Harper's* in December, 1887, soon after he entered that sanctum. Association with artists, sculptors, and architects, as well as with writers and journalists, had taught Howells that "the seeds of death are planted" in those who, like Angus Beaton, in *A Hazard of New Fortunes,* do not trust to their own observation; "they can produce only the stillborn, the academic." Critics and teachers, unfortunately, encourage the artists, and the writers as well, "to compare what they see and what they read, not with things that they have observed and known, but with the things that some other artist or writer has done." So strongly had Howells come to feel the importance of a direct relationship with the life "known to us all" that he made this "Editor's Study" the second section of *Criticism and Fiction* (1891) and basic to all that followed.

The sixth edition of *Venetian Life,* in which Howells had described what he had seen "by the light of the piazza," rather than by the instruction of the guidebooks, was issued in 1891, the same year in which *Criticism and Fiction,* addressing itself more directly to writers and critics, upheld the superiority of all creators to that "lowly caterpillar," the critic. "Sometimes it has seemed to me that the crudest expression of any creative art is better than the finest comment upon it," [1] wrote Howells, who, in his own work identified himself with all creative spirits.

Thirty years earlier Howells had wandered about the canals and piazzas, the churches and art galleries of Venice, guidebook in hand, and discovered that "the true standard of the arts is in every man's power." [2] As a novelist, Howells never tired of observing the usual things of life and sharing his sense of "the romance of the real" with a widening circle of readers. To convince ordinary people that "an easy observation of the most common, sometimes of the meanest things, in nature will give the truest lights" was the effort of Howells as an editor of *Harper's.* Though Howells frequently grew impatient with "the great mass of readers, now sunk in the foolish joys of mere fable" and freely admitted that readers stubbornly refused "to be lifted to an interest in the meaning of things through the faithful portrayal of life in fiction," he did not lose his faith in the ultimate good sense and good taste of the average reader, if not misled by the "false lights of critics and scholars." In his appreciation of fellow artists in other fields, Howells recognized a similarity of aim among artists, sculptors, painters, and illustrators.

Indeed, in the opening "Study" of January, 1886,[3] the new editor devoted several columns to a consideration of "the illustrated books with which the season loads the editor's table and the bookseller's counter." Howells' complaint was that the year's crop was so disappointingly similar to the harvest of former years. How do these volumes differ from the sumptuous holiday books of 1875 or 1865, he asked. He singled out for commendation an illustrated edition of the poetry of Holmes and another by Whittier; he admired a travel book, "Sketching Rambles in Holland," by G. H. Boughton, profusely illustrated by the author and E. A. Abbey— "they draw the meaning as well as the form of things." He playfully referred to "Mr. Howells' *Tuscan Cities"* by saying, "Mr. Pennell has done some of his best work, which is always gay, bright, honest, and expressive of the joy of doing," and he especially praised Howard Pyle's "quaint children's book, *Pepper and Salt."* Most of the other illustrated books were of the older tradition, Howells remarked, but Pyle "has gone to the useful Japanese for some hints in his amusing pictures, and in the test with which he has blended them, he has employed his own invention and that of the legend with equal charm." The relating of illustration to text, the subtle interplay of artist and writer, is what gives authenticity to the handsome holiday book. "Another year," Howells wrote in conclusion, "we would gladly see something still more authentic in the association of art with literature—something distinctive in our holiday books, as our illustrated magazines are distinctive and pertinent to our date and life." [4]

The "unreal editor" of the "Study," Howells announced, spent his days in an equally "unreal" study, the appointments of which were expressive of "cultivated pursuits." The real editor, however, could be sitting in a cloud of cigar smoke among piles of neglected manuscripts in "a narrow den at the top of the house," he wrote, while the imagined editor was "an airy, elusive abstraction" and was quite "fittingly circumstanced."

> Heavy rugs silence the foot upon his floor; nothing but the costliest masterpieces gleam from his walls; the best of the old literatures, in a subtly chorded harmony of bindings, make music to the eye from his shelves, and the freshest of the new load his richly carved mahogany table.

Moreover, the editor's "vast windows of flawless plate" looked out upon

> the confluent waters of the Hudson and the Charles, with expanses, in the middle distance, of the Mississippi, the Great Lakes, and the Golden Gate, and in the background the misty line of the Thames, with reaches of the remoter Seine, and glints of the Tiber's yellow tide.

As a "last secret," the editor admitted that the edifice of the publishing house with which he was associated was "an American architect's adaption of a design by the poet Ariosto." The building, he explained, "was originally in the Spanish taste, but the architect has added some touches of the new Renaissance and has done what he could to impart a colonial flavor to the whole." Amid these grand surroundings, the editor proposed to conduct "a sort of free parliament, but for the presiding officer only; or a symposium of one." Armed with a healthy supply of "prejudices and grudges," as well as "some opinions, honest as opinions go," the editor invited the reader to accept or reject the editor's views.[5]

That Howells' interest in the artists he had known in his Boston days carried over to his New York venture is suggested by a brief reference made by Edward Everett Hale in a letter to his wife of May 28, 1887. Having encountered Howells by chance in the Albany depot, Hale had breakfasted with him; afterwards, wrote Hale, "I showed him the way to the Hunt pictures and left him." [6] Howells had not forgotten the much-discussed frescoes that William Morris Hunt had painted a decade earlier on the dome of the state capitol in Albany, and he seized this opportunity to study them.

The help to literary criticism that the artists and writers together might render seemed a not impossible hope to the new encumbent of the "Study" at that time when painters such as Winslow Homer, John La Farge, Childe Hassam, Kenyon Cox, W. M. Chase, E. A. Abbey, John Singer Sargent, William Glackens, Joseph Pennell, John Sloan, and many others, assumed, as part of their roles as artists, the illustrations of the books of eminent writers.[7] Howells' faith in "the joint arts" was expressed characteristically in his review of *Old Songs,* which was illustrated by E. A. Abbey and Alfred Parsons. "It seemed to us," he wrote from the "Study," "that these illustrations were sometimes the last effect that the joint arts which produced them could ever give in that way." [8] In reviewing an edition of *She Stoops to Conquer* also illustrated by Abbey, Henry James paused to comment in similar terms on the happy combination of text and picture:

A charming story-teller indeed he would be who should write as Mr. Abbey draws. However, what is style for one art is style for another, so blessed is the fraternity that binds them together, and the worker in words may take a lesson from the picture-maker of "She Stoops to Conquer." It is true that what the verbal artist would like to do would be to find out the secret of the pictorial, to drink at the same fountain.[9]

Neither artist nor writer felt at this time that his art was belittled by the happy union of the two, for both "drank of the same fountain." It scarcely occurred to a critic of that day to suggest, for example, that Abbey's impressive frescoes in the Boston Public Library, were too "literary" to be true art.

Though Howells, with a certain mock modesty, habitually confined his comments of illustrations to their "literary quality," he nevertheless seldom failed to express his preferences among the artists.[10] In the spring of 1888, a "pretty book," written and illustrated by Mr. and Mrs. Joseph Pennell, came to his desk for review. After a discussion of the text, Howells turned to the illustrations. He must have recalled the earlier journey around the Tuscan cities when Pennell and he had learned from one another how related and yet how separate are the arts of painting and of writing.

In the pictures Mr. Pennell seems to be at his very best, and the sunny sweetness of his work is to be praised without qualification. The page, in fact, flashes to the eye in those gay, bright illustrations as with so many gleams of veritable sunshine; they impart precisely the sentiment of the glimpses of roads, fields, canals, cottages, peasants, garçons, gendarmes, chamber-maids, and soldiers which the artist himself caught, and of the different interiors with which his fortunes or misfortunes brought him acquainted. The reader perceives that we celebrate, as usual, only the literary quality in these pictures; again, as always in such cases, we leave their technical shortcomings, if they have any, to those who may deny themselves a good deal of pleasure in detecting them.[11]

Though Howells claimed to respond only to "the literary quality" of Pennell's sketches, it was the painterly qualities of the stories of Lafcadio Hearn that he particularly appreciated. In the latter years of the 1890's, Henry Mills Alden had engaged Hearn to write articles for *Harper's Monthly* describing life in the West Indies, and to these sketches, "Two Years in the French West Indies," Howells referred in the "Editor's Study" of September, 1890, when they were published as a book entitled *Youma.*

> In Mr. Hearn the public has learned to know an artist of those who think in color; and perhaps one doubts whether it might not be better for him to piant his sketches than to write them. As a painter he is of the most modern school: an impressionist who puts on pure color, and loves to render light in its fiercest and brightest and gayest tints; it is as a fictionist that he seems a reversion.[12]

"A Winter Journey to Japan," which appeared the following November in *Harper's Monthly,* illustrated Howells' views of Hearn as an Impressionist who painted prose pictures in light and color. A single sentence from the text evokes a painting in the reader's mind: "As the light slants and yellows with evening," wrote Hearn, "the vision of a sea becomes realized in every detail! For now the spaces between the snow waves become filled with those beautiful blue shadows peculiar to this winter world, and the edges of the crests alone remain gold-white." [13] Before the year was over, Lafcadio Hearn had quarreled with the house of Harper and had settled permanently in Japan.

The custom of teaming artists with writers was followed by *Harper's,* not only in their frequent travel series,[14] but also in their serialized fiction. The opening chapter of Howells' *A Hazard of New Fortunes,* appeared in *Harper's Weekly* with a cover drawing by the artist W. A. Rogers [15] depicting Basil March and Fulkerson, the editor of *Every Other Week,* standing before "the vast edifice beetling like a granite crag above them," which was the insurance company in Boston from which Basil was about to escape to a literary career. Rogers was one of the numerous young "artist fellows" associated with *Harper's* who, perhaps, contributed to Howells' concept of the "artist." Twelve drawings adorned the serial publication of *A Hazard,* and six of these were reproduced in the edition of the novel that appeared in November, 1889, soon after Howells had given up "the bigger life" of New York and moved his family into a flat at 184 Commonwealth Avenue, Boston. The "fine, old-fashioned apartment house" on Stuyvesant Square, New York, had become unbearable after the death of his daughter Winifred in March, 1889.

Howells' new home was, like all of his abodes, of immediate interest to the journalistic world. Lilian Whiting was commissioned by John Brisbane Walker, editor of the *Cosmopolitan,* to write an article entitled "Literary Boston" for the November, 1890, issue of that magazine. Perhaps because Walker was already in correspondence with Howells concerning a position on the staff of his new journalistic venture, Miss Whiting's article opened with an account of Howells' early career and then focused on "the Boston home" of the hero of her article. Though the "intensely modern" author of *A Hazard of New Fortunes* with "the heart of a philanthropist" was called "an earnest student of conditions and their tendencies" who was "looking deeply into life on every side," his dwelling was described by the admiring reporter as that of "a polished man of the world." Miss Whiting wrote:

> The Boston home of Mr. Howells is on that magnificent boulevard, Commonwealth Avenue. The drawing-room windows look out on this noble thoroughfare with its centre esplanade of trees and statues, that of Garrison being close at hand, and further to the westward stands Miss Anne Whitney's figure of Leif Erikson peering into the "Undiscovered Country" of a new continent. The rooms are poetic, with some old paintings from Florence on the walls; an original water-color by Fortuny, presented to Mr. Howells by a friend, with a little history of its own; there are Venetian views; a picture by Rossetti, and one by Alma-Tadema with "To my dear Howells" in the artist's writing in the corner, and many other bits of artistic value and association.[16]

Howells usually managed to live in surroundings characteristic of the rich, in spite of his "profound sympathy with humanity" and his concern for the problem of the poor. As Howells wrote to his father soon after he had moved to 184 Commonwealth Avenue, he and his wife were "theoretical socialists, and practical aristocrats." Always able to smile ruefully at his own inconsistencies, Howells added, "it is a comfort to be right theoretically, and to be ashamed of one's self practically"; and then, as if to illustrate his point, he described a recent dinner in New York that he had attended. Harpers had given the dinner in honor of the artist E. A. Abbey and invited to the feast the writers, the illustrators, and the reviewers then in the Harper orbit. As usual on these festive occasions, Howells had thoroughly enjoyed talking with the younger men just then making their way in the metropolis; and in his weekly letter he had described them to his father. "There I met, among many other artists, the one whose card I enclose." He was from Ohio, Howells explained, and once knew at school one of the younger Howells boys. "This artist is very talented and valued by the Harpers," Howells had added. "He is just going or gone to Japan for them. I have seldom met anyone I liked more on short notice." The artist was C. D. Weldon who was sent to the Orient with Lafcadio Hearn, whose essays Harpers had engaged him to illustrate.[17]

After a summer in Saratoga, where Howells gathered material for a gay little "idyl" to be written several years later,[18] Howells found himself back in the flat on Commonwealth Avenue, which, he wrote Henry James on September 25, 1890, he would gladly exchange for "a furnished house." "I look forward to the winter in Boston with a feeling of satiety towards the place," he remarked in this same letter. During this strained winter in Boston, Howells wrote and privately printed the brief and touching "Memoir" (1891) of his daughter Winifred; perhaps for this reason, his sympathies were drawn to "In Tenebras," a story concerning death by Howard Pyle, which the author had submitted to the editor for criticism.

Howells was at that time suffering from "fantastic and hideous" dreams about his daughter, which seemed to him a kind of punishment for his religious agnosticism, as he admitted to Pyle in a letter of December 22, 1890, thanking the author for his "romance." Howells described himself as "deeply thrilled" by Pyle's story of the life hereafter, which he considered "a reasonable conjecture" in spite of his own temperamental inability to maintain his belief in an afterlife. "For the greater part of the time I believe in nothing," he wrote sadly to this old friend who shared with him a Swedenborgian upbringing and hence was accustomed to brooding upon another world of ideal forms. However, Howells confessed, "When I awake at night the room seems dense with spirits"; Pyle's story interested him the more because Howells, too, had it in mind to "write a story of the future life, on an extended scale, using Swedenborg for my *entourage*." [19]

Though Howells never wrote any such novel, his thought at this period assumed a sort of mystical tone not unlike that suggested by the drawings of Howard Pyle. His own firm common sense and taste for the real prompted him to write to his more dreamy friend in April, 1890, "Sometimes I feel that I must live entirely on the earthly plane unless I wish to be an arrogant ass, and meddle with things above me," adding, "and yet I *must* meddle with them, both in my own defective conduct and in the imagined lives of others." [20] The book in which Howells had "meddled" with things above him and that Pyle had just been reading with interest was *The Shadow of a Dream*. In it the spirit of the dead husband exerted such a power over the lovers that marriage seemed at last impossible, in spite of the efforts of Dr. Wingate, the nerve specialist, to introduce a note of reason to the smitten pair. "Happy for all," wrote Howells of his characters at this most painful period of his life, "if they could die out of their difficulties! But even this is not permitted to many, to most. Perhaps we can only suffer into the truth, and live along, in doubt whether it was worth the suffering." [21] Undoubtedly Howells had discussed these psychological problems with Dr. Oliver Wendell Holmes, who had been his next-door neighbor on Beacon Street.

Howard Pyle's mystical brooding was expressed not only in his stories, but also in his drawings, some of which he dispatched to Howells as illustrative, perhaps, of the concepts toward which both men were struggling. "Your drawings came before your letter reached me," wrote Howells on January 30, 1891. He showed them at once to his wife and daughter, "and it seemed almost too good to be true that they were really meant for us. I say us, because they best knew how great it was." Like her mother before her, Mildred Howells occasionally drew pen and ink sketches very much in the style of Howard Pyle to accompany her father's writing,[22] and she must have gazed with particular interest at the batch of drawings in the morning mail. Howells modestly said of himself, "I can feel only the literary quality of pictures, but as yours are always full of this, the drawings were precious to me too." [23]

Howells' collection of poems, *Stops of Various Quills* (1895), profusely illustrated with drawings by Howard Pyle, perfectly indicated the harmony felt between the poet and the artist. Howells was correct in feeling that the drawings of Pyle were full of "literature" [24] and that they were especially "precious" to him because they caught the spirit of his own concern with death and suffering. Pyle's pen sketches accompanying every poem in the volume caught the melancholy, questioning, withdrawn mood into which Howells was thrown by the death of his daughter. Black-winged sphinx, shrouded figures lost in clouds, moonlight on rocky shores, dark cliffs overhanging open seas—the illustrator subtly reflected the spirit of the poet. Both Howells and Pyle, the one as a poet, the other as an artist, were exploring in *Stops of Various Quills* the mystical thought of Swedenborg. A striking illustration of the similarity of their thoughts on death was to appear in the May, 1900, issue of *Harper's*. Pyle, in "The Angel and the Child," and Howells, in "Father and Mother," treated in mystical terms the question of the return of the dead to the living.

Howells' contact with Pyle, who was at that time one of the many illustrators for the Harper publications, so possessed his imagination that a decade or more later Howells included an artist—possibly Pyle—among the little circle of friends who recounted or commented upon his series of "psychological" tales written for *Harper's Weekly* and *Monthly* in 1906 and 1907.[25] The bachelors who were accustomed to foregather in the "Turkish Room" of a certain dining club in lower New York were Wanhope, the psychologist, Minver, the artist, Rulledge, the sentimentalist, Newton, the stranger, and Acton, the writer (usually merely designated as "I"). "It was always a cosy place," the Turkish Room, wrote Acton, whether you entered it with cigars and coffee after dinner, or with "whatever liquid or solid appetiser you preferred" before dinner. Moreover, "it invited the philosophic mind to contemplation more than any other spot in the club." The nature of dreams, James's *Will to Believe,* loss of memory, life after death—these were the questions discussed by the thoughtful bachelors, who ventured toward the edge of the new psychological insights and, at the same time, held firmly to their customary urbanity and worldly skepticism. The three most defined personalities in the stories of 1906 and 1907 were those of the artist, the writer, and the psychologist, for during his two unhappy years in the early part of the 1890's, Howells' own inner conflict had been lightened by contact with Pyle and Holmes.

Before giving up the "Editor's Study," early in 1891, Howells, at the suggestion of Alden, gathered together a sheaf of "Study" essays and published them in a small white and gold volume entitled *Criticism and Fiction*. There readers discovered what Howells came to believe concerning the unity of the arts and the search for "truth" in the interest of the common man. But one must return to the original "Study" essays themselves, to become aware of the artists, illustrators, sculptors, and architects with whom the editor associated at the time. His contact with the larger life of New York brought him into touch with men of scientific interest, too, and he was quick to perceive the relationship between the artist and the scientist as well.

The concluding paragraph of *Criticism and Fiction,* which, several generations later, sounds strangely rhetorical, expressed a passionate belief in the importance of all the arts and the sciences in a civilization founded by and for the common man. The art that "disdains the office of teacher," Howells boldly asserted,

> is one of the last refuges of the aristocratic spirit which is disappearing from politics and society, and is now seeking to shelter itself in aesthetics. The pride of caste is become the pride of taste; but as before, it is averse to the mass of men; it consents to know them only in some conventionalized and artificial guise. It seeks to withdraw itself, to stand aloof; to be distinguished, and not to be identified.

Democracy in literature—and in the arts—"is the reverse of all this," he declared.

> . . . it wishes to know and to tell the truth, confident that consolation and delight are there; it does not care to paint the marvellous and impossible for the vulgar many, or to sentimentalize and falsify the actual for the vulgar few. Men are more like than unlike one another; let us make them know one another better, that they may be all humbled and strengthened with a sense of their fraternity.

The arts, then, are a form of communication. If they fail to reach the ordinary man, they fail as art.

Neither arts, nor letters, nor sciences, except as they some-how, clearly or obscurely, tend to make the race better and kinder, are to be regarded as serious interests; they are all lower than the rudest crafts that feed and house and clothe, for except they do this office they are idle; and they cannot do this except from and through the truth.[26]

Howells' conclusion as to the relation of "arts, letters, and science" returned the reader to the opening section of *Criticism and Fiction,* in which Howells restated the critical position of John Addington Symonds recently expressed in *The Renaissance in Italy.*[27] In that declaration of his aesthetic position, Symonds had expressed the hope that in the scientific spirit then prevalent men would give up the search for "the ideal" in art and would accept as valid nothing "but what is solid and positive." The "unity of taste in the future" should make men "more and more capable of living in the whole" and teach them their "place in the world." All men comprehend "with an instinctive certitude" what is "simple, natural and honest." It is "the task of a healthy person" to make himself acquainted with "the laws of evolution in art and society" and to rely on his own ability to discern, in any work of art, "the truth, sincerity, and natural vigor in it."

Howells accepted the word of John Addington Symonds, believed in the unity of the arts and in his own untrained power to discern the relation of various works of art to the common man, whom he had made the hero of his own literary expression. The terms in which Howells understood the purport of Symond's credo may best be studied in relation to Howells' contribution to the current debates over the paintings of William Powell Frith, James McNeill Whistler, and the social theories of art of William Morris. Both of these discussions were opened to the readers of the "Study" in 1888; the ideas expressed at that time, however, remained in Howells' mind and left their imprint on all of his writing in the 1890's.

NOTES

1. *Criticism and Fiction and Other Essays by W. D. Howells* (1959), p. 25.
2. *Ibid.,* p. 11. Quoted from Edmund Burke's "Essay on the Sublime and the Beautiful."

3. *Harper's Monthly,* LXXII (January, 1886), 325.

4. *Ibid.,* pp. 325–326.

5. *Ibid.,* p. 321.

6. Edward E. Hale, Jr. (ed.), *The Life and Letters of Edward Everett Hale.* Two vols. (1917), II, 328.

7. Childe Hassam illustrated Howells' *Venetian Life* (1903), and William Glackens drew the illustrations for *Letters Home* (1903). Joseph Pennell, Frank R. Stockton, Frederick Remington, John La Farge, and Henry James were both writers and artists.

8. *Harper's Monthly,* LXXVIII (April, 1889), p. 824.

9. James's review first appeared in *Harper's Weekly,* XXX (Dec. 4, 1886), pp. 786–787. It was reprinted in *Pictures and Texts* (1893).

10. See also by W. D. Howells, "Pictures from Don Quixote," *Century,* LVI (June, 1898) pp. 177–185; "Mr. Remington's Wild Men," *Literature,* n. s., I (February 17, 1899), pp. 121–122; New York *Herald Tribune,* January 14, 1894, p. 13.

11. *Harper's Monthly,* LXXVII (June, 1888), 155.

12. LXXXI, 642. See note 17 of this chapter.

13. LXXXI, 862.

14. Joseph Henry Harper described another such team. In 1892 Theodore Childs proposed to make a trip from Persia to India from which he hoped to collect material for articles for *Harper's* to be illustrated by E. L. Weeks, who accompanied Childs. See *House of Harper,* pp. 592–596.

15. XXXIII, 1. The twelve illustrations of *A Hazard* are to be found in the same volume on pp. 241, 261, 281, 301, 385, 409, 429, 517, 701, 757, 798, 829.

16. "Literary Boston," by Lillian Whiting. *Cosmopolitan* (November, 1890) p. 206. For the "little history" of the Fortuny painting, see Howells' "Meetings with King," in *Memoirs of Clarence King* (1904), pp. 144–145.

17. Letter dated Feb. 2, 1890. *Life in Letters,* II, 1–2. C. D. Weldon drew handsome sketches for two articles for *Harper's Weekly,* XXXV, both of which were signed "N. Amenomori," the pseudonym of Lafcadio Hearn. The first was entitled "The Chrysanthemum Show, Japan" (Jan. 24, 1891), p. 60, and the second "The Japanese Festival of Hoko Dashi" (June 27, 1891), p. 482. In *The House of Harper,* J. Henry Harper described the dinner at the Union Club given by Harpers in honor of E. A. Abbey. Hearn was led to the party by the watchful Alden and made a futile effort to escape even after he had been introduced to the assembly. After the guests had seated themselves at the table, Howells, who found himself beside Joseph Henry Harper, asked him who the diffident guest was. Harper reminded Howells that he had been introduced to Hearn and then added, "You surely know who Lafcadio Hearn is." Howells then "jumped up from his chair, and going round to Hearn, took his hand and remarked that the name Hearn meant nothing to him, but that there was only one Lafcadio Hearn, and that he felt so

pleased to meet him that he was impelled to shake hands with him again—a graceful act and one highly appreciated by Hearn." P. 586.

18. *An Open-Eyed Conspiracy* (1897). The hero of this tale was possibly suggested by Wolcott Balistier, of whom Howells remarked in his letter to James, "That youth made a gay time for us while he stayed with us in Saratoga." *Life in Letters,* II, 6.

19. *Life in Letters,* II, 9–11.

20. *Ibid.,* 11. Swedenborg's *Heaven and Its Wonders and Hell* (Latin, 1758). Appeared in English in 1887.

21. *Ibid.*

22. See "Race," a poem by Howells with illustrations by Mildred Howells. *Harper's Monthly,* LXXXVIII (April, 1894), 677. Reprinted in *Stops of Various Quills* (1895). See also "Life and Letters," *Harper's Weekly,* XL (Dec. 25, 1897), 1298.

23. *Life in Letters,* II, 14.

24. Howard Pyle also illustrated Holmes' *Autocrat of the Breakfast Table* in 1894.

25. The stories in which the group of characters appeared were: "The Eidolons of Brooks Alford," *Harper's Monthly,* CXIII (August, 1906), 377–397; "A Memory That Worked Overtime," *Ibid.,* CXV (August, 1906), 415–418; "A Case of Metaphantasmia," *Harper's Weekly,* XLIX (December 16, 1905), 20–22; "The Chick of the Easter Egg," *Ibid.,* L (April 14, 1906), 509–512; "Braybridge's Offer," *Harper's Monthly,* CXII (January, 1906), 229–236. These stories were republished in *Between the Dark and the Daylight* (1907). See also "Talking of Presentiments," *Harper's Monthly,* CXVI (December, 1907), 76–78, which was later included in *A Daughter of the Storage* (1916).

26. *Criticism and Fiction,* pp. xxviii, 87.

27. Stated by Symonds in Part V, pp. 230–321. This book was reviewed by Howells, *Harper's Monthly,* LXXV (November, 1887), 962–967.

· 2 ·

William Powell Frith:
A Novelist's Painter

Howells' review of *My Autobiography and Reminiscences* by William Powell Frith, makes it possible to reexamine the huge canvases of that most popular of nineteenth-century painters in the hope of discovering Howells' views on art as related to literature. For what Howells, as a novelist, meant by the term "realism" is illustrated by his appreciation of similar qualities in the paintings of Frith.

An Academician himself, Frith had hung his paintings in the Royal Academy in London year after year since 1840. Howells must have seen and admired these pictures when he visited the Exhibitions of 1882 and of 1883. Between these visits and the appearance of Frith's *Autobiography* in 1887, a controversy had raged on both sides of the Atlantic as to the true artistic merit of Frith's cheerful, narrative canvases. However, the paintings of family scenes, royal weddings, or railway stations continued to enchant the public in spite of the attacks of the critics.

What was Howells' position in the argument? Frith's *Autobiog-*

raphy [1] commended itself to Howells as it does to readers today, not so much for his philosophy of art as for the charm of his narrative style. Having known Turner, Dickens, Thackeray, Queen Victoria, and a wide variety of lesser personalities, Frith was willing and able to dazzle the reader by an amiable flow of anecdotes, both significant and trivial, that in the end left the reader with a clear impression of Frith's aims in art. As Howells observed in his review of March, 1888, "It is a delightful book, as autobiographies are apt to be, with signal merits of simplicity and honesty, and manifold attractions of gossip about art and artists and the world of London around them." [2] The talk of a London artist, Howells noted, had a wider range than that of a New York artist, for in London the world of art and the world of fashion were more closely related than in New York; and matters of taste therefore assumed an importance unknown to New Yorkers. Howells observed that Frith moved freely from studio to salon to drawing room, and as a critic noted, recorded, and judged. Although he modestly kept himself in the background, Frith, in writing his autobiography, felt free to give the reader the full benefit of his opinions and prejudices, his grievances and his triumphs. And why should he not have expressed his views frankly, since, in spite of the din of the art critics who criticized the crowded, realistic views of "Ramsgate Sands" (1854), "Derby Day" (1858), and "The Railway Station" (1862), Frith's canvases commanded exorbitant prices, were bought by the Queen,[3] and were hung in the National Gallery of London? In remarking that Frith dealt with "the every-day life about him, and loved above everything else to deal with it," and was "devoutly if not passionately faithful to it in his work," Howells showed his sympathy with a painter whose aims as an artist were similar to his own as a novelist.

Like Howells, Frith was a member of a large, hard-working family. His father was the landlord of a rambling, old inn, The Dragon, in Harrogate, near London; he recognized the special talent of his son when Frith was still a child, idly sketching drawings of the family dog before the fireplace of the inn. So confident was he of his son's ability that he sent Frith to live with his uncle in London—also an innkeeper—when he was about twelve years old, enrolling the boy in Mr. Sass's school for young artists in Charlotte Street.[4] Here Frith suffered from the discipline of having to sketch from wooden geometrical forms, but he soon found that he had time left over from his hours in Sass's studio to paint any live model whom he could persuade to sit for him. During these early years in London, the young Frith went frequently to the plays in Covent Garden and studied the gestures, facial expressions, and costumes of such actors as William Macready and Charles Kemble. Like Howells, Frith was always devoted to the theater and gained from the stage a sense of the importance of realistic details.

As a boy in London, Frith also studied the novels of Dickens and the sketches of his almost equally famous illustrator, George Cruik-shank. In the course of time Frith came to know Dickens personally and not only painted a number of the characters from his novels, but also the author himself. Again like Howells, Frith was nourished on the writings of Dickens, Thackeray, Goldsmith, Fielding; and, in a sense, he discovered his own individual means of expression by entering freely into the scenes opened up to him by these novelists. Self-educated, sociable, belonging to no clique or school, he was able to capture on canvas the very spirit of the imagined characters of the novelists, as well as that of the models whom he found on the streets of London. The enjoyment of literature did not prevent Frith or Howells from participating fully in the "commonplace" scenes around them. On the contrary, the creative expression of both men was enlivened by their appreciation of the worlds of Cervantes, Shakespeare, Scarron—or the latest melodrama in a nearby theater. Though Frith knew Sir Edwin Landseer, John Constable, Benjamin Haydon, Sir John Millais, the Rossettis, Oscar Wilde, and all the other artists of his day, he was singularly free from any art theory other than a good-humored belief in the pleasure of catching the tone of what appeared to him "real," whether from a play by Molière or a scene at the seashore.

Howells clearly perceived the critical quarrel at issue concerning Frith, for it was closely related to his "war" with his own critics, who accused him of being both "photographic" and "commonplace." "Simply stated," Howells wrote, "the quarrel is that Mr. Frith believed he saw the dramatic, the poetic, the beautiful, the sublime, the eternal, in the contemporary life of the London streets, the railway stations, the sea-side resorts, the race-courses, and his critics maintained that he saw only the commonplace, the vulgar, the trivial and the transitory." [5] The controversy over Frith's place as an artist was limited to the critics, however, and hardly affected the general public, which never seriously questioned Frith's artistic powers.[6] So great were the crowds that gathered around Frith's paintings at the annual exhibitions of the Royal Academy that barriers had to be erected before them and guards stationed nearby. Frith won the day with the public, if not with the critics, and Howells shrewdly suggested that "the criticism of the future will be kinder to him than that of his own time." Why, for example, should critics accept Hogarth's "Rake's Progress" and reject Frith's "Road to Ruin," which, according to Howells, was "so conscientiously studied and so tragically realized"?

In one of the series of five paintings entitled "The Road to Ruin" (1878), Frith depicted his hero wasting his time with a group of Oxford students intent over their game of cards as the dawn appeared in the sky behind the towers of Christ Church. One student was lying in a drunken stupor on the sofa, another was blowing out a guttering candle, and a third was standing moodily at the window as the six players vied for the basket of money on the table. The smoke-filled college room, the champagne bottles on the floor, the crossed rapiers over the marble mantelpiece, the shrewd faces of several of the players, were narrative in intent. The moral of the scene was clearly written on the countenances of the students on "the road to ruin." [7] Howells might have been referring to Frith's painting when he said in *Criticism and Fiction* that art and literature unconsciously affect the manners and morals of all who comprehend them. Frith's unabashed avowal of the moral purpose of his series of paintings depicting "The Road to Ruin" made perfect sense to Howells, and, indeed, to most unsophisticated art appreciators of the day, who had heard nothing of "art for art's sake." In his *Autobiography,* Frith freely described his narrative paintings of the downfall of a young man of the day; reflecting the views of the vast majority of the public of his day, Frith declared himself in favor of "art for the sake of the moral":

> For a long time I had the desire to paint a story in a series of pictures, and I began to make chalk-studies of the different groups for the five pictures called "The Road to Ruin."

Without any pretensions to do my work on the Hogarthian
lines, I thought I could show some of the evils of gambling;
my idea being a kind of gambler's progress, avoiding the
satirical vein of Hogarth, for which I knew myself unfitted. I
desired to trace the career of a youth from his college days to
his ruin and death—a victim to one of the most fatal vices.

These paintings were exhibited at the Royal Academy in 1878 and,
as usual with Frith's canvases, were immediately successful. "The
policemen and the rail were again required," Frith recalled, "and I
received many compliments, and no doubt much abuse." [8]
The popular applause and the critical abuse that marked the
careers of Howells and Frith taught both men to view with mistrust,
disdain, or amusement the words of self-appointed arbiters of taste.
In no uncertain terms Howells announced in *Criticism and Fiction*
that the crudest effort of any creative artist was superior to the
critic's finest comment upon it.[9] The difficulty with anonymous, de-
structive criticism, as Howells saw it, was that "the author, dramatist, painter, sculptor, whose book, play, picture, statue, has been
unfairly dealt with, as he believes, must make no effort to right himself with the public; he must bear his wrong in silence; he is even
expected to grin and bear it, as if it were funny," [10] for the public
blandly felt that the book, the play, the picture, or the statue provided a sufficient reply to the critic. Howells must surely have enjoyed the eloquent reply to his critics that Frith had supplied in his
enormous canvas, "The Private View," which Howells found hanging in the annual exhibition of the Royal Academy when he returned from a sojourn on the Continent in the summer of 1883.
With perfect composure and apparent innocence, Frith wrote of
"The Private View" in his *Autobiography:*

Beyond the desire of recording for posterity the aesthetic craze
as regards dress, I wished to hit the folly of listening to self-
elected critics in matters of taste, whether in dress or in art.
I therefore planned a group consisting of a well-known apostle
of the beautiful [Oscar Wilde], with a herd of eager worship-
pers surrounding him. He is supposed to be explaining his
theories to willing ears, taking some pictures on the Academy
walls for his text. A group of well-known artists are watching

the scene. On the left of the composition is a family of pure aesthetes absorbed in affected study of the pictures. Near them stands Anthony Trollope, whose homely figure affords a striking contrast to the eccentric forms near him.

The "eccentric forms" were those of the Pre-Raphaelites, of course, who were amusingly contrasted with the sturdy, bespectacled figure of the exponent of honest realism in the novel, Anthony Trollope, whom Howells also knew and admired. "The rest of the picture," continued Frith, "is made up of celebrities of all kinds, statesmen, poets, judges, philosophers, musicians, painters, actors, and others," the Archbishop of York, Gladstone, Mrs. Langtry, Browning, Huxley, Ellen Terry, Du Maurier, and other well-known personalities of the 1880's with whom both Howells and Frith found themselves conversing at dinner parties, at exhibitions, or on the terrace of Parliament during that cheerfully chaotic period in art history. The Exhibition of 1883 brought all the notables together, accompanied by their children and their poodles. As Frith modestly observed,

> Pictures composed of groups of well-known people are always very popular at the Academy, and "The Private View" was no exception to that rule, a guard being again found necessary to control the crowds of visitors.

"The temptation for a critic to cut fantastic tricks before high heaven in the full light of day," [11] which Howells complained of in *Criticism and Fiction,* was surely curbed by Frith's delightfully satiric canvas. With the gayety of Gilbert and Sullivan and the delicate sharpness of Max Beerbohm, Frith demonstrated to all that what the critics have to say should not be taken too seriously by the artist. Frith, like Howells, had learned that to be accepted and applauded by the public one need not be acclaimed by the critics.

In defending Frith's controversial book, Howells lent his support to a painter who was a representative of the Anecdotal school of painting. Howells took his stand with the painters exhibiting at the Royal Academy, as opposed to the followers of Whistler and the Impressionists, who were excluded from the annual exhibitions. "We have only the literary quality of the work in mind," Howells confessed. "Matters of technique we do not understand, and we gladly leave them to the art critics, who do not understand them either, if we may trust the artists." The artist to whom Howells appealed in his review of Frith's book was his friend, Saint-Gaudens, whom he quoted as saying, "in a recently reported interview,"

> Books on art are of no value. They are worse than useless and should be left alone. The pencil, the brush, and the modelling-stick should take their place, and be the student's constant companions.

Thus armed against the art critics with the words of an artist, Howells stated the problem raised on both sides of the Atlantic by the paintings of Frith. The reader, Howells pointed out, was familiar with the popular reproductions of these paintings and so had an opportunity of "judging between the artist and his critics in a quarrel which has been nearly life-long."

This controversy over Frith's paintings brought Howells to the conclusion that criticism itself, in the arts as well as in literature, was weak and needed to be enlivened by "the experience of every man who has done anything worth while in any of the arts." "The Study," Howells declared once more, was open to "any author, sculptor, painter, or architect who wishes to contribute to the evidence from his own experience." Perhaps criticism itself might be helped from such a comparison of experience, for certainly criticism had proved itself as unable to deal with problems of art in the modern world as "the Inquisition would be to deal with the problems of modern science."

Ample support for Howells' contention that the critics themselves were in a state of confusion appeared in the *Magazine of Art* of 1888. This handsomely bound, gilt-edged British publication of over five hundred pages reflected every angle of opinion, from that of the conservative Royal Academy to the views of the rival Grosvenor Gallery. Articles on old lace, Mr. Ruskin's museum, the lives of artists living or dead, the portraits of Napoleon I—all shades of attitudes on every aspect of "art" were to be found in that repository of comment on Victorian taste. Not only was Frith's *Autobiography* reviewed [12] as "one of the most entertaining books of recent years," but Frith himself was invited to give his views of Pre-

Raphaelitism and impressionism. In an article entitled "Crazes in Art," [13] adorned by a charming engraving of Frith at the age of thirty,[14] Frith freely expressed his ideas on painting.

What these modern painters of the avant-garde lacked, wrote Frith, was a knowledge of drawing. Sir Joshua Reynolds always lamented his want of skill in draughtsmanship, and, indeed, his paintings were, Frith said, weakened by the awkwardness of his drawing; he had, however, breadth of effect, superb coloring, and plenty of atmosphere. Just as serious painters were learning to view Reynolds with critical appreciation but to understand, through a careful study of Van Dyke and Titian, that every detail of a painting can be "almost photographically rendered, whilst the breadth of effect is fully preserved," there suddenly appeared "a band of young men who called themselves 'Pre-Raphaelite Brethren,' and who proceeded to prove the justice of their nomenclature by refusing the guidance of any painter who had the misfortune, in their wise young eyes, of being born after, or contemporary with Raphael." The Pre-Raphaelites were so enamored of an exaggerated form of "realism" that they painted the ugly heads of their angular saints so that you could count every hair. They were totally without the grace, beauty, and atmosphere that suffused the paintings of Reynolds. Members of an older school, such as that to which Frith adhered, were taunted with "the absence of honesty in our rendering of Nature: we were pretty, we were characterless, commonplace." However, this particular "craze," Frith declared, had passed and "another, far more dangerous, craze has come upon us"—impressionism.

According to Frith, this so-called impressionism, imported into England from France, was exactly opposite to the principles of the Pre-Raphaelites. "In the one we have overwrought details, in the other no details at all." As far as Frith's "feeble powers" enabled him to understand the Impressionist, such an artist claimed to reproduce an impression, probably momentary, that Nature had made on him. The only explanation of the paintings that resulted from this technique was that the receiver of the impression was "in a state of disease." After all, Frith remarked, "all art is impressionist in the true and wide sense of the term"; however, "the Impressionist's impressions" appeared to be merely "outrages on popular prejudice."

Why not recognize these painters as impostors and instead study the "impression" made on Van Dyke, for example, by Charles I? The Impressionists should not be encouraged to "play their pranks" in the Royal Academy Exhibitions any longer; too frequently a picture "simply true to Nature" had no chance against one in which the painter had "indulged in eccentricity." Buyers, unfortunately, were often attracted to a painting for the very reason that they could not understand it. "Nocturnes" and "symphonies" undoubtedly would continue to flourish for a while, in spite of this warning, Frith admitted, but at last the craze would "as assuredly pass away as everything foolish and false does sooner or later." Meanwhile, the student should know that his business was to learn to *paint,* "by which I mean to acquire the power of thoroughly and completely representing—as the great masters did—the object before him, whether it be a human figure or any other model."

The fact that clearly observed and skillfully executed realism, both in painting and in novel-writing, seems not only to appeal to a later generation but to survive the changes of taste, has always caused the critics to pause and wonder. Sydney Armytage, writing in the 1870's, observed that "in any exhibition of pictures, Frith's always drew the largest crowd"—and not because his paintings were merely fashionable and cheerful. Frith was interested in poor little London waifs, one of whom he painted in "The Crossing Sweeper," as well as in the overdressed men and women depicted in "Derby Day." Of the former, Armytage wrote, "The picture presents to us an episode of the social history of our time; and what a history that is, when it descends into the lower depths of the community, is known only to those who have wandered through the regions of poverty, destitution, and crime, whence come the hundreds of juvenile Arabs who throng our streets." [15] Of the latter, Walter Sickert observed in the *Burlington Magazine* of December, 1922,[16]

Of the masterpieces of British art, Frith's "Derby Day" remains, since the memory of man, the most popular, as it is certainly the most unaffectedly enjoyed painting in the National Gallery. It is said, and there is nothing astonishing in the fact, that it accounts for more sixpences at the turnstile than all the other pictures put together.

With a detachment derived from a humane and often humorous interest in the daily existence of ordinary persons, both rich and poor, Howells and Frith turned with ease from one social class to another and presented a thoughtful—or satiric—study of the common man in every walk of life. Both novelist and artist put their faith in the skillful use of pen and brush and eschewed the crazes of their day. Henry James might lament that Howells did not become the American Zola, break from his sustained contemplation of ordinary life, and write a naturalistic novel of darker, if exaggerated, implications; William Michael Rossetti might grudgingly remark on the "cheerful, lounging, recreating" quality of Frith's "Ramsgate Sands," and ask in despair, "Could no more be made pictorially of life at the seaside?" [17] But neither James nor Rossetti could alter the artistic habits of two such devotees of the simple, daily truth as were Howells and Frith.

Howells' attitudes toward "crazes in art" were reflected in two novels of the 1880's, *A Woman's Reason* and *April Hopes*.[18] Helen Harkness, of *A Woman's Reason* (1883), was given to drawing and painting in the Pre-Raphaelite manner. Near Helen's dressing table in her room on the top floor of the substantial old family mansion at 9 Beacon Steps, Boston, were reminders of the period when, as a child, "she had thought herself wedded to art." In this remote chamber "there were certain charcoal sketches pinned against the wall, and in one corner, not very definite at first glance under the draperies tossed upon it from time to time, was her easel." Her father, too, was interested in art, but of another period. "Among the many pictures on the walls (there were too many), there were three Stuarts, the rest were of very indifferent merit; large figure paintings, or allegorical landscapes, after the taste of Cole and Poussin, in great carved and scrolly frames." Helen had from time to time thought of "making a raid upon these enemies of art," and redecorating the parlors "in conformity to the recent feelings in such matters," which were, of course, prevailingly Pre-Raphaelite in spirit and tone. The death of her mother and the illness of her father, however, prevented Helen from carrying out her ideas; indeed, "she had not got further than some golden-rod and mullein-stalks upon the panels of her own chamber door," [19] when her father also died and left her with the problem of disposing of the stately old mansion and all its

*William Dean Howells in Venice
(1863)*

Elinor Mead Howells

Casa Falier, where Consul Howells lived in Venice

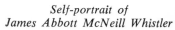

AN APPEAL TO THE LAW.

NAUGHTY CRITIC, TO USE BAD LANGUAGE!   SILLY PAINTER, TO GO TO LAW ABOUT IT!

Punch's *comment on the quarrel between Whistler and Ruskin*

John Ruskin

Self-portrait of
James Abbott McNeill Whistler

Illustration by W. T. Smedley for Howells'
The Landlord at Lion's Head

William Powell Frith's "The Road to Ruin"

Ohio artist J. Q. A. Ward's "The Indian Hunter"

The new home of The Century Club in 1889, on Forty-third Street west of Fifth Avenue, from the drawing of the architects, McKim, Mead, and White

contents. When she learned that her father, whom she had supposed wealthy, had left her penniless, Helen sold the family Copleys to the Museum of Fine Arts [20] and went forth to earn her living by painting china and Christmas calendars, and by trimming bonnets. Howells recognized the dangers that lie in wait for "artistic" daughters whose devoted fathers are unable to provide for them.

April Hopes (1888), written at the time when Howells was enjoying Frith's *Autobiography*, presented readers with a young hero named Dan Mavering, who, like Helen, possessed an "artistic temperament" that almost caused his downfall. A Harvard senior, Dan had decided not to go into his father's wallpapering business and had made up his mind, he thought, to become an artist. Though the paper that the elder Mavering produced was "aesthetic" in the William Morris style, the paper mills in Ponkwasset Falls, New Hampshire, represented to Dan the standards of business, rather than those of art. Not only was Dan confused as to whether he wished to earn money or paint pictures, he was still further puzzled as to the limits his gay and charming temperament should (and could) set to his philandering impulses. Clearly, Dan had an "artistic temperament," rather than the temperament of a genuine artist.

Opening the novel with a Harvard Class Day, taking his characters to the summer hotels of Campobello, and finally leading them through the official receptions of a new President in Washington, Howells drew, as a novelist, a series of "scenes" that might be labeled "The Road to [almost] Ruin." The very Harvard room in which Dan lived resembled the Oxford chamber of the hero of Frith's series of paintings that Howells chose for particular comment. Dan's room, where he led his guests for a Class Day "spread," had "the deep window nooks and easy-chairs upholstered in the leather that seems sacred alike to the seats and shelves of libraries; the aesthetic bookcases, low and topped with bric-à-brac; the etchings and prints on the walls . . . the foils crossed over the chimney, and the mantel with its pipes, and its photographs of celebrities tilted about over it," of a typical Harvard senior—symbols of the new generation that were calculated to stir "obscure misgivings of the sort which an older generation always likes to feel concerning the younger." [21] Was Dan, indeed, started on his "Road to Ruin"?

That was the problem that Howells put, with ironic humor, before the reader.

Whether or not the hero met "ruin" at the end remains an open question. Dan not only accepted his father's offer of a position in his factory, but he also married the rather exciting Pre-Raphaelite beauty, Alice Pasmer, who was as unsmiling, heroic and handsome, in her pale, sage-green costumes, as a figure in a Rossetti painting. However, the story of Dan's previous flirtation with Julia Anderson was not divulged in the curtained barouche as it drove away from his wedding. When the bride earnestly urged the groom henceforth to be always "frank and open with me and tell me everything," Dan leaned over and kissed her. "I will, Alice! I will indeed!" he replied. "I won't keep anything from you after this." But Alice did not seem to be in just the frame of mind at this time to hear his story; moreover, Dan musingly wondered whether he himself understood what he really meant by his rash promise to Alice. The moral of Howells' scenes from the life of an "artistic" young man was briefly and ironically stated in the final paragraph:

> If he had been different she would not have asked him to be frank and open; if she had been different, he might have been frank and open. This was the beginning of their married life.[22]

In Howells' "Road to Ruin," as in Frith's, the moral was as simple as the carefully sketched scenes were complex. Howell's delightful verbal canvases, like Frith's, achieved a unity and harmony in terms of movement and confusion that never impaired their serenity. The occasion itself, whether it was Class Day at Harvard or Derby Day at Epsom, lent to the many divergent personalities a oneness of interest and a harmony of feeling. At the same time, the highlight was cast upon the central characters, who were themselves caught up in the Day, whatever it was. There were, for example, Dan and Alice soon after their first meeting, emerging from the entrance of the Harvard Gymnasium at the close of the opening ceremony of a Harvard Class Day. Dan had led Alice through the vestibule, banked with pots of ferns and palms, and they moved

> down the steps into the glare of the Cambridge sunshine, blown full, as is the case on Class Day, of fine Cambridge

dust, which had thrown a delicate grey veil over the grass of the Gymnasium lawn, and mounted in light clouds from the wheels powdering it finer and finer in the street. Along the sidewalks dusty hacks and carriages were ranged, and others were driving up to let people dismount at the entrances to the college yard. Within the temporary picket-fences, secluding a part of the grounds for the students and their friends, were seen stretching from dormitory to dormitory long lines of Chinese lanterns, to be lit after nightfall, swung between the elms. Groups of ladies came and went, nearly always under the escort of some student; the caterers' carts, disburdened of their ice-creams and salads, were withdrawn under the shade in the street, and their drivers lounged or drowsed upon the seats; now and then a black waiter, brilliant as a bobolink in his white jacket and apron, appeared on some errand; the large, mild Cambridge policemen kept the entrances to the yard with a benevolent vigilance which was not harsh with the little Irish children coming up from the Marsh in their best to enjoy the sight of other people's pleasure.

June light viewed through the dust of carriages, strolling ladies glimpsed between festoons of Chinese lanterns, white-jacketed waiters darting expertly through the good-natured throng gathered under the elms—Frith might well have sketched that Harvard Class Day of the 1870's on one of his large canvases.

Just as the painter might have thrown the light on the handsome young couple as they moved down the steps, so Howells centered his reader's attention on the pair by the following dialogue, which took place after they had traversed the Square:

"Isn't it a perfect Class Day?" cried the young Mavering, as he crossed Kirkland Street with Miss Pasmer, and glanced down its vaulted perspective of elms, through which the sunlight broke, and lay in the road in pools and washes as far as the eye reached. "Did you ever see anything bluer than the sky today?" [23]

Miss Pasmer, with a flatness her beauty belied, asked simply, "Is it the usual Class Day weather?" "You spoil everything by asking that," cried the young man. By this simple exchange, the reader perceived, that, in fact, Dan's natural exuberance and Alice's serious literalness were in danger of "spoiling everything" for life.

Howells' genuine appreciation of Frith's *Autobiography,* as expressed in the "Editor's Study" of March, 1888, came, then, from his own recognition of the common language of painter and novelist. Without passing to philosophy, both shared a sense of the richness and meaning to be found in varied scenes of ordinary men and women going about their daily business and pleasure. Not tempted to exaggerate, both painter and novelist perceived the latent drama before them with the observant eye of the realist.

In 1951 the Whitechapel Art Gallery of London held "An Exhibition of Paintings by William Powell Frith, R.A., 1819–1909." In a Foreword to the Catalogue, James Lever declared that "any competent artist who faithfully reflects his contemporary scene is sure of revival, and even of a kind of immortality." Such an artist, remarked Lever, was Frith:

> . . . and now that the Victorian Period has outlived the indifference of the Edwardians and the contempt of the nineteen-twenties, we find ourselves looking at his pictures with a new interest. While the Rossettis were wandering in a dream world of their own which we may or may not find attractive . . . Frith was painting "The Railway Station" and "Derby Day," and giving us the very form and pressure of the time.

After he had read Howells' first novel, *Their Wedding Journey,* Henry Adams remarked that a student of a future age could find in this story a more accurate account of how life really was than in any other book, and hence that its immortality was assured.[24] Thomas Hardy wrote of the first few chapters of *A Hazard of New Fortunes,* "I like the opening; one seems to see New York, and hear it, and smell it." [25] Whereas William Powell Frith was "a novelist's painter," Howells with equal truth might be called "a painter's novelist"; both painter and novelist worked in sympathy with the realism popular in their day and increasingly appreciated in ours.

"Would to God," exclaimed Roger Fry, when contemplating the artists who attempted to revive the ancient glories of the Middle Ages or of Greece, "Would to God they had been Friths instead of

Alma-Tademas." [26] While sympathizing with Roger Fry's anguished cry, today one must remember that Howells was as delighted with the paintings of Alma-Tadema as with those of Frith, that, in fact, he returned from England in the autumn of 1883 with one of Alma-Tadema's small pictures presented to him by the artist as well as a painting by Rossetti. These hung on his living room wall, together with his Fortuny, for many years. Much as Howells enjoyed the works of Frith and understood the point of view behind them, he made no claim to a critical view of painting. Always an amateur in his comments on painting, sculptor, or architecture, he perceived the interrelationship of all the arts and their ultimate dependence on "reality" as understood by the ordinary observer. Moreover, Howells' own novels were immeasurably enriched by the insight he gained into other arts.

With engaging modesty, Frith told in his *Autobiography* the story of his extraordinary rise to fame more in terms of anecdote than of art theory. Like Howells, he put his trust in accurate drawing, a feeling for the unity and diversity of large scenes, a respect for detail and, above all, a delight in the human beings swarming about a railroad station, a picture gallery, or a horse race. Like Howells, Frith seemed to derive his pleasure in the diversity of humanity as much from the reading of literature, from Cervantes, Goldsmith, Fielding, Dickens, and Thackeray as from the streets and drawing rooms of London. The sheer joy of creation brought to both Howells and Frith such a hearty popular response that they could afford to disregard that "little caterpillar, the critic." Later generations have turned to these men to rediscover in all its fullness how people of another period actually looked and felt. The fact that neither Frith nor Howells actively allied himself with any clique or school but maintained a certain cool detachment, as well as a genial pleasure in the passing show, made them faithful observers and reporters of their age, as well as genuine artists.[27]

NOTES

1. First published in England in 1887; Harper & Brothers brought it out in this country in 1888. Frith's *Autobiography* was edited by Nevil Wallis and reissued in 1957 in condensed form as *A Victorian Canvas, The Memoirs of W. P. Frith, R.A.*

2. "Editor's Study," *Harper's Monthly*, LXXVI (March, 1888), 643.

3. "The Marriage of the Prince of Wales" (1865) was painted by command of the Queen.

4. Described by Thackeray in *The Newcombs*, Chapter XVIII.

5. *Harper's Monthly*, LXXVI (March, 1888), 643.

6. See "English Art and Society, Recollections of a Successful Painter." *My Autobiography and Reminiscences*, New York *Tribune*, Dec. 18, 1887.

7. Cf. similar scenes described by Edgar Allan Poe in *William Wilson* and by William Makepeace Thackeray in *Pendennis*, Chapters XVIII–XX. Chapter XX of the latter is entitled "Rake's Progress."

8. *My Autobiography and Reminiscences*, Chapter III, pp. 346–347.

9. *Criticism and Fiction and Other Essays*, p. 25.

10. *Ibid.*, p. 30.

11. *Ibid.*, p. 31.

12. Pp. 71–72.

13. *Ibid.*, pp. 187–192.

14. From a painting by Augustus L. Egg, R.A.

15. Sydney Armytage, *Beautiful Pictures by British Artists, 1800–1870*, pp. 31–32.

16. "Derby Day," XLI, 276–277.

17. *Fine Art, Chiefly Contemporary* (1867), p. 263.

18. Howells' interest in the Pre-Raphaelites is also reflected in *A Little Girl Among the Old Masters, With Introduction and Comment by W. D. Howells*, issued in 1884 by Howells' publisher, James R. Osgood. The book proved to be a delightful reflection of Mildred Howells' imaginative pleasure in the Italian paintings her mother and father had taken her to see in Florence, Siena, and Venice. Howells' Introduction assures readers that the drawings were made "without instruction, without suggestion from any one else," that "they are simply the reflection, in a child's soul, of the sweetness and loveliness of early Italian art." After a morning spent gazing at the paintings of Botticelli, Fra Angelico, or Titian, Mildred would curl up in an armchair with her drawing pad on her lap, or spread her papers on the dining room table, and produce her interpretation of Italian art. However, as readers examine the pages of that charming book of sketches by a gifted child, they could hardly fail to be struck by the impression that all of her angels, cherubs, and Madonnas turn out to be strictly Pre-Raphaelite in posture, facial expression, and decorative detail. Howells admits that Mildred probably would not have been moved to draw at least one of her sketches had she not been taken to see Rossetti's picture, "The Loving Cup," in London the previous summer.

19. Pp. 27–28.

20. P. 99.

21. Pp. 35–36.

22. P. 484.

23. Pp. 26–27.

24. *North American Review,* CXIV (April, 1872), 444.

25. Unpublished letter of May 10, 1892. Houghton Library, Harvard.

26. Quoted by James Lever in the *Whitehall Art Gallery Catalogue* (1951).

27. Shifts in taste in novel-writing and in painting were not infrequently allied in the reviews of the day. T. S. Perry, for example, in his review of Lockhart's *Life of Sir Walter Scott* (1879), observed that many readers regarded Scott as old fashioned, for styles in painting and in novels had changed. Scott's successors "no longer choose large canvases. Where he took a whole century and packed it full of living people, the novelists of to-day busy themselves with a sort of literary Pre-Raphaelitism. They take a brief period and, generally, commonplace people, and describe a few tepid passions that flourish in every block of the street. Where Scott drew inspiration from spoken or written history, some of the novels of to-day read as if they were based on that record of contemporary history, the newspaper. . . . [T]he principal unromantic fetish of the present day is for scientific exactness. . . . [Scott's] novels have a sort of old-fashioned air; they are set in frames, as it were, like works of art, and nowadays novels are what someone has called slices of life." *Atlantic Monthly,* XLVI (September, 1880), 313–319.

· 3 ·

Whistler v. *Ruskin:*
Howells' View

Howells' rather guarded review of Whistler's *Gentle Art of Making Enemies* (1890), which appeared in the January, 1891, issue of *Harper's,* must have exasperated and intrigued the readers of its day by its ambiguity. The elusiveness of Howells' comment was due in part to the fact that Whistler hardly needed to be introduced to *Harper's* readers, for this witty maker of enemies had kept himself in the forefront of the art news ever since the serio-comic case of *Whistler* v. *Ruskin* of 1878 and his controversial "Ten O'Clock Lecture" of 1885.

In *The Gentle Art* both the lawsuit and the lecture were ironically reconsidered by Whistler, by then known on both sides of the Atlantic as an Impressionist whose subdued "harmonies" and "nocturnes" exemplified the newest movement in painting. Howells reviewed Whistler's explosive book with a certain hesitancy, perhaps because he himself was committed to a sturdier realism. Howells' view of the Whistler-Ruskin controversy is of particular interest as a reflection of the novelist's growing awareness of impressionism in art and its relation to a parallel movement in literature.

James McNeill Whistler, expatriated American painter, dedicated the "pathetic Papers" (as he called them) included in *The Gentle Art of Making Enemies* to "The rare Few, who, early in Life, have rid Themselves of the Friendship of the Many"; and above the dedication he sketched his well-known signature, an airy butterfly. The book opened with a page addressed to "Messieurs Les Ennemis!" on which appeared another little butterfly, this one looking more like a small devil than a harmless insect. The first enemy to be held up for ridicule was John Ruskin, and the method used by Whistler was simply to dramatize the case of *Whistler* v. *Ruskin* by slightly altering the newspaper accounts of the court scenes and inserting in the margins his own sardonic comments, which he called "Reflections."

In his reveiw of *The Gentle Art,* Howells referred to the trial only obliquely, devoting most of his space to the longest single essay in the book, "Mr. Whistler's 'Ten O'Clock,' " which he commended "above everything else in the queer volume" before him. Since Whistler's famous lecture [1] delivered in London, Oxford, and Cambridge grew out of the earlier trial and the extensive newspaper controversy that followed the decision, one must, before turning to the "Ten O'Clock," recapture both the absurdity and the significance of Whistler's suit against the aging and enormously influential art critic, John Ruskin.

The facts are these: Ruskin returned to London in 1877 from one of his many trips to Italy, just in time for the opening of the new Grosvenor Gallery. There he saw and studied the paintings of Alma-Tadema, Watts, Holman Hunt, Burne-Jones, Millais—and Whistler. "Nocturne in Black and Gold: The Falling Rocket," Whistler's brilliant study of fireworks in Cremone Park, London,[2] had dazzled the public attending this first exhibition at the Grosvenor, both by its fiery colors and its use of the new technique of impressionism. It remained for the accepted arbiter of taste to speak. Ruskin at once recognized Whistler as a challenge to his authority. In the July 2, 1877, issue of Ruskin's letters to workingmen, *Fors Clavigera,* he extravagantly praised the Pre-Raphaelite painters, especially Burne-Jones, and then wrote a caustic page or two about the upstart exhibitor, Whistler—who immediately sued Ruskin for libel, and, to the surprise of the public, won the case.

As a "Prologue" to the "Action" of the trial, which he presented in *The Gentle Art of Making Enemies,* Whistler quoted the words of Ruskin on which he had based his libel suit twelve years earlier:

> For Mr. Whistler's own sake, no less than for the protection of the purchaser, Sir Coutts Lindsay ought not to have admitted works into the gallery in which the ill-educated conceit of the artist so nearly approached the aspect of willful imposture. I have seen, and heard, much of cockney impudence before now; but never expected to hear a coxcomb ask two hundred guineas for flinging a pot of paint in the public's face.[3]

Ruskin was only one among many critics to express disapproval. Before Ruskin's letter appeared in *Fors Clavigera,* the young Henry James had written his views of the opening exhibition at the new Grosvenor Gallery for the *Nation* of May 31, 1877.[4] Like Ruskin, James praised the eight canvases of Burne-Jones as "the most brilliant work offered at present by any painter to the London public" and then turned his attention to the display of canvases by his compatriot, whom he patronized as follows:

> Mr. Whistler presents half a dozen canvases which I must take care not to mention as pictures; they are, according to the catalogue, "nocturnes," "arrangements" and "harmonies." Since our business is with pictures, it were better, I suppose, not to speak of these things; but, after all, their material is paint and canvas, and they are framed and hung upon a wall. I have never seen any combination of these ingredients which has struck me as less profitable.

Since James himself at that time was producing in prose just such "nocturnes," "arrangements," and "harmonies" in his travel sketches and novels, it is somewhat surprising to discover that he apparently recognized no relationship between the "new way of painting" and "the new way of writing."[5] Had Whistler read them, James's words in the *Nation* might have been almost as offensive to him as Ruskin's. America's young art critic wrote concerning Whistler's "impressionism":

Mr. Whistler, it is known, is an "impressionist"; one of his nocturnes is his impression of Mr. Henry Irving, and another his impression of Miss Ellen Terry. It may be good to be an impressionist; but I should say on this evidence that it were vastly better to be an expressionist. Mr. Whistler's productions are, in the very nature of the case, uninteresting; they belong to the closet, not to the world. They may be good studio-jokes, or even useful studio-experiments, but they illustrate only what one may call the self-complacency of technicality.

James surely spoke like an old-line Academician when he brought his condemnation of Whistler's impressionism to a close with the firm remark that, "To people who stand on their own two feet and look at a reproduction of life with their two eyes, [Whistler's canvases] appeal with no persuasive force whatever."

The case of *Whistler* v. *Ruskin* was heard in the Court of the Exchequer Division on November 25 and 26, 1878; [6] the plaintiff claimed £1,000 damages; he won the suit and was awarded one farthing. Ruskin and Whistler were made to bear the cost of the trial; however, the wealthy Ruskin was relieved of the burden of debt by his friends, while Whistler—though he won the verdict—soon found himself bankrupt as a result of this trial. Howells observed in his review of *The Gentle Art of Making Enemies,* "This art scarcely deserved so much study as is there given it," since, besides being ruinously expensive, the "art of making enemies" is not permanently important.

> To make enemies is perfectly easy; the difficult thing is to keep them; the first you know they are no longer hating you. That seems to deprive Mr. Whistler's controversial sarcasms of importance; to leave them faded, as they were already ephemeral.[7]

Clearly, Howells never mastered "the gentle art of making enemies"!

An excellent example of how Whistler impaled his contemporaries—even those who did not deserve to be listed among his enemies—with the sharp pin of his wit, may be noticed in his garbled, one-page account of the testimony of William Powell Frith, one of the three witnesses for Ruskin.[8] Though Frith was entirely out of sympathy with all new art movements, he was, nevertheless, a much more gifted painter than Whistler would admit. On the margin of *The Gentle Art,* Whistler impishly quoted a sentence from Frith's *Autobiography* in which Frith had remarked that "it was just a toss up whether I became an Artist or an Auctioneer"; then Whistler added the "Reflection," "He must have tossed up."

Frith was in some confusion when he took the witness stand. Though he did not care for Whistler as an artist, neither did he like the pontificating Ruskin, whom he thought mistaken in his defense of the Pre-Raphaelites. Ruskin had chosen Frith as a witness, in fact, because he was known to be opposed to most of Ruskin's theories of art, and thus would not be predisposed to support Ruskin's cause. "You attend here very much against your will?" asked Sergeant Parry, the examining counsel, when Frith was called as a witness. "Yes," replied Frith, "it is a very painful thing to give evidence against a brother-artist. I am here on sub-poena." [9]

At the time of the trial, Whistler had never exhibited at the Royal Academy, nor had Frith exhibited at the Grosvenor, and Whistler welcomed the chance to sharpen the difference in attitude between Frith, the elderly Academician, and himself. He, therefore, cheerfully edited Frith's testimony for *The Gentle Art:* "I am an R. A. [Royal Academician]," Whistler quoted Frith as saying, "and have devoted my life to painting. I am the author of the 'Railway Station,' 'Derby Day,' and 'Rake's Progress.' " (Note the designation of Frith as an "author," rather than an "artist"!) Omitting the examiner's questions, Whistler summarized Frith's remarks in one paragraph:

"I have seen Mr. Whistler's pictures, and in my opinion they are not serious works of art. The nocturne in black and gold is not a serious work to me. I cannot see anything of the true representation of water and atmosphere in the painting of 'Battersea Bridge.' There is a pretty colour which pleases the eye, but there is nothing more. To my thinking, the description of moonlight is not true. The picture is not worth two hundred guineas. Composition and detail are most important matters in a picture. In our profession men of equal merit differ as to the character of a picture. One may blame, while another praises, a work. I have not exhibited at the Grosvenor

Gallery. I have read Mr. Ruskin's works." Mr. Frith here got down.

Whistler's "Reflection" in the margin of the page read: "A decidedly honest man—I have not heard of him since." [10] It was followed by a tiny butterfly, resembling a sprite turning a somersault in its amusement over Frith's total inability to comprehend the meaning of impressionism.

Apparently Henry James attended the trial, for he wrote it up for the *Nation* within a week after the decision was rendered. "The verdict, of course, satisfied neither party," he noted, and he added that he found "the crudity of levity of the whole affair . . . decidedly painful." Had the trial taken place in "some Western American town," James remarked, it would have been cited as "an incident of a low civilization." However, James was interested, at least, in the attitudes toward painting that were brought out in the course of the trial after "the painter's singular canvases were handed about in court." He commented with approval that "Mr. Ruskin had the honor of having his estimate of them substantiated by Mr. Frith," whose testimony James accepted.[11]

The trial aroused further thoughts in James's mind. Should a critic, he wondered, even so eminent a one as Ruskin, be allowed to damn the work of an artist, even an inferior one? The question was important to James, for at that time he also was suffering from the unfriendly reviews of critics. "Mr. Ruskin's language quite transgresses the decencies of criticism," James wrote to his American readers, adding reflectively, "and he has been laying about him for some years past with such promiscuous violence that it gratifies one's sense of justice to see him brought up as a disorderly character." As a slight concession, perhaps, to this friend of his own friend C. E. Norton, James concluded his words on the rights of critics by saying of Ruskin, "He is a chartered libertine—he has possessed himself by prescription of the function of general scold. His literary bad manners are recognised."

Though Ruskin attempted to write to Norton of the trial with casual nonchalance,[12] he never completely recovered from the loss of prestige that followed the verdict, and he soon resigned his position as Slade Professor of Art at Oxford, which he had held since 1870.

Whistler, on the other hand, though bankrupt, was undaunted. James's next communication to the *Nation,* on February 18, 1879,[13] was chiefly concerned with a little pamphlet, published by Whistler, "in which he delivered himself on the subject of art-criticism." The pamphlet, James reported, was "prettily-printed," and was already in its sixth edition.[14] It sold for a shilling, he said, and could be seen "in most of the shop-windows."

> It is very characteristic of the painter, and highly entertaining; but I am not sure that it will have rendered appreciable service to the cause which he has at heart. The cause that Mr. Whistler has at heart is the absolute suppression and extinction of the art-critic and his function. According to Mr. Whistler the art-critic is an impertinence, a nuisance, a monstrosity—and usually, into the bargain, an arrant fool.

And James added thoughtfully, "What greater sarcasm can Mr. Ruskin pass upon himself than that he preaches to young men what he cannot perform?"

However, Whistler's "little diatribe against the critics is suggestive," James remarked. So suggestive, in fact, was this small pamphlet that it affected the tenor of thought of its day. It is now looked upon as an amusing but important statement of the art-for-art's-sake views, which were finally to silence the art-for-morality's-sake or the art-for-religion's-sake—or art-for-the-narrative's-sake—views of an earlier generation of Victorian England.

Whistler made this 17-page pamphlet of 1878 the basis of his famous "Ten O'Clock Lecture," in 1885 and gave it a prominent place in *The Gentle Art of Making Enemies.* Howells commended this essay especially, for many of the arresting ideas expressed by Whistler were precisely those that Howells had been attempting to hammer into the minds of his *Harper's* readers ever since he moved into the "Study" in 1886.

Though Howells enjoyed, admired, and learned from the canvases of Frith—which he appreciated as he did the novels of Dickens—he had long ago become aware of a new and fresh way of painting and writing. Watching George Fuller bending over his easel in his studio on Tremont Street, studying the exhibitions of early Impressionists in Boston in the seventies, talking with Henry James, whom he invited to comment on the current art shows for the *Atlantic*—these influences, among others, had made Howells conscious of the new ideas that were causing the ethical-religious art concepts of Ruskin and others to seem outmoded.

Howells had expressed his notion of "the new way of writing" in "Henry James, Jr.," his essay for the November, 1882, *Century Magazine,* in terms that suggested Whistler's statements concerning "the new way of painting" in his "Ten O'Clock Lecture." Howells thus was prepared to welcome the lecture when it reappeared in *The Gentle Art,* which he introduced to his readers the following year with this brief summary:

> "Listen," says Mr. James McNeill Whistler in that "Ten O'Clock" lecture of his which must have made his hearers feel very much lectured indeed, not to say browbeaten—"Listen! There never was an artistic period. There never was an art-loving nation" . . . Some such thing we understand Mr. Whistler to teach us in those dazzling fireworks of his which scale the heavens as stars, and come down javelins on the heads and breasts of enemies. Art arose because some artist was born with the need to beautify the useful, and other men used the beautiful things he created while they were off killing and tilling, because there were no others to use when they got back; they *had* to drink out of decorated cups and dwell in noble palaces.

Nobody questioned the propriety of using the beautiful goblets made by the artists, wrote Whistler; nobody asked for rugs or garments or javelins other than those offered by the artists, "for the artist alone produced" in the days before the invention of machinery. But, Whistler wrote, we have entered the period of "the tawdry, the common, the geegaw"; the people are just as content to accept these machine-made objects of the modern age as they once were to make use of the products of the artists. The manufacturer and the huckster are taking the place of the artist whose occupation is almost gone. What then of the artist, with art relegated to the curiosity shop? The artist, as always, suddenly appears in our midst and is a law unto himself. He must pick, and choose, and group as he will, the elements of color and form which he sees around him. Nature, unaided, never succeeds in producing a picture, nor should the critic demand that the artist be "realistic." The artist knows that "Nature is usually wrong"; he shuns the glare of the daily scene, and is guided by his own "impression" according to temperament. This is the artist's "truth."

> And when the evening mist clothes the riverside with poetry, as with a veil, and the poor buildings lose themselves in the dim sky, and the tall chimneys become campanili, and the warehouses are palaces in the night, and the whole city hangs in the heavens, and fairy-land is before us—then the wayfarer hastens home; the working man and the cultured one, the wise man and the one of pleasure, cease to understand, as they have ceased to see, and Nature, who, for once, has sung in tune, sings her exquisite song to the artist alone, her son and her master—her son in that he loves her, her master in that he knows her.[15]

Whistler's prose nocturne might have been written by Howells, looking out of his study window at sunset across the Charles River at the dark outline of the Cambridge factories and smokestacks, reminiscent to him of evenings in Venice. Or it might have been a paragraph from James's *Princess Casamassima*, describing Hyacinth Robinson's lonely evening walk through the dimly lit streets of London to his looming tenement. For Howells and James, in their poetic interpretation of "realism," were attempting, like Whistler, to catch the light and shadow of the actual scene as it appeared to the beholder. As Howells said, artists had to put aside "such deadly old engravings as 'Washington Irving and His Friends' "[16] and learn to see with new eyes. For the writer of the new school "competes with his brother the painter in *his* attempt to render the look of things, the look that conveys the meaning, to catch the color, the relief, the expression, the surface, the substance of the human spectacle."[17] Just as, according to Whistler, art is essentially the impression of the artist, so, according to James and Howells, "the capacity for receiving straight impressions"[18] is the first requisite of the novelist. Therein lies the essential "moral" of the painting or the novel

—does it truly reflect the impression made on the mind of its creator? Nor is the intrusive, noncreative critic in a position to have an opinion on the subject. "Countless, indeed, the horde of pretenders" to this knowledge, groaned Whistler, while Howells likened the critic to a man "who is given a gun, and told to shoot at some passer from behind a hedge." [19] Fortunately, "Art seeks the Artist alone," said Whistler, and pays no attention to the "intoxicated mob of mediocrity, whose leaders prate and counsel, and call aloud, where the Gods once spoke in whisper!" [20]

Though James still referred to Whistler as "the buffoon of the Grosvenor, the laughing-stock of the critics," his essay for the August, 1882, issue of the *Atlantic* indicated that he had relented in his attitude toward the "extremely peculiar" Mr. Whistler.[21] After studying the seven paintings by Whistler hanging at the Grosvenor that summer, James wrote: "Mr. Whistler is a votary of 'tone'; his manner of painting is to breathe upon a canvas. It is not too much to say that he has, to a certain point, the creative afflatus." Moreover, the wearisome British paintings in that same exhibit were illustrative of "no striking experiments," though the usual number of tables, chairs, mantelpieces, and waddling geese were to be seen, for these were the "stock properties of British art," which was sadly "Philistine."

Howells, too, during this exciting summer in London, was not only studying the paintings at the Grosvenor and the Royal Academy—no doubt under the guidance of James—but he was also enjoying delightful personal association with Edward Burne-Jones, Lawrence Alma-Tadema, Hubert Herkomer and George Henry Boughton,[22] each of whom James discussed at some length in his August essay for the *Atlantic*.

Ten years after Howells' summer in London, and a year or two after his review of Whistler's *Gentle Art* for *Harper's,* his thoughts on the Impressionists had sifted through his mind sufficiently to reappear in a slight but amusing novel, *The Coast of Bohemia* (1893).[23] In that story, Frank Ludlow, the twenty-one-year-old hero, was an artist recently returned from study in France. He found himself, on a sweltering day in September, attending the forty-sixth annual fair of the Pymantoning County Agricultural Society of his home state, Ohio. Roaming through the milling crowd near the horsetrack, with paintings of the Impressionists fresh in his mind, he sought with youthful earnestness to transform the dusty scene before him into the kind of painting he had been trained to appreciate in his Paris studio. "The spectacle had the importance which multitude gives," he noticed, and this "he hoped to get again in his impression." Ludlow "saw the deep purples which he looked to see with eyes trained by the French masters of his school to find them, and the indigo blues, the intense greens, the rainbow oranges and scarlets; he knew just how he should give them. In the light of this vast afternoon sky, cloudless, crystalline in its clearness, no brilliancy of rendering could be too bold." [24]

Like Howells after his years in Venice, Ludlow felt that his European experience should be used to enhance his vision of the American scene. The fair, he thought, "could be reported on his canvas with all its native character; and yet it could be made to appeal to the enlightened eye with the charm of a French subject, and impressionism could be fully justified of its follower in Pymantoning as well as in Paris." The following description convinces one that Howells, if not Ludlow, had profited by studying the paintings to be seen in Paris and London:

> The golden dust along the track; the level tops of the buggies drawn up within its ellipse, and the groups scattered about in gypsy gayety on the grass there; the dark blur of men behind the barrier; the women, with their bright hats and parasols, massed flower-like,—all made him long to express them in lines and dots and breadths of pure color.

Ludlow had "caught the vital effect of the whole," and this he resolved to interpret at least to those who "had received the light of the new faith in painting, who believed in the prismatic colors as in the ten commandments, and hoped to be saved by tone-contrasts." Ludlow had become "too fanatical an impressionist to care" for the opinion of those who had not been converted. A certain "lingering doubt" of the subject, rather than of his own powers, had kept him from bringing a canvas with him to the Fair, in order to record his "precious first glimpse" of the scene. But as he wandered through the long, barnlike buildings with their inadequate attempts at decorations, his vision faded until he began to doubt "whether people tasteless enough to produce these inanities and imagine them artistic, could form even the subjects of art."

Ludlow spent "a very miserable time in the Fine Arts Department of the Pymantoning County Agricultural Fair; and in a kind of horrible fascination began to review the collection in detail"— the crazy quilts, the photographs, the "round brass plaques painted with flowers, and little satin banners painted with birds or autumn leaves, and gilt rolling-pins with vines." Could those village girls, "so prettily gowned and picturesquely hatted on the benches out there by the race-course, could it have been they who committed those atrocities?" Exasperated as well as pained, Ludlow was, like the hero of Gilbert and Sullivan's "Patience," a "Greenery-yallery Grosvenor Gallery" young man, to whom "the worship of beauty was a sort of religion" and the acceptance of ugliness "a sort of blasphemy."

Needless to say, Howells' unhappy young artist, who had drunk deep of the art philosophy of the decade, had yet to learn that a fifteen-year-old girl, in tears because her sketches had not won a "premium," might herself be more interesting than her childish drawings. Howells, having profited from his study of Whistler and other Impressionists, could only smile ironically at the delusions of the artists who supposed "aesthetic cultivation," rather than human understanding, was the end of life.[25] Ludlow was guilty of that "pride of taste" against which Howells had spoken in *Criticism and Fiction*. However, after encountering Cornelia Saunders, Ludlow gradually "descended from the high horse which he saw it was really useless for him to ride in that simple presence." [26] Instead of thinking of "our farm folks" in terms of "Millet and his Barbizon peasants," [27] Ludlow was called upon to deal with the much more difficult problem presented by a talented country girl as an art student in New York City. Throughout her adventure, Cornelia remained, of course, on the "*coast* of Bohemia." Who knows into what dark forests she might have wandered had she not found herself guided at last into marriage with Ludlow?

In June, 1894, the year after the publication of his study of the art student in New York, Howells visited his son in Paris. John

Howells was at that time pursuing his architectural studies at the Beaux Arts and living in a studio-apartment on the Rue du Bac overlooking the garden of Whistler. The familiar figure of the painter, bird cage in hand, clad in white duck trousers, blue jacket, and wide straw hat, could be seen from John's window as Whistler strolled about among his flowers.

Having made Whistler's acquaintance some ten years earlier, Howells and his two children, John and Mildred, were soon invited to the Whistler "breakfasts" in the blue and white dining-room of 110 Rue du Bac, where Howells had an opportunity to brood—though briefly—over the Paris version of "the coast of Bohemia." According to Joseph Pennell, Howells attended the Whistler gatherings "once or twice," with his daughter, of whom Whistler made a lithograph.[28]

Mrs. Pennell later recalled the occasions when she and her husband were "one of the gay company at the long table with its blue-and-white, its excellent *menu,* its good wine, above all with Whistler presiding, talking as only he could talk and giving to his historic 'Ha! Ha!' a friendliness undreamed of by the outside world." Mrs. Pennell remembered, too, that after breakfast the company enjoyed "the freedom of the garden with its cool shade of trees and the solemn chanting of monks on the other side of the high wall." The talk in the garden was subdued, "the years had made a *chèr maître* of the once much feared collector of scalps." [29] In this enchanting atmosphere Howells met the artists and writers he had known in New York and London—the Abbeys, John Sargent, Aubrey Beardsley, the Pennells, all of whom were welcomed by the Whistlers in their ground-floor apartment. But before the month was over, Howells was summoned home by the illness of his father.

What, precisely, Howells thought of his Parisian experience when he returned to America, is difficult to say; his rather confused feelings, however, are suggested by the letter he wrote to his son from Saratoga, New York, on July 27, 1894. "Perhaps it was as well I was called home," he mused. "The poison of Europe was getting into my soul. You must look out for that. They live much more fully than we do. Life here is still for the future,—it is a land of Emersons—and I like a little present moment in mine. When I think of the Whistler garden!—But Saratoga amuses somewhat." [30]

Through a mutual friend, Jonathan Sturges, Henry James heard of Howells' visits to the Whistler apartment and wrote in his notebook the younger man's impression of Howells in Paris. "He seemed sad—rather brooding" Sturges had told James. "He laid his hand on my shoulder and said, *à propos* of some remark of mine: 'Oh, you are young, you are young—be glad of it; be glad of it and *live*. This place makes it all come over me. I see it now. I haven't done so—and now I'm old. It's too late. It has gone past me—I've lost it. You have time. You are young. Live!' " [31]

Jonathan Sturges' report of the "five words" Howells said to him one day in Whistler's garden caused James to perceive in them "the faint vague germ, the mere point of the start of a subject." Whether Lambert Strether, the subject of *The Ambassadors* was, indeed, Howells—as James protested he was not—is impossible to say. Strether, in the final summing up of his elderly adventure in Paris, remembered a painting he had seen in a "maroon-coloured, sky-lighted inner shrine of Tremont Street." This "small Lambinet had charmed him, long years before, at a Boston dealer's," had caused him to turn and twist "the possibilities for an hour" before he decided, for lack of funds, to forego "the only adventure in his life in connection with the purchase of a work of art." [32] Surely at this point in the novel Strether was, not Howells, but James himself, thinking back to his days in Boston when, as art critic for the *Atlantic,* he was eagerly studying the Impressionist displayed in the show rooms on Tremont Street. Though both Howells and James took issue with—and borrowed—the art-for-art's-sake ideas of their day, they were not only deeply affected by the new attitudes of the art movement in their own poetic-realism, but they were personally moved by their glimpse of Bohemia, if only from the coast.

In April, 1895, after Howells' hasty trip to Paris, he was asked by *Harper's Weekly* to comment on the Spring Exhibition of the Society of American Artists. Childe Hassam,[33] John Twachtman, J. Alden Weir, and other American Impressionists were to be seen that year, and after Howells' view of them, he wrote, in terms reminiscent of Whistler, "All that form and color gave a sense of bloom such as might remain from some stroll through a gardened landscape in a happy hour of the fullblown spring. It is like that, or it is like the sense of music which one has heard once or twice; and perhaps that is enough; perhaps form and color that insist upon saying something more articulate make the appeal that literature ought to make." Impressionism, and especially that of Whistler's paintings, had taught Howells to look for color and harmony of form in a painting, rather than story. "The world looks much lighter and brighter and more positive for it," he wrote, "and if it will not continue to look always and everywhere so light and bright and positive as impressionism has seen it, still we shall have been shown that it does sometimes somewhere look so." [34]

In 1896, *Harper's Weekly* invited Howells to attend the two important New York exhibitions—that of the American Artists and that of the National Academy. In his column, "Life and Letters," of April 18, 1896, Howells evenly divided his compliments between the two shows, for he enjoyed the old and the new in art, just as he delighted in the paintings of Frith as well as in those of Whistler. "At the Artists everything was fresher, moderner, newer," he wrote, "but it wanted the pathos of the old-fashioned work, which I found very great in some of the Academy pieces." Howells, however, was aware that, in art as well as in literature, there had taken place a subtle change in popular taste that both artist and writer disregarded at their peril. "A picture of 1856 painted in 1856 will have a certain claim to one's admiration," he wrote, "but a picture of 1856 painted in 1896 can appeal only to one's compassion." At the National Academy "the heart was wrung for the art that had outlived its time."

Howells' sensitive response to the new in literature and in art prompted him to welcome the little volume of *The Poetry of Emily Dickinson* when it first appeared in 1891, and to link it, in his "Study" of January, 1891, with Whistler's *Gentle Art,* since both announced a fresh outlook. When Howells came to know the young writer Stephen Crane during the nineties, he encouraged him, not only by helping him find a publisher, but also by reading aloud to him the poetry of Emily Dickinson. The result was another small volume of "strange poems," *Black Riders,* written by Crane who, with Howells' aid, found his own mode of expression, which was closely akin to the impressionism of Emily Dickinson's poetry and to Whistler's painting.[35] Howells reviewed *Black Riders* favorably when it appeared in 1896, not because he altogether approved of

Crane's free verse, but because he felt "sympathy keen and eager with all who are trying to utter life in any form."

NOTES

1. Twenty-five copies were printed for private use in 1885, republished in 1888.

2. See Howells' comment on this painting in "The Editor's Study," *Harper's Monthly Magazine,* LXXXII (January, 1891), 321.

3. "Prologue," p. 1. Sir Coutts Lindsay was a wealthy Scotsman who in 1877 opened the Grosvenor Gallery, often referred to as a British "Salon des Repusées."

4. "The Grosvenor Gallery and the Royal Academy," unsigned article datelined, "London, May 9, 1877," *Nation,* LXXVII (May 31, 1877), 320–321.

5. See "James and Whistler at the Grosvenor Gallery," Donald M. Murray. *American Quarterly,* IV (Spring, 1952), 49–65.

6. In *The Gentle Art of Making Enemies,* Whistler gave the date of the trial as November 15, 1878, which was incorrect. See Hasketh Pearson, *The Man Whistler* (1952), p. 107.

7. *Harper's,* LXXXII (January, 1891), 321.

8. The other two witnesses for Ruskin were Edward Bourne-Jones and Tom Taylor. Witnesses for Whistler were William Michael Rossetti, William G. Wills, and Albert Moore.

9. Quoted by Hesketh Pearson, *op. cit.,* p. 116.

10. *The Gentle Art of Making Enemies,* p. 17.

11. "Contemporary Notes of Whistler vs. Ruskin," *Nation,* LXXVIII (Dec. 19, 1878) 385. Reprinted in Le Roy Phillips (ed.), *Views and Reviews* (1908).

12. Ruskin wrote to Norton on November 26, 1878, "Today, (Monday-date guessed above), I believe the comic Whistler lawsuit is to be decided." *Letters of John Ruskin to C. E. Norton* (1905) II, 152.

13. Vol. LXXIX, p. 119.

14. "Whistler vs. Ruskin," 1878.

15. *The Gentle Art,* p. 144.

16. *Criticism and Fiction,* p. 63.

17. Henry James, *The Art of Fiction* (1884). Leon Edel (ed.), *The Future of the Novel* (1956), p. 14.

18. *Ibid.,* p. 21.

19. *Criticism and Fiction,* p. 28.

20. *The Gentle Art,* p. 152.

21. "London Pictures and London Plays," *Atlantic Monthly,* L (August, 1882), 253–263.

22. See Part Two, Chapter I of this book.

23. Illustrated by F. O. Crawford.

24. *The Coast of Bohemia* (1893), pp. 1–3.

25. *Ibid.,* pp. 7–9.

26. *Ibid.,* p. 16.

27. *Ibid.,* p. 6.

28. This lithograph is in the possession of the Howells family. E. R. and J. Pennell, *The Life of James McNeill Whistler* (1911), p. 317.

29. Elizabeth Robins Pennell, *Whistler, the Friend* (1930), p. 179.

30. *Life in Letters,* II, 52.

31. Oct. 31, 1895. F. O. Matthiessen and Kenneth Murdock (eds.), *The Notebooks of Henry James* (1961), pp. 226–228.

32. *The Ambassadors* (1909), II, 245–246.

33. Childe Hassam illustrated Howells' *Venetian Life* (1907).

34. "At the American Artists'," by W. D. Howells. *Harper's Weekly,* XXXIX (Apr. 6, 1895), 318. For a list of the exhibiting artists, see "Spring Art Exhibitions: The Society of American Artists." Unsigned article, *Ibid.,* p. 318.

35. Joseph J. Kwiat, "Stephen Crane & Painting," *American Quarterly,* IV (Winter, 1952), 331–338.

· 4 ·

Art and Society

Though Howells' concept of realism was modified by his deepening sense of the implications for fiction-writing that were to be found in the paintings of the Impressionists, it was to William Morris, craftsman and socialist, that he turned for his idea of the place of art in an ideal community. William Morris called his "Chapters From a Utopian Romance" *News From Nowhere* (1891); Howells named his utopian "Romance" *A Traveler From Altruria* (1894).

Morris' Guest and Howells' Traveler brought back from Nowhere and Altruria the essentially romantic news that, by doing away with both the idea of classes and of money, human beings might escape from commercialism, competition, and the tyranny of the machine. Morris' Guest was merely a nineteenth-century Englishman dreaming of how the banks of the Thames, marred by factories and dingy towns, might be restored to their medieval beauty. Howells' Traveler was, in fact, an enlightened American—though he claimed to have come from a remote island near Greece—who imagined a democracy based on a respect for the rights of every citizen to "life, liberty and the pursuit of happiness." Both men suffered from the labor strife, the class distinctions, and, above all, from the ugliness of the competitive society of their day. In the beautiful, serene lands of Nowhere and Altruria, men and women clad in brightly colored garments of classic design happily worked in their shops or studios, contentedly tilled the soil, or idly fished in clear streams.

In both of these utopias the principles of beauty were considered so much more important than the principle of gain that money, machinery, strikes, and all the other woes of a commercial society were regarded as dimly remembered nightmares, done away with by the Revolution (Morris) or by the Evolution (Howells). *News From Nowhere* (1891) was written, according to Morris, in reply to Edward Bellamy's *Looking Backward* (1888); Howells' *Traveler From Altruria* (1894) was deeply affected by Morris' concept of a society founded on a belief in man's need for creative expression. Bellamy's dream of a materialistic society, overflowing with machine-made gadgets, appealed to neither man.

As far as is known, Howells and Morris never met to talk over their ideas, nor did they correspond. Howells, indeed, did not at first sympathize with the poetry or painting of Morris. Though Howells wrote in *My Literary Passions* (1895) [1] that he had read the poetry of Morris in the 1870's "with a pleasure little less than passionate," a rereading of Howells' review of "Love Is Enough" suggests that he found Morris' poetry very dull indeed. After quoting a lengthy passage from the poem, Howells confided to the reader that this was the best he could find in "the whole skillfully attenuated triviality from which we take it, and which is otherwise too dull for any words of ours to tell; nobody but Mr. Morris could give a just sense of its inexorable dreariness, its unrelenting lengthiness, and serious vacuity." [2]

Two years later Howells attempted a review of Morris' poem, "The Defense of Guinevere"—concerning which he later professed a "passionate" pleasure—but he found it "a somewhat perplexing affair," increasing his "besetting doubt" as to whether "it is quite worth while to do the things he does so well." [3] At that time, Morris was not only an ardent member of the Pre-Raphaelite Brotherhood, but he had set up a shop in Red Lion's Square, London, where, with several members of the group, he had for more than ten years been making and designing wall-paper, hangings, chintzes, carpets, stained-glass windows, and metal work of all kinds. In 1875 the company dissolved, and Morris continued the business as sole manager of a thriving group of workmen. He did not, however, become thoroughly imbued with socialistic thought until the 1880's, and therefore his taste for medievalism, as it was reflected in his poetry of the seventies, seemed to Howells merely tiresome. "From first to last," he wrote, at that time there was in him a sort of "prepense return to former mental conditions and feelings," and this tendency Howells emphatically deplored. To read the poetry of Morris,[4] he mused, was rather "like looking through a modern house"

> equipped with Eastlake furniture, adorned with tiles, and painted in the Pompeiian style, or hung with Mr. Morris' own admirable wall-papers; it is all very pretty indeed; charming; but it is consciously mediaeval, consciously Greek, and it is so well aware of its quaintness, that, on the whole, one would rather not live in it.

Howells, who, when he wrote this review,[5] had only recently moved into his new home on Concord Avenue in Cambridge, had a fresher attitude toward modern living, as well as modern art and literature, than the older man. Could it be that Morris' poetry was merely "a kind of decorative, household art"? he asked, noting that the first four poems in the little book

> are the sort of thing that one would like to have painted on large, movable screens. As it is, they are rather painted than written, and might perhaps serve the desired purpose of decoration if pasted on the screens.

Howells expressed, in this early review of Morris' poetry, an intuitive mistrust of painterly poetry and poetic painting. He recognized clearly that any such superficial relationship is disastrous to true painting, as well as to true poetry. Thus falsely related, they both became merely "decorative." Morris' art seemed dull to Howells until Morris, like Howells, was caught up into the deepening stream of social thought of the 1880's.

It is not surprising that Howells did not encounter Morris during the two summers he spent in London (1882–83), for at that time Morris was an ardent member of the Socialists Democratic Federation, writing "Chants For Socialists," and making speeches, up and down England, on such subjects as "Art, Wealth and Riches." This lecture was delivered in 1883 at the Manchester Art Museum; it aroused such interest that a discussion of its attack on "the mean, the shabby and the dirty" was continued in the Manchester *Examiner*. One letter to the *Examiner* suggested, with anxious disapproval, that Morris discussed in his address more than "mere art."

Morris, no doubt, welcomed the letter, for it gave him an opportunity to express again his social philosophy based on his belief in popular art. His reply indicated that Morris, as well as Whistler, was aware of the dangers to art of the machine age, which provides us only "the tawdry, the common, the gee-gaw" in art. However, the conclusions he reached as to the relation of the artist to society were the reverse of Whistler's notion of the supreme individuality of the artist. "Art for art's sake" seemed to Morris "mere art," but in his lecture Morris raised another question, of wider implication. He especially wished to point out that art is not individualistic but social, "involving the happiness or misery of the greater part of the community." In earlier times all art was popular art, said Morris; since the machine has deprived men of this fundamental relationship with production, our society suffers all the resultant evils of a class society.

> The absence of popular art from modern times is more disquieting and grievous to bear for this reason than for any other, that it betokens the fatal division of men into the cultivated and the degraded classes which competitive commerce has bred and fosters; popular art has no chance of a healthy life, or, indeed, of a life at all, till we are on the way to fill up this terrible gulf between riches and poverty . . . [W]hat business have we with art at all unless all can share it? [6]

Five years later, in the December, 1888, "Study," [7] Howells commented in the same spirit, on "the conditions" of modern life, especially in America, where "vast masses of men are sunk in misery that must grow every day more hopeless, or embroiled in a struggle for mere life that must end in enslaving and imbruting them." The answer to the question of how "to be saved from the curse that is on selfishness" Howells found in the doctrine of popular art that was expressed in the writing of William Morris and John Ruskin. Quoting from Morris' lecture, "Art and Socialism," [8] Howells wrote:

> Art, indeed, is beginning to find out that if it does not make friends with Need it must perish. It perceives that to take itself from the many and leave them no joy in their work, and to give itself to the few whom it can bring no joy in their idleness, is an error that kills. This has long been the burden of Ruskin's message: and if we can believe William Morris, the common people have heard him gladly, and have felt the truth of what he says . . . [that] the men and women who do the hard work of the world have learned from him and from Morris that they have a right to pleasure in their toil.

Howells included this passage from the "Study" in the final section of *Criticism and Fiction* several years later, for a belief in the social obligation of art had by then become a fundamental part of his philosophy. As a result of the social awakening that, in the 1880's, changed the outlook of both Howells and Morris, Howells grew to understand and appreciate the views of the British socialist and artist. Howells then read Morris so "passionately" that he seemed to forget his earlier judgment of Morris' poetry and painting as merely "decorative."

News From Nowhere, written at the end of a decade of strenuous writing and lecturing on the subject, was a summing up of Morris' views on art and society, after he had become an avowed socialist; in Howells' Altrurian essays he expressed his conclusion concerning democratic art. Like all of Howells' writing, these essays were uniquely his own: they were, however, colored by the socialistic aesthetics of Morris' utopian dream. Howells advanced no definite political platform as did Morris. In order to understand how similar —and how different—were the social dreams of Morris and Howells, as expressed in *News From Nowhere* and *A Traveler From Altruria,* one must glance back to the mid-1880's, and observe the parallel paths that led the two men to their conclusions.

In 1885, the year when Whistler delivered his three "Ten

O'Clock" lectures and Howells agreed to take over the "Study" of *Harper's,* Morris undertook the editorship of *Commonweal,* the official paper of the newly organized Socialist League. "As to the conduct of The Commonweal," Morris wrote in the opening issue, "it must be remembered that it has one aim—the propagation of Socialism." [9] Edward Aveling was announced as the "Sub-Editor," and Eleanor Marx Aveling, the daughter of Karl Marx, was a contributor. Until 1891, when Morris became discouraged by the communistic tendencies of the staff of the *Commonweal,* he wrote editorials, poems, reviews, imaginary tales of all sorts for its columns, edited it almost alone, and, indeed, paid for its publication from his own pocket. Though Morris himself was inclined to write articles on "The Aims of Art," or "Genius," he also wrote an editorial on the trial of the Chicago anarchists [10]—which he called "One of those pieces of bloodshed which are the natural results of driving oppressed men into a corner"—as well as on "Christianity and Socialism," the "Fabian Essays," and "The 'Eight Hours.'" Morris' "Dream of John Ball" and his "News From Nowhere" appeared in the *Commonweal* [11] before he withdrew from the whole socialist movement and retired to his printing press at Kelmscott a few years before his death in 1896.

News From Nowhere came out in book form in 1891, just at the time when Morris retired; Howells then returned to New York after two years in Boston, where he had become deeply immersed in the activities of the Christian Socialists.[12] Though there was no official connection between the *Dawn,* the organ of that short-lived left-wing American movement, and the *Commonweal,* it is to be remarked that both publications reflected the ideas of Tolstoy, Henry George, Laurence Gronlund, Edward Bellamy, the Fabian Society; both were concerned with the place of the church in modern society; both considered art in relation to the regeneration of society as a whole. Mr. and Mrs. Edward Aveling [13] visited America in the winter of 1886–87, during which they visited with members of the staff of the *Dawn* and reported in *Commonweal* on "Socialism in America." [14] Henry George lectured in London and Boston and wrote for the two papers. The range of ideas, the tone of the editorials, the very make-up of the two publications, were similar, the chief—and important—difference being that, whereas the *Com-monweal* stressed revolution, the *Dawn* advocated evolution, or the gradual change through education and the vote. Neither to Morris nor to Howells, however, were the political issues so important as the social reorganization of society, which was described by both men in terms of the psychological needs of the common man for beauty.

Morris' sense of these needs and of the impossibility of finding room for their expression in the age of machinery finally drove him to give up the exhausting effort he had made, through lecturing and writing, to bring about a Socialist revolution. Being neither "a professional economist nor a professional politician," but merely "a man busily engaged in the arts," Morris wrote in the Preface to *Signs of Change* (1888),[15] he had endeavored to "repulse pessimism" by persuading himself that "the ugly disgraces of civilization might be got rid of by the conscious will of intelligent people." This effort he at last found to have been misplaced; "as I strove to stir up people to this reform, I found that the causes of the vulgarities of civilization lay deeper than I had thought." Step by step Morris "was driven to the conclusion that all these uglinesses are but the outward expression of the innate moral baseness into which we are forced by our present form of society, and that it is futile to attempt to deal with them from the outside." Therefore, Morris gathered a number of his earlier lectures, some of which had been published in the *Commonweal,* and addressed them to any of his readers "who have found themselves hard-pressed by the sordidness of civilization."

Howells, who was also "busily engaged in the arts," and was certainly neither a politician nor an economist, found in these essays the germ of the thought that, a few years later, he embedded in the Traveler's description of Altruria. "In one of his lectures," Howells wrote in the January, 1890, "Study,"

> Mr. Morris asks his hearer to go through the streets of any city and consider the windows of the shops, how they are heaped with cheap and vulgar and tawdry and foolish gim-cracks, which men's lives have been worn out in making, and other men's lives in selling, and yet other men's lives in getting

money to waste upon, and which are finally to be cast out of our houses and swept into our dust-bins.

These "sham-needs" Morris described in "The Aims of Art." [16] To educate young people, not in the arts of moneymaking, but in the lost pleasure of creative work, should be the aim of popular art. Morris, Howells observed, instances the demand for machine-made art, rather than the craftsman's product, as "one of the great sham-needs which the exigencies of competition have created." Art can only be redeemed from the curse of machinery by "the cooperative society of the future," where "excellence" and not "commercial success" will be "the aim of artistic endeavor."

Howells found Morris' position in this lecture "interesting"; however, he remarked sadly, Morris "hardly takes account of the aesthetic immaturity" of the public. As Morris had tried throughout the eighties to make the purchaser consider the true beauty of a pitcher or a table, which is made with a real sense of purpose by an individual and not by a machine, so Howells from the "Study" of *Harper's* had from month to month urged his readers to cultivate a taste for the "real" in literature, as opposed to the romantic and stereotyped. By the end of the decade, Howells, as well as Morris, despaired of his efforts. As Howells put the matter in his comment on Morris' lecture, "Some of us like to see life in literature as it is; but far more like to see it in circus dress, with spangled tights, riding three barebacked horses at once." The tawdry in art Howells found akin to the romantic in literature, and both were a seemingly inevitable accompaniment of the "civilization" based on "selfish greed" and "ceaseless contention," rather than on "brotherhood and cooperation." [17]

At the opening of the new decade, January, 1890, when Howells was musing on Morris' unattainable hopes for popular art, he was about to resign from his position on *Harper's Monthly,* having finally conceded that he had lost the battle for realism. "When the Study opens its windows and sees the cattle on a thousand hills, how contentedly they munch away at the grass," the Editor has to admit that "choice and delicate fruits" are not appropriate. "Mere fodder in all the arts" is what "those honest oxen, those amiable sheep, those worthy donkeys" require; he despaired for the moment, of popular art, other than the romantic and the machine-made.

The three social novels that Howells wrote in the second half of the 1880's—*The Minister's Charge, Annie Kilburn,* and *A Hazard of New Fortunes*—all reflected Howells' own frustrated thinking on how the "amiable sheep" of modern American society might be helped by those from the "cultivated" classes to escape from their impoverished lives. In these three novels, neither the minister, who attempted to aid a poor young poet; nor the social-minded Annie Kilburn, who tried to bring leisure and drama to the factory girls; nor the journalist, who coped with the conflicting issues of a strike, succeeded in his efforts. Howells' next two years in Boston (1889–91), where he associated with old friends such as Norton, Holmes, and Hale, and new ones such as Bellamy, Bliss, and Garland, enabled him to share with more confidence the idealistic thoughts on social progress. Morris' *News From Nowhere* supplied the belief in popular art that inspired Howells' *Traveler From Altruria.*

The speech of the Altrurian describing to the guests of a New Hampshire hotel, the "conditions" in Altruria "before the time of the Evolution," closely paralleled Hammond's account of "The Great Change," [18] which was brought about by the revolution in Nowhere. Howells believed in evolution, and Morris advocated revolution; however, their basic concepts of production in the machine age were so similar that the Altrurian's words on "the ugly and stupid and foolish things" of an earlier period moved the professor in the group listening to the Altrurian's speech to whisper to his neighbor "He has got *that* out of William Morris. Depend upon it, the man is a humbug. He is not an Altrurian at all." [19] The professor was surely correct in his recognition of Morris as the source of the Altrurian's concept of the false relationship of the worker and his product in the Age of Accumulation from which Altruria had evolved. "We dwelt in the old competitive and monopolistic forms after the life had gone out of them," the Altrurian told his listeners, in words which might have been quoted from *Commonweal:*

That is, we continued to live in populous cities, and we toiled to heap up riches for the moth to corrupt, and we slaved on in making utterly useless things, merely because we had the habit of making them to sell. For a while we made the old sham things, which pretended to be useful things and were worse than the confessedly useless things.[20]

Once rescued from "the old slavery" and "dedicated to beauty," the product that was "honest and useful became, by the operation of a natural law, a beautiful thing," said the Altrurian. When the stress and strain of overproducing "false and hideous things to sell," is removed, there is plenty of leisure to make the beautiful things the overworked slaves of the Age of Accumulation only dreamed of. The artist, the man of genius, then becomes the "normal man," for, "in the measure of his ability and of his calling," each man works "in the spirit of the artist." The Evolution gives the people of this enlightened land *time,* said the Altrurian, so that there is "not a furrow driven or a swath mown, not a hammer struck on house or ship, not a temple raised or an engine built," that is not done "with an eye to beauty as well as to use." [21]

And might we not in America "work out an Altruria of our own?" asked the banker in the group. Need this change be brought about by revolution? To be sure, remarked the banker, a person quite as well read as the professor, "There's a little tract of William Morris's thought—I forget just what he calls it—that is full of curious and interesting speculation on this point. He thinks that if we keep the road we are now going, the last state of labor will be like its first, and it will be owned." The banker was impressed by Morris' solution of the labor question—"I'm a kind of Altrurian myself," he admitted—but revolution struck him as "Un-American." "And how came you to decide that labor should own capital?" he asked the Traveler. "We voted it" was the reply.[22]

Morris believed that the struggle of the socialist for a better society would grow "sharper and bitterer day by day, until it should break out openly at last into the slaughter of men by actual warfare instead of by the slower and crueler methods of 'peaceful' commerce," [23] and Howells concluded that among all the labor agitators of his day, "the socialists are the only fellows among them who propose to vote their ideas into laws." [24] Both men agreed that the fundamental cause of social unrest lay in the fact that the machine had deprived the worker of his right to create, slowly and lovingly, objects which were "useful" and hence necessarily "beautiful." In our planning for a better and happier society, Morris said, "We must begin to build up the ornamental part of life—its pleasures, bodily and mental, scientific and artistic, social and individual—on the basis of work undertaken willingly and cheerfully, with the consciousness of benefitting ourselves and our neighbors by it." [25] This, declared Morris, is the true meaning of "Popular Art," which "no longer exists now, having been killed by commercialism." [26]

Howells, too, dreamed of a complete rebirth of society, from hamlet to city, based on economic equality, which should grow out of respect for all forms of labor. The Altrurian's remarks on the cultural centers of Altruria, were a reflection of Howells' love of the great metropolises of the United States—Boston, New York, Chicago—which seemed to him to be growing dirtier, more commercial, and more ruthless year by year. In Altruria, on the contrary, "the capitals are the centers of all the arts, which we consider the chief of our public affairs, they are oftenest frequented by poets, actors, painters, sculptors, musicians and architects." [27] But no such rejuvenation can be brought about unless the artist himself is looked upon, not as an adjunct to business or journalism, but as, in fact, central to the development of a democracy. In Altruria—or in Howells' vision of America—"We regard all artists, who are in a sort creators, as the human type which is likest the divine, and we try to conform our whole industrial life to the artistic temperament." The artist is not necessarily one who is recognized as preeminent in his chosen work; he is any craftsman in any art who has the impulse to do well what he is happy in doing. "Even in the labors of the field and shop, which are obligatory upon all, we study the inspirations of this temperament, and in the voluntary pursuits we allow it full control." [28] Perhaps with Tolstoy in mind, Howells wrote, "We do not like to distinguish men by their callings; we do not speak of the poet This or the shoemaker That, for the poet may very likely be a shoemaker in the obligatories, and the shoemaker a poet in the voluntaries." [29]

When the Altrurian came to the end of his lengthy account of Altruria, "the rustic and ruder" part of the crowd gathered about him and "cheered and cheered till the mountain echoes answered," whereas the guests of the hotel quietly "broke away and went toward the house, over the long shadows of the meadow," murmuring their disapproval. "Well, did you ever hear more disgusting rigmarole?" asked one of the visitors of the professor in an undertone. He replied, citing an array of possible sources of Howells' utopian concepts, "With all those imaginary commonwealths to draw upon, from Plato, through More, Bacon, and Campanella, down to Bellamy and Morris, he has constructed the shakiest effigy ever made of old clothes stuffed with straw." The banker was more thoughtful. "I don't know," he mused, "that frank declaration that Altruria was all these pretty soap-bubble worlds solidified, was rather fine," [30] and thus expressed Howells' approval of the "soap-bubbles" of Morris' vision of Nowhere.

Though "the more cultivated people who had met him . . . continued of two minds," both about the existence of the country the Traveler described and the reality of the Altrurian himself, the "lower classes" remained "devout in the faith that there was such a commonwealth as Altruria, and that he was really an Altrurian." [31] It is possible that Howells himself was of two minds concerning his utopian dream, that he joined in the cheers of the rustics and also participated in the doubts of the cultivated summer guests. Having himself been a country boy in Ohio and having spent many years in Boston and New York, the two cities from which these sophisticated visitors came, Howells found some difficulty in believing the Altrurian's assertion that, in his country,[32] "our capitals are as clean and quiet and healthful as the country." Vindication for this beautiful vision he found in Morris' *News From Nowhere,* for Morris, like Howells, dreamed of noble cities where all might enjoy drama, music, art, as well as rolling country blessed by fertile fields and apple orchards.

Cherishing the hope that progress could be made toward transforming America into Altruria, Howells continued, when the *Traveler From Altruria* came to an end, to address his readers through his imagined Traveler, first by means of *The Letters of an Altrurian Traveler,*[33] and then by continuing the "romance" of the Altrurian in *Through the Eye of the Needle.*[34] In formulating his utopian concepts for these two series of essays, Howells seems to have depended less on literary sources than on direct contact with Chicago and New York. Howells, like the Altrurian, theorized about the country but loved the life of the metropolis, for, as the Altrurian pointed out, "in the capitals are the universities, theaters, galleries, museums, cathedrals, laboratories and conservatories, and the appliances of every art and science, as well as the administration buildings; and beauty as well as use is studied in every edifice."

As a citizen of New York, Howells enjoyed his strolls through parks and streets at all seasons of the year, finding as much pleasure in "the tenement streets" as in Central Park. To a realist, an after-theater drive through the Bowery was interesting, but in May one might find "pleasure in the mere climate of New York," especially if one lived in one of the older squares. In a charming paper for *Harper's Weekly*,[35] Howells told his readers of "a walk eastward as far as the river, and back through the tenement streets between lofty house fronts, all garlanded with fire-escapes, to the leafy spaces of Stuyvesant Square." Since it was seven o'clock of a May morning when he set forth, "there was a sort of English coolness in the sun-shot air, and a sort of London quaintness and oldness in the keeping of the neighborhood." The foliage was dense enough in the park to deepen for him the "illusion of an alien remoteness," which always pleased him. Then there were other things to interest one; there was, for instance, "St. George's Church, which is always fine for its Gothic's sake"; there was "the Friend's Meeting-House, with its brick-work and white paint of Georgian classicity." There were also the cats to observe, and the workmen setting out in the mornings, and even the spring blossoms strewing the asphalt paths. "I made Grace Church my objective," wrote Howells, "not merely because I meant to breakfast at the famous café under its shadow, but because it is always a consolation and refuge to dwell upon its beauty amidst the architectural chaos of the street." As Howells made his way to his morning coffee he did not fail to notice two beggars still asleep in a doorway and a line of silent men waiting to apply for one job announced on a dirty store window, for he was the kind of "realist" who never lost sight of the interrelation of "Art and Society."[36]

NOTES

1. Pp. 237–238.
2. *Atlantic Monthly*, XXXI (March, 1873), 359–360.
3. *Ibid.*, XXXVI (August, 1875), 243.
4. "The Defense of Guinevere," "King Arthur's Tomb," "Sir Galahad," "The Chapel of Lyonesse."
5. *Atlantic Monthly* (August, 1875), p. 243.
6. Sydney Cockerell (ed.), *Life of William Morris* (1949), p. 105.
7. LXVIII, 159–160.
8. *Collected Works*, XXIII (1915), 202.
9. I (February, 1885), 1.
10. *Commonweal*, II, No. 18 (May 15, 1885), 1. Howells was not mentioned in this editorial.
11. *Ibid.*, November 2, 1886, to January 15, 1887.
12. "Howells and the Church of the Carpenter," Clara and Rudolf Kirk. *New England Quarterly*, XXXII, No. 2 (June, 1959), 185–206.
13. See letter from Eleanor Marx Aveling to Howells, London, 1889. Letter, Houghton Library, Harvard.
14. *Commonweal*, III–IV (January 29, 1887), p. 39.
15. Francis Watts Lee (ed.), *William Morris, Poet, Artist, Socialist* (1890), pp. 132–133.
16. This essay, Morris tells us in his Preface to *Signs of Change*, was first delivered as a lecture and then circulated as a pamphlet.
17. "The Hopes of Civilization," *Signs of Change*, p. 176.
18. *Ibid.*, Chapter XVII.
19. *A Traveler from Altruria* (1894), p. 277.
20. *Ibid.*, p. 274.
21. *Ibid.*, pp. 278–279. Compare Chapters XV and XVI of *News From Nowhere*.
22. *Ibid.*, pp. 227–229. The tract was probably "Useful Work *Versus* Useless Toil." This was later included as the last essay in *Signs of Change*.
23. "Useful Work *Versus* Useless Toil," p. 233.
24. *A Traveler from Altruria*, p. 226.
25. "Useless Work *Versus* Useless Toil," p. 223.
26. *Ibid.*, p. 226.
27. *Ibid.*, p. 283.
28. *A Traveler from Altruria*, p. 284.
29. *Ibid.*, pp. 285–286.
30. *Ibid.*, p. 312.
31. *A Traveler from Altruria*, p. 318.
32. *Ibid.*, p. 284.

33. *Cosmopolitan*, XVI–XVII (November, 1893–September, 1894). See *Letters of an Altrurian Traveller* (1961).
34. *Through the Eye of the Needle, a Romance*, 1907.
35. "Life and Letters," *Harper's Weekly*, XLI (June 12, 1897), 590–591.
36. See Appendix IV of this book for Howells' view of Mrs. Gardner's attitude toward the workmen at Fenway Court.

PART

FOUR

Altruria in Chicago

In September, 1893, Howells visited the Chicago Exposition as the personal guest of the director, Daniel H. Burnham. Howells' delighted response to the beautiful White City, which had sprung up as though by magic on the shores of Lake Michigan, is to be found in a single, long letter the Altrurian wrote to a friend in Altruria.[1] This letter, like all the letters of the Altrurian, reflected Howells' own response to the society around him.

Early in the month the Traveler, like the other guests in his New Hampshire hotel, had returned to New York; there he had again been caught up in the "fantastic" nightmare of a city where things happen "without law and without reason," as they do in one's sleep. A description of New York, which, the Altrurian wrote, was "tardily repeating in the nineteenth century the errors we committed in the tenth," constituted the first of "The Letters of an Altrurian Traveller." His second letter, dated September 28, 1893, was written from Chicago and reflected the visitor's hope for the passing of the madly competitive society of America still lost in the Age of Accumulation. "After seeing the World's Fair City here," he wrote,

> I feel as if I had caught a glimpse of the glorious capitals which will whiten the hills and shores of the east and the borderless plains of the west, when the New York and the Newer York of today shall seem to all the future Americans as impossible as they would seem to any Altrurian now.

To these "glorious capitals" trainloads of farmers, schoolteachers, businessmen, workers with their children and their lunch baskets were flocking from every state in the Union. The great objective of the Fair was to give all classes a chance to glimpse the wonders of the world of tomorrow built firmly on the foundation of the noblest monuments of the past. The humblest American could stroll among buildings modeled on those of Athens, drift in gondolas on a lagoon as romantic as the canals of Venice, gaze at paintings gathered from Paris, London, Rome, and New York [2]—or, if he preferred, drink beer in a delightful little German village built on the Midway. The White City seemed to Howells as beautiful as the capitals described by Morris in *News From Nowhere.* Clearly, however, Morris erred when he wrote that "the price to be paid for so making the world happy is *Revolution.*" [3] Behold—here, on the outskirts of a very raw and ugly American city, this wonderful dream-city had come about through *Cooperation.* It marked, said the Traveler, "the first great triumph of Altrurian principles among this people in a work of peace," and had grown clearly from a luminous sense "of the true relations of the arts and the interests" of business. The recognition by the men and women who planned the Exposition that cooperation might supplant competition was a forecast of the American Altruria toward which, according to the Traveler, the artists themselves were leading the country. The Altrurian continued,

> The notion of a competition among the artists, which is the practical American's notion of the way to get the best art, was at length rejected by these most practical Americans, and one mind large enough to conceive the true means and strong enough to give its conception effect was empowered to invite

the free cooperation of the arts through the foremost artists
of the country.

Tears filled the eyes of the Altrurian as he gazed; "the pillared
porches" swam before his vision, in the presence of "the visible, tangible result" of this gigantic undertaking, "which was carried on in
the true Altrurian spirit, so far as the capitalists and artists were
concerned, and with a joy like ours in seeing nature yield herself
to the enlightened will of men." What the ax and the saw of earlier
days could not have achieved was there accomplished by the "powerful machinery" and "modern methods" well known in Altruria.
Though trees had been ruthlessly dragged from the soil, morasses
effaced, and streams turned from their courses, these happily coop-
erating Americans, inspired by a new sense of civic beauty, had
caused "the wastes of sand" on the shores of Lake Michigan "to
smile with the verdure that now forms the most enchanting feature
of their normal cities." Unlike Morris, who dreamed of the restored
beauty of Nowhere, Howells, as he strolled through the wooded
avenues of the White City, had his mind focused on Somewhere. He
was able to imagine that, guided by the freely given labors of artists,
America might in the future build civic centers of Grecian design
with the full use of modern machinery and business capital. The
White City of the Exposition seemed to him definitely a model for
other American cities—to be attained by the willing cooperation of
all classes.[4]

Howells had been present at the great dinner given for Burnham,
the year before the Fair was opened, as the grand opening of the
cooperative effort that was to result in the most beautiful exposition
this country had ever known. Among the architects and artists who
had contributed to the Fair had been his two brothers-in-law, Rutherford and Larkin Mead, his friends, Augustus Saint-Gaudens and
John La Farge, not to mention writers and publishers whom he
knew as colleagues or acquaintances. In Madison Square Hall,
around tables heaped with red roses, had been gathered, not only
the gifted, but also the wealthy—the Morgans, the Vanderbilts, and
the Astors—who had contributed to the undertaking designed to
raise the American public to a new level of taste.

Contemplating, in his second Altrurian letter, the results of his visit to the Exposition the following September, Howells thought he envisaged the harmonious cooperation of artist and millionaire on a genuinely creative basis. This, he thought, was sure to mean a better society for the art-starved, humble Americans living in city tenements and on lonely prairies. The Exposition of 1893 was, in fact, an embodiment of Howells' idea of progress, which must be at once social, economic, and aesthetic. Above all else, the Fair taught the gazer that the artists themselves, by working together for ends not associated with material gain, could encourage businessmen and all other workers to make their contribution to a common goal. "For the different buildings to be erected, different architects were chosen," wrote Howells, thinking, no doubt, of the contribution made to the Exposition by the firm of McKim, Mead, and White. Thus, "for the first time since the great ages, since the beauty of antiquity and the elegance of the Renaissance, the arts were reunited."

> The greatest landscape gardeners, architects, sculptors and painters, gathered at Chicago for a joyous interchange of ideas and criticisms; and the miracle of beauty which they have wrought grew openly in their breath and under their hands. Each did his work and had his way with it, but in this congress of gifted minds, of sensitive spirits, each profited by the censure of all.

The dazzling result of Grecian colonnades by the side of lagoons shimmering in the light of thousands of colored "electrics" was not brought about by the quiet labors of many craftsmen, as in the utopia of Morris, but it was designed and executed by the "gifted minds" of outstanding artists with whom Howells had for many years associated. Richard Morris Hunt, known to Howells through the Jameses, was the architect of the Administration Building dominating the whole; Lucia Fairchild, family friend and one-time Belmont neighbor, exhibited a painting of Mildred Howells in the Women's Building; Larkin Mead designed the pediment of the Agriculture Building; Frederick Law Olmsted, whom Howells knew as a friend and contributor to the *Atlantic,* was the landscape gardener of the entire Exposition; "the exquisite peristyle," which Howells particularly admired, was the work of Daniel C. French and several others with whom he associated in New York. These men, Howells knew, labored for little or nothing; moreover, their wealthy business-men backers willingly supported the whole undertaking. Howells seemed to be speaking in his own voice, rather than in that of the Altrurian, when he wrote that, in erecting the White City, "the artists gave their talents" as freely as the millionaires gave their money.

> These great artists willingly accepted a fifth, a tenth, of the gain which they could have commanded in a private enterprise, and lavished their time upon the opportunity afforded them, for the pleasure of it, the pride of it, the pure good of it.

The Altrurian—and Howells—recognized that in a truly utopian society the millionaires do not have to step into the breach and supply the funds to support a civic undertaking. However, commented the Altrurian, in America, "as yet, the governmental function is so weak here that the national part in the work [of building the Fair] was chiefly obstructive, and finally nil." Therefore, wrote the Altrurian, "an opportunity for the arts, unlimited as to means and unhampered by conditions," was offered for wealthy business-men to work with gifted artists for the public good. And thus, by the slow but certain *evolution* of a partially civilized democracy, America might become the Altruria of the future.

Meanwhile, how raw and crude the Americans at the Fair seemed to the cultivated Altrurian! He was painfully aware of "the hard nasal American tones of the speech of the milling crowds in the Midway"; he smiled at the "different versions of the Paris fashions" worn by the tired farmers' wives, which he mentally contrasted with "the gay tints of our own simple costume"; [5] he glanced sympathetically at "the careworn masks of the competitive crowds" in museums and restaurants and thought of "the peace, the *rest* of the dear Altrurian face." But in spite of these reminders of a competitive, money-minded society, "the illusion of Altruria was very vivid at many moments in the Fair City," where the Traveler spent the happiest days of his stay in America. When the Altrurian contemplated the Court of Honor, the Agricultural Building, the "Perfect Greek of the Art Building," he could hardly believe "that so foul a thing as money could have been even the means of its creation." Though "merely sketched in stucco," and not "executed in marble," as were the public buildings in Altruria, the White City was nevertheless "divinely beautiful." The curves of bridges, the "glorious peristyle, serene, pure, silent," groups of statuary on quay or cornice, the "pillared spaces" relieving the masses of the buildings —"all was harmonized to one effect of beauty, as if a symbol of the concentered impulses which had created it." Indeed, the Altrurian admitted, "in grandeur of design and freedom of expression," the buildings were "perhaps even nobler than the public edifices" in some of "the Regionic capitals" of his own country. The Altrurian was astonished that "a design, the effect of a principle," could have been evolved in the buildings on the shores of Lake Michigan in marked contrast to "the straggling and shapeless accretion of accident" that the Altrurian had seen in Boston and New York. Alas, the Americans themselves hardly seemed to understand "the moral value" of what they beheld at the Fair! Admitting "the practical perfection of the scheme," the Americans to whom the Altrurian addressed himself assured him that the White City "would never do for a business city, where there was something going on besides the pleasure of the eyes and the edification of the mind." The Altrurian's hopes for a utopian society in America, a society in which cultural values would supplant materialistic aims, would founder, they said, on the rocks of our rapidly evolving business world.

The Altrurian's old friend of the previous summer, the banker from Boston, made the position of the average American businessman clear to the Traveler. The two met by chance in Old Vienna, a quaint little restaurant in the Plaisance, and discussed the puzzling question of "who pays the piper" for such an Exposition when all the fun is over, and their talk extended far into the starlit night. But the banker remained blandly unconvinced. In response to the Altrurian's account of the beautiful cities in his own country built and maintained without the use of money, the banker merely smiled. "Oh, come now!" he exclaimed with obvious disbelief; without the "warfare of competition" without money as the reward, there would be no millionaires to support such displays as the Exposition itself. The Altrurian was quick to point out that the White City was, in fact, a proof of the possibility that cooperation might replace competition. Obviously, he said, "there *is* no competition among you a moment longer than you can help." As soon as Americans are convinced of the importance of an undertaking, "then you have monopoly, which even upon the limited scale it exists here is the only vital and fruitful principle, as you all see." Monopoly is only another word for intelligent cooperation for a common cause in an evolving capitalistic society, said the Altrurian; now, however, "you are afraid to have it upon the largest possible scale, the national scale, the scale commensurate with the whole body politic, which implicates care for every citizen as the liege of the collectivity." When Americans really grasp the meaning for the future suggested by the Exposition, then "money will cease to have any office among you, and such a beautiful creation as this will have effect from a consensus of the common wills and wishes."

The banker listened to the familiar ideas of the Altrurian patiently and amiably. "I'll own," he said, "that you have rather knocked the notion of competition on the head." But doesn't monopoly in any form destroy individuality, and hasn't "the individuality of the several captialists, up or down, to the individuality of the several artists" something to do with "the creation of all this beauty?" he innocently asked. The banker's questions provided the Altrurian with a chance to express in full his view of the importance of individuality, "the most precious gift of the Deity," and to lament "the wholesale effacement, the heartbreaking obliteration of individuality" in American society. Everyone knows the names of the "munificent millionaires . . . whose largess made this splendor possible and the name of every artist they freed to such a glorious opportunity." But who knows the names of "the artisans of every kind and degree, whose patience and skill realized their ideals? Where will you find *their* names?" "You are very easily answered," the banker laughingly replied. "You will find *their* names on the pay-roll." And how do you manage to honor the craftsmen in Altruria, he inquired. In Altruria, the Traveler vehemently responded, the true individuality of the maker is unconsciously inscribed on all parts of his work. "Every man who drove a nail, or stretched a line, or laid a trowel upon such a work, would have his name somehow inscribed upon it," but in America the contribution of the workman is lost in oblivion, both in "these public works of artistic cooperation, or the exhibits of your monopolistic competition." Having wandered through "these vast edifices" of the Fair for a week, the Traveler decided at last that "the whole mighty display" was essentially "dehumanized" and "impersonal." "You are hopelessly unbusiness-like," responded the banker mildly, "but I like your unpracticality. There is something charming in it."

Unconsciously vindicating the Altrurian's comment on the ordinary American's lack of individuality, the banker glanced over the throngs still filling the Midway and observed, "What a serious, and peaceful, and gentle crowd it is! . . . mainly a western and south-western crowd, a Mississippi Valley crowd." Dressed in their clothing-store outfits, and munching sandwiches from their paper bags, "they look pathetically good!" remarked the banker with the faint patronage of the wealthy. "When I think of how hard-worked they all are, and what lonely lives most of them live on their solitary farms, I wonder they don't descend upon me with the whoop of savages." The "vast level" of the people seemed to the banker as dreary as the endless plains over which they had traveled to find inspiration in this magical center of culture.

Of course there were many "of the more cultivated visitors" who studied the exhibits at the Fair with more insight than these simple country folk. C. E. Norton was entranced with what he saw, especially with his observations of the people themselves. Henry Adams visited the Exposition more than once to stand in philosophic wonder before the dynamo in the Hall of Machinery. But it was "the vast bulk" of visitors, "the massed members of that immense equality," inoffensive, reserved, and patient, that interested the Altrurian. The banker, having been rendered more thoughtful by his talk with his idealistic friend, said that, for his part, he hoped that the sights of the Fair would have "an esthetic effect" on the people and not give them "any fresh impulse in material enterprise, which he thought the country did not need." There were already inventions enough, prosperity enough; now what "the great mass of the people . . . needed was some standard of taste," and that, he triumphantly pointed out, was the object of the Fair. The very sight of the beautiful Greek stucco building "should at once have a great influence upon architecture, and sober and refine the artists who were to house the people," and thus justify the hopes of the millionaires who financed the Fair.

The Altrurian "heartily agreed" with the banker in his criticism of American taste and American architecture, and "tried to make him observe that the simplicity of Greek architecture came out of the simplicity of Greek life," where preference was given "to art over business." The example of the Fair City would merely make classicism "a fad with the rich man and a folly with the poor, and not a real taste with either class," unless the moral of the Exposition, as an example of how men might reconceive their entire society, was understood. As far as the Altrurian had observed, "The whole competitive world," with "the exception of a few artists," seemed to have lost the sense of beauty—if, indeed, Americans, "as a people," ever had had it. The Fair, he concluded, would not "have any lasting effect with you unless you become Altrurianized," by which he meant that "the quality of self-sacrifice in the capitalists who gave their money and in the artists who gave their talent without hope of material gain" must be understood and shared by all until a new, superior, Altrurian America evolved.

"Ah, my dear fellow, you must realize this [Columbian Exposition] was only a spurt," sighed the banker. "It could be done once, but it couldn't be kept up." "Why not?" asked the Altrurian. "Because people have got to live, even capitalists and artists have got to live, and they couldn't live by giving away wealth and giving away work, in our conditions." "But you will change the conditions!" the Altrurian exclaimed patiently. "I doubt it," said the banker with another laugh, and parted genially from his strange companion.

With thoughts not unlike those of the Altrurian, Hamlin Garland had surveyed this same Chicago crowd, and, indeed, had lectured to it in July of the summer of 1893. Ten years earlier, Garland had himself emerged from one of those forlorn farmsteads with a windmill beside it that had made the Altrurian melancholy as he studied the dull uniformity of the landscape from the window of his train. In *Main-Travelled Roads* (1891), Garland had gathered together stories of his family and neighbors in South Dakota. Howells had come to know Garland during his two years in Boston and had encouraged him to write the lives "of the men who hopelessly and cheerlessly make the wealth that enriches the alien and the idler, and impoverishes the producer." Howells described Garland's "robust and terribly serious" book in the "Editor's Study" of September, 1891, adding that the tales "are full of those gaunt, grim, sordid, pathetic, ferocious figures . . . whose blind groping for fairer conditions is so grotesque to the newspapers and so menacing to the politicians." In *Criticism and Fiction,*[6] which Garland accepted as a guide for his literary program, Howells had already expressed his views on how these "blind gropings for fairer conditions" might be directed if only the place of the artist in society were more generally understood. Garland succeeded in bringing to a focus the questions that concerned the literary man and the artist.

In his lecture at the Literary Congress, held in July, 1893, in conjunction with the Columbian Exposition, Garland repeated with his characteristic vehemence [7] Howells' hope for democratic art. This lecture, "Local Color in Fiction," was later included in the small iconoclastic volume, *Crumbling Idols* (1894). Dedicated "To the men and women of America who have the courage to be artists," these twelve essays on literature and paintings were a plea for a stronger belief in the latent creative power of the country, especially of the West. Like Howells, Garland believed that the "common man" had somehow been cheated of his birthright by the old "idols" of an aristocratic order that were "crumbling." "America is not yet democratic in art, whatever it may claim to be in politics," [8] declared Garland at the time when Howells was hopefully illustrating the saving grace of democratic art in his Altrurian essays.

"As impressionism has already transformed painting," [9] wrote Garland, so "veritism" [10]—Garland's word for "realism"—has "changed the current of literature." It discards the old "idols" of plot complications, familiar character types, happy endings. Instead, "it deals with life face to face, and swiftly and surely and always from the individual artist's standpoint." Several years ago, Garland pointed out, "when Mr. Howells remarked upon this . . . the walls of Jericho were apparently shaken down, to judge from the dust and noise of reverberating explosion." Howells' defense of realism in *Harper's Monthly,* said Garland, made him "a literary issue" throughout the country.

Perhaps Garland also had in mind "the dust and noise" caused by the "explosion" on the public of Stephen Crane's *Maggie* in the same year in which *Crumbling Idols* and *A Traveler From Altruria* appeared. Garland's discussion of "the novel of the slums," in terms of the poetry of Whitman and the painting of Monet,[11] reminds one that earlier in the year Crane's story of "A Girl of the Streets" had been recognized by both Garland and Howells as a striking example of a new kind of realism, different from either Howells' realism or Garland's veritism. It was clearly related to the impressionistic paintings, but the relationship was not merely a matter of color, the use of light, the apparent casualness of arrangement. Garland suggested in "The Local Novel" that the individual "impression" was as important to the novelist as to the painter. "The novel of the slums must be written by one who has played there as a child," he said, "and taken part in all its amusements; not out of curiosity, but out of pleasure seeking." To such a writer, the scene will be neither "strange" nor "picturesque," but "all will be familiar, and full of significance or beauty." When a writer is giving his own impression, without seeking for effect; when he is writing from the inside and neither from above nor from the outside, then he is voicing "the real utterance of a city." [12] No matter how sordid the surroundings, beauty is perceived because of the intensity of the vision of the writer.

"The Local Novel," which Garland included in *Crumbling Idols* as among his papers read at the Fair, was first delivered in Avon-by-the-Sea, New Jersey, in the summer of 1891.[13] Among those who listened to Garland was a young reporter of the New York *Tribune*,[14] Stephen Crane, who introduced himself to the speaker after the address was ended and asked for the manuscript to help him with his article for the *Tribune*. Thus began a fruitful friendship between Garland and Crane that soon included Howells, for all three were affected by the movement in art and literature called impressionism, though that term was seldom used.[15] It was, indeed, Howells' definition of realism in *Criticism and Fiction* that Garland made use of in the lecture to which Crane listened so eagerly. Crane's interpretation of the term added an intensity and an immediacy to the word "realism." "I decided," he wrote, "that the nearer a writer gets to life the greater he becomes as an artist, and most of my prose writings have been toward the goal partially described by that misunderstood and abused word, realism." [16]

Before Garland delivered his lectures on impressionism, veritism, and realism at the Chicago Exposition, he had learned that Howells had tried in vain to find a publisher for *Maggie,* which Richard Watson Gilder of the *Century* considered altogether too grim to print. Perhaps Garland's futile effort through Howells to help his gifted young friend added a certain vehemence to his insistence in *Crumbling Idols* on the definition of the artist and writer as "truth-staters" who are always at war with "the conservatives" who fear change. All creative spirits recognize that "life is the model" and "life is always changing," declared Garland. Hence painting and literature are always a reflection of the creator's *"impassioned personal outlook on life."* [17] Among the exponents of "the mighty literary movements of his own time," Garland listed Ibsen, Tolstoy, Björnson, Howells, and Whitman; [18] among the artists, he commented on Monet, Pissarro, Zorn, Inness, Rousseau, Millet, and many artists now forgotten as examples of painters who were a part of the movement of their own times. But the lesson Garland derived from his study of paintings at the Exposition was the same he had already learned from conversations with Howells and Crane, that is, that both art and literature are aspects of the "inexorable march" of civilization, and therefore never remain static. The Impressionists themselves know that "the final word will never be spoken upon art" and that "the dead must give way to the living" in every generation.[19]

The lesson that Howells learned from the Fair the following September was, as we have seen, fully expressed in his Altrurian essays that began to appear in the *Cosmopolitan* in November, 1892. He continued for the next two years to put before his readers the hope that the abyss between the very rich and the very poor might be healed through a renewed appreciation of the place of art in society. Like the citizens of Altruria, Americans could be taught to substitute a joy in cooperative artistic expression for the tiresome competitive game of moneymaking. The marvelously beautiful Columbian Exposition was a triumphant example of such a united effort on the part of millionaires and gifted artists. But the Fair was only a beginning, the first step in moving toward a society that would make use of the highly individual artistic potential of every citizen; this the Altrurian attempted to explain to the banker, who still subscribed to the American illusion that enlightenment must be bestowed upon the poor by the wealthy.

Though Hamlin Garland in *Crumbling Idols* seemed to approach the problems of art, literature, and society from an angle quite different from that of Howells in the Altrurian's letter from the Fair, both men agreed that art and literature belong to the common man, and that they must come to grips with truth, no matter how many idols crumbled in the quest. According to Garland, Howells, a tireless truth-seeker, belonged to a group of writers and artists who were continually testing their powers and trusting more to their individual impression of their day and generation than to tradition. "Realism," said Garland to his audience at the Fair, "is not a theory, it is a condition of mind, of sensibility," [20] characteristic of both artists and writers of the new school. "Mr. Howells," he observed, "represents truthful treatment of the cities of Boston and New York." [21] Garland, no doubt, was here reflecting upon the remarkably "truthful" picture of Boston that Howells had painted in *The Rise of Silas Lapham* and *The Minister's Charge;* he must also have had in mind Howells' still more ambitious presentation of New York in *A Hazard of New Fortunes*. To this modern Babylon the Altrurian reluctantly returned after "a fortnight's stay in that vision of Altruria at the great Fair in Chicago." The vision had given to Howells, and to Garland as well, a vivid insight into the relationship between painting, architecture, and literature in a vital society.

NOTES

1. *Letters of an Altrurian Traveller,* pp. 20–34. Howells spelled the word "traveller" in that series of essays. I have, however, spelled it with one "l" except when the word was originally used as a part of a title. These letters (November, 1893—September, 1894) began to appear in the *Cosmopolitan* as soon as the series of essays called "A Traveler From Altruria" (November, 1892—October, 1893) came to a close.

2. Julian Hawthorne wrote that "There are more utterly exhausted people in the Fine Arts Building than in all the rest of the Exposition put together." *Humors of the Fair* (1893), Illustrated by Will E. Chapin, p. 114. See also Gustave Geffroy, "French Art at Chicago," *Cosmopolitan,* XVI (January, 1894), 371–372.

3. *William Morris, Poet, Artist, Socialist,* p. 286.

4. See Chapter V, "The Columbian Exposition," *W. D. Howells, Traveler from Altruria, 1889–1894,* Clara Marburg Kirk (1962).

5. The National Council of Women put on a popular exhibit of "Rational Dress for Women" in the Women's Building. See "The Rational Dress Movement, A Symposium," *Arena,* I (February, 1894), 305–326. "The nearest approach to comfort in skirt form is the Grecian robe," wrote Hattie C. Flower, p. 326.

6. *Criticism and Fiction* (1891) was a collection of essays from the "Study" which had appeared between 1886 and 1891 in *Harper's Monthly Magazine.* These essays Garland had studied during his years in Boston and had discussed them with Howells.

7. Donald Pizer, "A Summer Campaign in Chicago: Hamlin Garland Defends a Native Art," *Western Humanities Review,* XIII (Autumn, 1959), 375–382.

8. "Provincialism," Robert E. Spiller (ed.), *Crumbling Idols* (1952), p. 8.

9. "The Drift of the Drama," *ibid.,* p. 94.

10. Garland derived this word from Eugène Véron's *Aesthetics.* See *Criticism and Fiction and Other Essays by W. D. Howells,* pp. 256–259.

11. "The Local Novel," *Crumbling Idols,* pp. 72–73.

12. *Ibid.,* p. 72.

13. *Roadside Meetings* (1950), pp. 189–206. Garland tells the story again in "Stephen Crane as I Knew Him," *Yale Review,* n.s. 3 (June, 1914), 494–506. Garland wrote: "Crane was living at this time with a group of artists or art students ('Indians,' he called them) in an old building on East 23rd St. . . . They all slept on the floor, dined off buns and sardines, and painted on towels and wrapping paper for lack of canvas." p. 497.

14. Stephen Crane, "Howells Discussed at Avon-By-The-Sea," New York *Tribune,* Aug. 18, 1891.

15. Many critics of the day were to show the relationship between realism and impressionism in painting and literature. See, for example, W. C. Brownell, "French Art—III: Realistic Painting," *Scribner's,* XII (December, 1892), 604–627. He observed that "Monet first gave us this sense of reality in a measure comparable with that which successively Balzac, Flaubert and Zola gave to the readers of their books—a sense of actuality and vividness beside which the traditionary practice seemed absolutely fanciful and mechanical," p. 623. See also Gustave Geffroy, "French Art at Chicago," *Cosmopolitan,* XVI (January, 1894), 371–372.

16. Introduction to Max J. Herzberg (ed.), *The Red Badge of Courage* (1926), pp. vi–vii.

17. *Crumbling Idols,* p. 77. The italics in the sentence quoted are Garland's.

18. *Ibid.,* p. 9.

19. *Ibid.,* p. 141.

20. *Ibid.,* p. 118.

21. *Ibid.,* p. 33.

· 2 ·

Plutocratic New York

Though the Altrurian and the banker might argue until the sun came up over the lagoon of the White City and still not agree as to the interplay of work, art, and money in an ideal society, Howells himself had clear views of their actual relationship in the society he knew in the 1890's. In October, 1893—the very month when "A Traveler" came to an end in the *Cosmopolitan* and several months before the Altrurian's letter on the Fair appeared in that magazine—Howells published in *Scribner's* an essay entitled "The Man of Letters as a Man of Business." [1] He opened his comments on that difficult subject with the remark, "I think that every man ought to work for his living, without exception, and that, when he has once avouched his willingness to work, society should provide him with work and warrant him a living. I do not think any man ought to live by an art."

Even in "the grotesque confusion of our economic being," Howells observed, people in our society feel that "a man's art should be his privilege" after he has proved his ability as an artist and has managed to earn his daily bread by some other means. Moreover, what the artist creates should be free to all, without payment; "people feel that there is something profane, something impious, in taking money for a picture, or a poem, or a statue."

Just as the Altrurians had concluded centuries earlier, Howells felt that money, as payment, hardly compensates the artist for his gift to society, and, further, that the artist is humiliated by having to sell his work: "Most of all, the artist himself feels this." Though "he puts on a bold front with the world" and attempts to "brazen it out as Business," he is quite aware of the fact that there is "something false and vulgar" in the transactions, for "the work which cannot be truly priced in money cannot be truly paid in money." But the artist also has learned the bitter truth that "unless he sells his art he cannot live, that society will leave him to starve if he does not hit its fancy in a picture, or a poem, or a statue." Under what Howells refers to as "the conditions" of our society, the artist is forced to accept whatever payment is offered him. "All the same, the sin and the shame remain, and the averted eye sees them still, with its inward vision." When the writer has to be a "huckster" of his own wares "the scandal is greater than when a painter has sold a picture to a patron, or a sculptor has modelled a statue to order," for the work of these artists is less personal than that of the writer; "they are more exterior to their work," and therefore "part with less of themselves in the dicker." This distinction between the writer and other artists is inevitable because of the very nature of literature, which is

> at once the most intimate and the most articulate of the arts. It cannot impart its effect through the senses or the nerves as the other arts can; it is beautiful only through the intelligence; it is the mind speaking to the mind; until it has been put into absolute terms, of an invariable significance, it does not exist at all.[2]

The whole story of how a young writer, Percy Bysshe Shelley Ray, had come to New York from Ohio and attempted to sell his wares to unsympathetic editors and publishers was told by Howells in *The World of Chance*,[3] which appeared in book form six months before his article, "The Man of Letters as a Man of Business." When, the following December on the shore of Lake Michigan, the Traveler lectured the banker on the unholy alliance between the artist and the millionaire, he spoke from the depths of Howells' own experience as "a man of letters" who labored under the necessity of being, at the same time, "a man of business." Before writers and artists can make their full contribution to society, "the world of chance"—or, as the Altrurian would say, "the conditions" of competition—must be replaced by a planned economy that would free the individual from the desperate struggle for subsistence. Howells expressed this same thought both in the "Letters of an Altrurian" and in his novel, *The World of Chance.*

When Ray first approached New York by the ferryboat from Jersey City, he saw only the picturesque beauty of the scene. With the manuscript of a novel in his bag and $500 in his pocket, Ray gazed in awestruck admiration "with a sense of the beauty struggling through the grotesqueness of the huge panorama, and evoking itself somehow from the grossest details" and saw nothing amiss. Like the solitary figure in "The Wake of the Ferry," painted by John Sloan, ten years later, Ray leaned over the railing and drank in the busy confusion of canal boats loaded with freight trains, dirty sloops with half-filled sails, coastwise steamboats "like fantastic villas."

> The mean, ugly fronts and roofs of the buildings beyond, and hulking high overhead in the further distance in vast bulks and clumsy towers, the masses of those ten-storied edifices which are the necessity of commerce and the despair of art, only helped to compose the brutal and stupid body of the thing, whose soul was collectively expressed in an incredible picturesqueness. Ray saw nothing amiss in it. This agglomeration of warring forms, feebly typifying the ugliness of the warring interests with them, did not repulse him. He was not afraid.[4]

Ray had yet to learn—as did Howells, too, when he first came to live in New York—that the "warring forms" of the architecture of the great city were symbolic of the "warring interests" of those who lived in dark tenements and in Fifth Avenue mansions. Ray's discovery of these disconcerting economic facts is the theme of this novel concerning the writer's attempt to market his manuscript. His conclusion that modern society is merely a "World of Chance" was the conclusion that the Altrurian had come to after a year's study of American cities. What the Traveler attempted to explain to the banker over their supper on the Midway was that the astonishing beauty of the White City was hardly more than a mirage, for architecture is always a reflection of society, which builds inevitably according to its attitudes toward the relationship of the rich and the poor.

After a few weeks in Chicago contemplating an architectural dream suggestive of the capitals of his own land, the Altrurian returned to New York or "Babylon" in 1893, at the beginning of a prolonged depression, and found further vindication of his belief that no great metropolis can possibly achieve architectural harmony and beauty under competitive economic conditions. What he thought of the sights and sounds and smells of New York the Traveler expressed in three long letters to his distant friend in Altruria that appeared in the *Cosmopolitan* early in 1894.[5] That these views of the city to which Howells had moved were his own, as well as the Altrurian's, is made clear by the fact that, in 1896, Howells, merely by changing "he" to "I," transformed three letters into two essays, "Glimpses of Central Park" and "New York Streets," and included them in a volume entitled *Impressions and Experiences*.[6] At the same time, he joined the newly organized Social Reform Club of New York; Howells, who was by nature a nonjoiner, apparently approved of the purpose of this Club, which was to bring professional men and workmen together in order "to discuss practical measures for improving industrial and social conditions." [7]

Like the young Ray on his first sight of New York, Howells, too, was tempted to enjoy the picturesqueness of "New York Streets" (the title of one of his essays) "with a callous indifference to that ruin, or that defeat, which must so largely constitute the charm of the picturesque." A street of tenement houses is sure to be more interesting to the artist or the writer than a sedate thoroughfare of brownstone mansions, especially in summer, when the streets are swarming with children and pushcarts. Here Howells found fresh literary material, and so also did the painters of the Ashcan school, such as Henri and Luks. Though these "wretched quarters" are indeed "blotches of disease upon the civic body," the scene possesses, at the same time, an attractive quality that, Howells perceived, "in a picture" would be "pleasingly effective, for then you could be in it, and yet have the distance on it which it needs." [8]

How suggestive, indeed, of John Sloan's painting of the fences and clotheslines he saw from his window in Greenwich Village is Howells' description of the tenements he enjoyed at the very moment when he was describing them as "loathsome sores, destined to eat deeper and deeper" into society. "The fronts of the edifices," he wrote,

> are decorated with the iron balconies and ladders of the fire-escapes, and have in the perspective a false air of gayety, which is travestied in their rear by the lines thickly woven from the windows to the tall poles set between the backs of the houses and fluttering with drying clothes as with banners. [9]

On an autumnal evening in 1894, Howells strolled over to the East River through streets lined with tenement houses "just as the soft night was beginning to fall" in a haze of beauty. As "the afterglow died from the river," Howells hung over a parapet and experienced an "artistic delight" akin to that which Whistler sought to paint "in the aspect of the long prison island which breaks the expanse of the Channel." Knowing very well that the buildings were prisons and that the men and women in them "were doomed to a life of outlawry and crime," Howells was glad not to be able to see, in the waning light, "the barred windows of those hells." "I could only see the trees along their walks"; he wrote, "their dim lawns and gardens, and the castellated forms of the prisons; and the aesthetic sense, which is careful to keep itself pure from pity, was tickled with an agreeable impression of something old and fair." As "the dusk thickened," great steamboats passed silently through Long Island Sound to the city. They swept by the quiet observer on the parapet above, "luminous masses on the black water." Howells could see

> their lights aloft at bow and stern, floated with them like lambent planets; the lights of lesser craft dipped by, and came and went in the distance; the lamps of the nearer and farther

shores twinkled into sight, and a peace that ignored all the misery of it, fell upon the scene.[10]

New York, that "mighty city," though it is "the parent of such misery," is also the parent of astonishing beauty. This Howells had learned from his study of painting, and this he no doubt helped to teach the Ashcan school of painters, such as Henri, Luks, and Sloan. The ships in the East River, wrote Howells, "look happy and free, in the stream, but they are of the overworked world, too, as well as the houses; and let them spread their wings ever so widely, they still bear with them the sorrows of the poor." [11] Clearly, Howells saw something in these scenes other than their picturesqueness.

Like the parapet over the East River, the Third Avenue Elevated had for Howells the magical power of lending distance to scenes of misery. Those who are enjoying the "airy swiftness" of the elevated trains cannot observe much of the shabbiness of the streets below, "which is pitilessly open to the eyes in the avenues which have only horse-car tracks in them." Though "men and women are indecently crushed together" in these trains, without regard to personal dignity, and though "horrible accidents" sometimes happen, Howells recognized, as did Sloan in many of his paintings, that "the elevated roads are always picturesque, with here and there a sweeping curve that might almost be called beautiful." [12]

Howells did not fail to observe, however, that, in their aesthetic enjoyment of the light and shadow of these swiftly flying trains, New Yorkers had long since forgotten the "moral offense" involved in the fact that private enterprise had put up these tracks for private gain, to the utter disregard of the rights of the people who lived in the houses on the four avenues in front of which the Elevated ran. No compensation had been offered to the home-owners along the route, for in an unplanned economy the rights of the individual to peace and quiet, as well as life and limb, were blandly disregarded. In America, "private enterprise is allowed to violate the rights of private property." [13] Howells, in spite of his sense of the picturesque beauty to be enjoyed in East-side streets, the river at night, and the curves of the Elevated tracks, never forgot the people who actually lived under "the conditions" of the ruthless, crowded, selfish city.

Among the essays included in *Impressions and Experiences* was "An East-Side Ramble." Since this is the only essay in the collection that was being published for the first time, we may conclude that it was written not long before the publication of the book in 1896. We may surmise further that the "friend" who accompanied Howells on this ramble was Stephen Crane; no doubt they were inspired to make this plunge into the East side because of Howells' interest in the manuscript of *Maggie,* for which he had at last succeeded in finding a publisher. Crane had lived for a time in the Bowery while gathering material for his story; he was, therefore, as perfect a guide as "the most anxious philosopher" could desire.[14]

During that Christmas season, Howells, who had been accustomed to leaving his calling card with the liveried servant of "the well-to-do" on Fifth Avenue, resolved, instead, to accompany his "friend" on a series of calls on "the ill-to-do." Though Howells had long enjoyed walking city streets, especially those of New York, this ramble took him beyond his usual circuit. "The friend who went with me on my calls," he wrote, "led me across the usual surface tracks, under the usual elevated tracks, and suddenly dodged before me into an alleyway about two feet wide." This narrow passage "crept under houses fronting on the squalid street" from which they had entered and led them into a long, narrow court, surrounded by buildings "low and very old." One of these was "a stable, which contributed its stench to the odors that rose from the reeking pavement and from the closets filling an end of the court, with a corner left beside them for the hydrant that supplied the water of the whole inclosure." [15] Howells' guide led him up rickety stairs and knocked at random on any door, entering without ceremony other than "the robust 'Good-morning!' " that seemed to account for their presence. Though somewhat abashed by the direct approach of his friend, Howells was fascinated by this close view of the tenements from which Maggie might have emerged. In one of these abodes they found the family sitting in complete darkness; there was nothing in the room but several chairs, a table and an unlit stove. Howells' companion

struck a match and held it to the cavernous mouth of an inner cellar half as large as the room we were in, where it winked and paled so soon that I had only a glimpse of the bed, with the rounded heap of bedding on it; but out of this hole, as if she had been a rat, scared from it by the light, a young girl came, rubbing her eyes and vaguely smiling, and vanished up-stairs somewhere.[16]

To Stephen Crane, this girl buried under a heap of filthy bed-clothing might well have suggested another Maggie; to Howells she was a reminder that "all life is a hopeless tangle . . . especially in economical affairs." [17] This Howells had recognized for many years and had attempted to express through Basil March in *A Hazard of New Fortunes*. Having seen at first hand the "loathsomeness" of the East-side tenements and talked with "the inmates of the dens and lairs" he visited, he was ready to conclude that a "week's sojourn" in the Bowery, "with no more hope of a better lot than they could have, would make anarchists of the best people in the city." [18]

Instead of turning Howells into an anarchist, however, this contact with Stephen Crane made Howells feel even more the writer's obligation to truth. Though Richard Watson Gilder of the *Century* had been alarmed by "the damns and the curse yehs" of *Maggie,* Howells admired the story for the very reason that "it embodied perhaps the best tough dialect which has yet found its way into print." Such "parlance," Howells observed, might seem impossible "to cultured ears," but it may be heard, he assured his readers, "by any listener in the streets of certain quarters of the city." [19] However, since New Yorkers from Fifth Avenue seldom stroll so far as the Bowery, they neither know nor wish to know the truth concerning the lives of those who live in the slums of their city. Similarly, these same New Yorkers prefer the "romantic" tales of Rider Haggard and "Ouïda" to the "realistic" accounts of human experience that Howells had defended since he first moved into the "Study" of *Harper's Monthly*. Crane, several years later in a newspaper interview [20] with his older friend, put to him a question as to the future of realism in literature. Howells admitted that he had felt "a change in the literary pulse of the country" recently and that he was aware that readers were again turning toward the romantic in novels in spite of his battle for realism in all the arts.

When Howells asserted in *Criticism and Fiction* that "in the whole range of literature" he knew of "no true picture of life . . . which is not also a masterpiece of literature," [21] he laid down a principle of aesthetics that led him to investigate for himself "the picture of life" presented by Crane. Believing, as he did, that all the arts are interrelated and that they reflect the "conditions" of economic and social concepts, Howells extended the thought that "there is no greatness, no beauty which does not come from truth," to his comment on architecture. Corroboration of his view that untruth is as fatal to buildings as to books Howells found in *Aesthetic Principles* by Henry Rutgers Marshall, which he reviewed in the August 31, 1895, issue of *Harper's Weekly*. Marshall, Howells wrote, deplored "the merely decorative use of structural forms in architecture," and he quoted the author as writing that "there rings out a false note in the scheme; there is a violation of our negative canon which tells us to avoid untruth." His further analysis of the thought of the author shows just how Howells himself related his critical appraisal of literature and architecture. He wrote, of Marshall's "negative canon":

> I daresay this negative canon is the same as my notion of a tacit virtue, and that the avoidance of untruth is mainly the proof of an artist. Possibly it is more largely in this than in any other way that the truth is manifested, the joy of it imparted; for as this author goes on to say "untruth gives a shock that is fatal to beauty." In fact, the moment that you come upon the false, in book or in building, your pleasure is gone, and all the literary or architectural virtuosity will not recall it. It is for this reason that I cannot give myself away with the romanticistic novel which asks me to believe that something happened impossible in the circumstances supposed by the author. It is not merely my illusion that is spoiled, but my faith is undermined, and I cannot trust myself to the author.

The "shock of American conditions," where dark tenements are to be seen immediately behind the ornate Renaissance mansions of Fifth Avenue, are fully described in the letters the Altrurian wrote to his friend. The Traveler, like Howells, linked the moral and the physical ugliness of Babylon in his comment to Cyril. "I have seen what might be, in the Fair City," he wrote, "and I shrank [on my return to New York] not only from the moral, but the physical ugliness of the thing." Again like Howells, the Traveler moved into an apartment on Fifty-ninth Street overlooking Central Park and attempted to withstand the "impact" of "Plutocratic New York," as he called it, by strolling every fine morning through the shaded walks of the Park, where he enjoyed "A Bit of Altruria" in the midst of the metropolis.

Howells republished this letter in *Impressions and Experiences* because the Altrurian's concept of the significance of Central Park as "a prophecy of the truer state which . . . America is destined yet to see established" was at that time of particular relevance. Since 1894, the question of a charter for Greater New York had been under discussion. How to beautify and improve the rapidly growing metropolis was the subject of many newspaper and magazine articles [22] before the change of name became effective on January 1, 1898. Howells' contribution to the discussion was couched in his usual oblique style in "Glimpses of Central Park." These wooded acres, he remarked, will surely suggest to "the countless thousands who continually visit" the Park the question as to why "the whole of life should not be as generous and just as this part of it." [23]

Here, in the Park, said Howells, he was able to forget for awhile the misery of the city and give himself "wholly up to the delight of the place." He preferred these wooded pathways to the city streets for his afternoon walks for the contrasts between the rich and the poor are not here "so frequent, if they are glaring still." Howells had an eye both for "the sodden tramps" whom he met now and then on the paths and for the "gentleman driving a four-in-hand, with everything to minister to his vanity." [24] Neither they, nor any of the other pedestrians, horsemen, or bicyclists, pause to consider the "kindly and poetic genius" of the man who designed this "American woodland" in the heart of the city, "giving to the city-prisoned poor an image of what the free country still is, everywhere." Howells, no doubt, had in mind his friend, Frederick Law Olmsted, who had helped in the planning of the Boston Common, the parkways of Washington, Philadelphia, and Chicago. He again paid a tribute to Olmsted when he observed that, though genuine artists are seldom given a chance by our plutocratic society "to serve the community," nevertheless, "when this chance offers . . . it finds the right man to profit by it, as in the system of parks at Chicago, the gardened spaces at Washington, and the Central Park in New York." However, not only enjoyed the civic spirit behind the Park, but also the fact that "all has been done to beautify it." The wide expanse is "brightened with pools and ponds lurking among rude masses of rock, and gleaming between leafy knolls and grassy levels," for the designer fully realized that the Park should not be "taken away from nature," but "rendered back to her" to remind those who live in tenements and apartments "of the land as it was before the havoc of the city began." [25] Howells forgave Olmsted his asphalt walks and the well-kept drives but had less tolerance for "the decorative features," which, he felt, were endangering the rustic simplicity of the "simple woodland paths."

Having, many years earlier, strolled through the Royal Garden of "A Little German Capital," and having studied the fountains, the statues, the terraces of "Tuscan Cities," Howells was eager to be pleased by an American attempt to adorn its public parks. "I like to mount some steps graded in the rock at one place," he wrote, "and come upon a plinth supporting the bust of a poet, as I might in an old Italian garden." [26] Unfortunately, however, most of "the decorative features" of the Park seemed to Howells lamentably poor. There was very little attempt at gardening; there was "an excess in the viaduct, with its sweeping stairways and carven freestone massiveness," and "the sculpture is often foolish or worse." [27] In fact, wrote Howells, "there is only one thoroughly good piece of sculpture in the Park," and that is the "Indian Hunter" by J. Q. A. Ward. "An American Indian hunting with his dog, as the Indians must have hunted through the wilds here before the white man came," Howells found "in sympathy with the primeval suggestiveness of the landscape-gardening." [28]

Howells' long association with Olmsted and Ward made him sensitive to the harmony between sculptured group and curving path. However, what he particularly appreciated was that "the Park imparts something of its peace to every one"; he liked to observe the "pairs of beautiful deer" in the zoo, to come upon "that expanse in the heart of the woods where the tennis-players have stretched their nets" and to walk "on the edge of the lawns" where "the art students have set up their easels." Above all, he liked, as he strolled along,

> to note the quiet comfort which the elder people take in this domain of theirs, as they sit on the benches in the woodland ways, or under the arching trees of the Mall, unmolested by the company of some of the worst of all the bad statues in the world.[29]

Just as Howells could put up with "bad statues" if the people in the Park found enough benches under "the arching trees" for their evening rest, so he studied with misgiving "good" art born of social oppression. Howells considered, ironically, the aesthetic and social implications of "the Egyptian obelisk, which the Khedive gave us some years ago, and which we have set up here in one of the finest eminences of the Park." The Khedive, he noted, had "no moral right to rob his miserable land of any one of its characteristic monuments." But perhaps it might as well be in New York as in Alexandria; perhaps "its heart of stone" feels "the continuity of conditions" and is quite aware of "the essential unity of the civilizations beside the Nile and beside the Hudson"; had Cleopatra's Needle really an eye, it would surely see that neither is "truly civic." [30]

Howells' contemplation of the Needle in Central Park brought him to conclusions closely resembling Thorstein Veblen's in *Theory of a Leisure Class* (1899), which Howells reviewed when it appeared several years later.[31] Standing at the base of the obelisk, Howells at that time, watched "dissatisfied and weary wealth" roll by "in the fantastic variety of its equipages" and wondered whether the Needle noticed much difference between the occupants of these carriages and those who had swept beneath it in chariots in the capital of the Ptolemies more than two thousand years before. "I can imagine it at times winking such an eye and cocking in derision the gilded cap with which the New-Yorkers have lately crowned it." For the Needle must recognize, in the elegant vehicles which sped by her on the Hudson, the same "spirit of that atrocious waste" that she had known on the Nile.

These ironic musings on Cleopatra's Needle were, when they first appeared in the January, 1894, issue of the *Cosmopolitan,* attributed to the Altrurian; when they reappeared in *Impressions and Experiences,* in September, 1896, Howells claimed them as his own "Glimpses of Central Park," for he and the Altrurian were, though not identical, closely related. He shared the Altrurian's dream, the fulfillment of which he had glimpsed at the Chicago Fair, that all men have within them a latent love of beauty that might, under more ideal conditions, do away with the concept of classes. Doubts concerning the future of "Plutocratic New York" accosted both Howells and the Altrurian as they stood (singly or together?) at the crossroads in Central Park near the Needle and contemplated the barouches, the four-in-hands, the buggies, the wagons that streamed along on the drive before them, unmindful of the need of the poor who were also enjoying the Park.

Howells' own understanding of the relationship between city planning and the lives of the rich and the poor who live in mansions and tenements had been deepened by his contact with Stephen Crane and Abraham Cahan. His indebtedness to these two men he amply repaid by introducing them to a larger audience. Just as Howells had encouraged Crane in his writing, so he had made Cahan feel that he, too, might be "an important force in American literature." Not only did Howells persuade D. Appleton and Company to publish both *Maggie* and *Yekl* in 1896, he also reviewed them for the New York *World* of July 26, 1896. The review, with a large picture of Howells in the center, filled an entire page of the *World.* The article is effectively summed up in the inch-high heading, "New York Low Life in Fiction," and the subheading, "The great novelist hails Abraham Cahan, the author of 'Yekl,' as a new star of realism, and says that he and Stephen Crane have drawn the truest pictures of east side life."

Howells' review, which was a sensation in its day, was also the means by which Crane and Cahan came to know one another. Several months later, in September, 1896, the Lantern Club of New York gave its first dinner of the season to these two exponents of realism. The gathering of the Club in a huge garret of an old mansion on William Street was such a new and exciting experience to the Russian-born Cahan that he described the occasion fully in his

Autobiography. The room, he wrote, was "decorated in a most interesting manner. Original paintings and drawings hung on the walls. The furniture—indeed, the entire appearance of the place—smacked of the artistic temperament and the artistic freedom from formality. Forty or fifty American writers, journalists, painters, and sculptors met there. They drank whiskey, ate sandwiches, made speeches, and cracked jokes. Compliments to Crane and myself were interspersed in the speeches. (Hamlin Garland came late.) They kibitzed us about our next works. The affair was lively and interesting." [32] Howells, Cahan reported, was not present, though he and his work were discussed during the evening.

It was proper that Howells should not have shared in "the friendly laughter" and the speeches, interrupted by "thunderous ovation," that marked that evening at the Lantern Club. For his three protégés, Garland and Crane and Cahan, were of another generation and were familiar with another vocabulary, which attempted to define realism in terms of veritism, impressionism, or social conditions. These three men, whom Howells knew and befriended during the years when he was writing his Altrurian essays, were in their stories living illustrations of how creative artists help to bridge the gulf between the very rich and the very poor. In the authors of *Main-Travelled Road, Maggie,* and *Yekl,* Howells found the "extraordinary" persons who could say with Emerson, "I ask not for the great, the remote, the romantic . . . I embrace the common; I sit at the feet of the familiar and the low."

In America, Howells had observed in *Criticism and Fiction,* "we are all, or nearly all, struggling to be distinguished from the mass, and to be set apart in select circles and upper classes like the fine people we have read about. We are really a mixture of the plebeian ingredients of the whole world; but that is not bad; our vulgarity consists in trying to ignore 'the worth of the vulgar.' " [33] The three younger writers whom Howells came to know, to their profit and to his, illustrated to him the ways in which the old term "realism" had been interpreted by three men who bespoke the cause of the masses in their writing. The Altrurian, for his part, tried to persuade that distinguished friend of his, the banker, that in Altruria no one is so vulgar as to try to be distinguished; they find, indeed, their fullest reward in whatever form of creativeness is natural to them. Moreover, they discover that select circles and upper classes are essentially sterile. When the banker asked the Altrurian who, in his country, was considered the really great man, the Traveler replied that the honored man in Altruria was he who could "give the greatest happiness to the greatest number—some artist or poet, or inventor or physician." The arts in an ideal world, which Howells "glimpsed" in Central Park, seemed to be "for the relief of man's estate" as truly as the skills of the engineer or the scientist. Could plutocratic New Yorkers be persuaded to build their city in harmony with the Altrurian dream? Could they turn their attention from imaginary romances to the realism of "New York Low-Life in Fiction"? The two questions were related in Howells' mind as he looked out of the window of his Fifty-ninth Street apartment at Central Park and the rapidly changing skyline of New York and pondered these perennial questions.

More important than the social questions, however, were those that involved an understanding of new movements in art. When Howells reviewed Crane's *Open Boat* for *Literature* (May 7, 1898) it was the Impressionists who supplied for him the clue to Crane's style.

> As far as we can judge—and Mr. Crane has not as yet written a great deal—his position in literature is in some ways peculiar. He has in a very unusual degree the power of bringing a scene, no matter what, before our eyes by a few graphic phrases. His subjects are not always interesting; it is his way of presenting them that is everything. In this respect he resembles those painters who care little for the subject but more for the method of their art, and are called for want of a better term, Impressionists. To this extent, with his carefully chosen details, his insistence on the main theme, and his avoidance of irrelevance, Mr. Crane is an Impressionist, and not a mere descriptive writer. His book must not be regarded as a collection of short stories. They are incidents rather than stories, and are selected, not for their dramatic interest, which the author apparently wishes to exclude, but as a vehicle for the telling touches in which he paints aspects of nature, or analyses human nature . . . The sketches are complete in themselves . . . nor do they seem to contain raw material that might be further developed.

"In my own poor way I have always liked the truth," Howells observed in the June 4, 1898, issue of this same magazine, "and in times past I am afraid that I have helped make it odious to those who believed beauty was something different." Impressionism in painting and in writing suggested to Howells a new method of getting at truth. In his contact with Stephen Crane, Howells perceived that social questions and aesthetic techniques seemed to converge; but Howells' understanding of Crane's aim in writing grew from his deeper interest in the growth of great cities in the United States, particularly "Plutocratic New York."

NOTES

1. *Scribner's Magazine*, XIV (October, 1893), 429–445, reprinted in *Literature and Life* (1902).

2. *Ibid.*, p. 429.

3. "The World of Chance" came out in *Harper's* between March and November, 1892, and was brought out as a book by Harper's in March, 1893.

4. *The World of Chance* (1893), pp. 12–13.

5. *Cosmopolitan*, XVI (January, February, March) 259–277, 415–425, 558–569. See also *Letters of an Altrurian Traveller*.

6. For an analysis of the relationship of the "Letters of an Altrurian Traveler," and their reappearance as two essays in *Impressions and Experiences*, see *Letters of an Altrurian Traveller*.

7. *Club Men of New York,* first issue, 1893; fourth issue, 1901. Howells was listed in 1901 as belonging to two clubs, the Century and the Social Reform Club.

8. *Impressions and Experiences* (1896), pp. 251–255. Many of Sloan's paintings seem almost to be illustrations of Howells' essay. See, for example, "6th Avenue and 13th St." (1907), "Pigeons" (1910), "Bleecker Street, Saturday Night" (1918).

9. *Ibid.* Compare Sloan's painting, "Women's Work" (1911).

10. *Ibid.*, pp. 256–257.

11. *Ibid.*, pp. 255–256.

12. *Ibid.*, p. 261.

13. *Ibid.*, p. 260.

14. Joseph J. Kwiat, "Stephen Crane and Painting," *American Quarterly*, IV (1942), 331–338. Garland described Crane's "Indians" in "Stephen Crane as I Knew Him." It is possible that the "older man" to whom Crane referred in his introductory dialogue to "An Experiment in Misery" (1895) was Howells himself. Howells' casual remark in the essay, that the people on whom he and his "companion" called did not

speak to them in Yiddish because they knew it "would be wasted on us," lets us know that Abraham Cahan, the editor of the *Arbeiter Zeitung,* was not "the friend" who led Howells on his visits in December, 1895.

15. *Impressions and Experiences,* pp. 130–131.

16. *Ibid.,* pp. 141–142.

17. *Ibid.,* p. 133.

18. *Ibid.,* p. 139.

19. "Life and Letters," *Harper's Weekly,* XXXIX (June 8, 1895), 532–533.

20. New York *Times,* October 28, 1894. George Arms and William M. Gibson (eds.), *Five Interviews with William Dean Howells* (1943), p. 273.

21. P. 49.

22. See, for example, William C. DeWitt, "Molding the New Metropolis," *Munsey Magazine,* XVII (September, 1897), 923. "Parks and the People," *Harper's Weekly,* XLI (Apr. 17, 1897), 379; "The Greater New York," *ibid.,* pp. 385–391; illustrated articles on the new buildings in New York are to be found in many issues of *Harper's Weekly* in 1897.

23. *Impressions and Experiences,* p. 225.

24. *Ibid.,* pp. 226, 239.

25. *Ibid.,* p. 227.

26. *Ibid.,* p. 228.

27. *Ibid.,* p. 227.

28. *Ibid.,* p. 228.

29. *Ibid.,* pp. 230–231.

30. *Ibid.,* p. 238.

31. *Literature,* n.s. I (Apr. 28, May 5, 1899), 361–362, 385–386.

32. In 1889, before Cahan made the acquaintance of Howells, he delivered a lecture on "Realism" in which he used Tolstoy and Howells as examples of realism in literature and the Russian artist, Verestchagin, as an example of realism in art. Both novelists and artist, said Cahan, attempted to give us a "real" picture of society, i.e., a study of social conditions. See "Abraham Cahan and William Dean Howells," Clara and Rudolf Kirk, "W. D. Howells: The Story of a Friendship," *American Jewish Historical Quarterly,* LII (September, 1962), 28–29. In an article entitled "Realism in Literature and Art," *Arena,* X (December, 1893), 98–113, Clarence S. Darrow made a similar distinction and also used Tolstoy, Howells, and Verestchagin as examples.

33. Pp. 40–41. In "Life and Letters," *Harper's Weekly,* XL (February, 1896), p. 150, Howells suggested, ironically, that titles are needed in the United States, "especially in New York, where millionaires have now become so common from the tendency of the new fortunes to centre in the metropolis from all parts of the country, that to be a millionaire here is not to be anybody in particular." Howells considered the possibility of the city granting a franchise to a Standard Title Company. "This plan," he pointed out, "would enable a number of rich men to grow richer at the expense of their fellow plutocrats, and would involve none

of the hardships to the poorer classes which monopolies are supposed usually to work." One of the most bitter expressions of Howells' resentment of American society's lack of appreciation of the artist is to be found in "Some Suggestions from Mr. McCarthy," *Literature*, XXVIII, n.s. (July 21, 1899), 33. Here Howells remarked that "At its best, society is an enlightened anarchy, an embodiment of free volitions, animated by a tendency to the equality which is the ideal of happiness. Society is communism realised without legislation, in compliance with an unwritten code which everyone is eager to ascertain and obey. Art, on the contrary, and above all, literary art, is the quintessence of individualism . . . art can now apparently have no place in good society, unless the artist is, as he almost never is, born in good society, and enured all his life to sacrifices of personal consciousness for the common enjoyment."

· 3 ·

The Philistine
and the Artist

Howells' visit to the Columbian Exposition, which he gazed at through the eyes of the Altrurian Traveler, and his return to the architectural and social chaos of an expanding New York, which he studied in all of its aspects with the clear eyes of a "realist," brought him to several somewhat ironic conclusions. That he himself was undoubtedly a Philistine in relation to painting, architecture, and sculpture he gladly admitted; that he was an artist in relation to his own literary aims was equally true. Should, then, the Philistine be educated in his tastes by the artist, or should the artist study more carefully the popular response to his efforts and learn to modify his expression in order to communicate with the common man, who is, eventually, the final arbiter of taste?

In an article for *Harper's Weekly*,[1] written soon after Howells' "East-side Ramble" with Stephen Crane, he discussed "The What and How of Art,"[2] on which he had long been meditating. In the opening paragraph Howells placed before the reader the question that constantly haunted his mind—the relation between the Philistine [3] in art and the artist himself:

> One of the things always enforcing itself upon the consciousness of the artist in any sort is the fact that those whom artists work for rarely care for their work artistically. They care for it morally, personally, partially. I suspect that criticism itself has rather a muddled preference for the what over the how, and that it is always haunted by a philistine question of the material when it should, aesthetically speaking, be concerned solely with the form.

Howells was "put upon thinking" of the whole question by viewing a melodrama at the theater,[4] where the audience, which "filled the gallery to the roof," called for the actor who took the part of "the black-hearted villain" and hissed him across the stage between the acts. The hisses were not meant for the actor personally, of course, but were criticism of the character he portrayed. The question of art never occurred to the spectators of this melodrama. "The attitude of the audience towards this deplorable reprobate is," said Howells, "really the attitude of most readers of books, lookers at pictures and statues, listeners to music, and so on through the whole list of the arts. It is absolutely different from the artist's attitude, from the connoisseur's attitude; it is quite irreconcilable with their attitude." And yet, dismaying as this may be, isn't it just this spontaneous response which the artist works for? "Art is not produced for artists, or even for connoisseurs"; clearly, "it is produced for the general, who can never view it otherwise than morally, personally, partially, from their associations and preconceptions." At least the artist does not finally succeed without popular approbation. "Their brute liking or misliking is the final test; it is universal suffrage that elects, after all," said Howells, who, like his friend Henry James, was never on the best-seller list. If the artist or writer is beaten, he ought "to ponder the causes of his defeat, and question how he has failed to touch the chord of universal interest." Obviously, "he is in the world to make beauty and truth evident to his fellow-men, who are as a rule incredibly stupid and ignorant of both, but whose judgment he must nevertheless not despise." Whether the crowd cheers or hisses, the artist "may well have his misgivings" as to the true artistic worth of the painting or poem. And here, of course, "the paradox lies in wait . . . to confound us." Recognition of the dilemma is sufficiently humiliating to our artist-pride, for

> we talk, for instance, of poetry for poets, and we fondly imagine that this is different from talking of cookery for cooks. Poetry is not made for poets; they have enough of their own, but it is made for people who are not poets. If it does not please these, it may still be poetry, but it is poetry which has failed of its truest office. It is none the less its truest office because some very wretched verse seems often to do it.

Nor is it the "logic of such a fact" that the poet should write doggerel; it is, rather, "that he should study how and where and why the beauty and the truth he has made manifest are wanting in universal interest, in human appeal."

> The painter, sculptor, or author who pleases the polite only has a success to be proud of as far as it goes, and to be ashamed of that it goes no farther. He need not shrink from giving pleasure to the vulgar because bad art pleases them. It is part of his reason for being that he should please them, too; and if he does not it is a proof that he is wanting in force, however much he abounds in fineness. Who would not wish his picture to draw a crowd about it? Who would not wish his novel to sell five hundred thousand copies, for reasons besides the sordid love of gain which I am told governs novelists? One would not really wish it any the less because chromos and romances are popular.

The paradox to be resolved by the creative artist in any medium is the same: how to communicate to ordinary people the inner sense of truth to which the artist is committed and at the same time retain the approval of "the masses." That Howells discussed this question with the "artist fellows" of his acquaintance he reported in another paragraph of this essay.

> Not long ago I was talking about pictures with a painter, a very great painter, to my thinking; one whose pieces give me the same feeling I have from reading poetry . . . I said that

I could enjoy pictures only on the literary side, and could get no answer from my soul to those excellences of handling and execution which seemed chiefly to interest painters. He replied that it was a confession of weakness in a painter if he appealed merely or mainly to technical knowledge in the spectator; that he narrowed his field and dwarfed his work by it; and that if he painted for painters merely, or for the connoisseurs of painting, he was denying his office, which was to say something clear and appreciable to all sorts of men in terms of art. He even insisted that a picture ought to tell a story.

Since many of Howells' painter-friends were at that time engaged in illustrating books, decorating public buildings, and exhibiting at the Academy, the American Artists, or the School of Design, we cannot be sure of the identity of "the very great painter" with whom Howells had been talking. William Morris Hunt's paintings for the capitol in Albany, John La Farge's altarpiece for the Church of the Ascension, E. A. Abbey's and John Sargent's series of frescoes for the Boston Public Library, the various panels and friezes then being designed for the Library of Congress—all were expressions of popular art at that time. Each of these murals "told a story" and was suffused with poetry readily understood by the ordinary observer. Not only had Howells stood before these paintings and talked with the artists, but he had seen and studied further examples of their work at the Chicago fair to which these men contributed with no fear of vulgarizing their art by appealing to the crowds.

It seems more probable, however, that the "very great painter" whom Howells had in mind when he wrote "The What and How of Art" was Howard Pyle, who not only illustrated Howells' volume of poetry, *Stops of Various Quills,* which had recently been brought out by Harper's,[5] but also was an old friend with whom Howells had corresponded for years.[6] Pyle, himself a writer as well as an artist, entered fully into the mystical mood of Howells' poetry, conferred with him as to their Swedenborgian implications, and supplemented the story element suggested by the poetry. Pyle's illustrations for his own retelling of the Robin Hood stories were then appearing in *Harper's Monthly* and adding vastly to the popular appeal of that magazine, which had achieved its position of prestige partly through the hearty cooperation of artist and writer.

Henry Mills Alden, editor of *Harper's Monthly,* described in "Fifty Years of Harper's Magazine" [7] this flourishing period of its history, when the most distinguished artists of the day worked in the Harper workshop on illustrations for the stories and essays of the most eminent writers with the avowed intention of winning popular favor for the magazine. "As a popular magazine," Alden wrote, *Harper's* could not compete with the *Atlantic Monthly,* then shining brilliantly in "the literary heavens" of Boston, unless it defined a new path and engaged the best story writers and the best artists.[8] Though Alden recognized that he could not hope to survive in "honorable competition" if he depended on "Emerson's essays or Lowell's critical papers," he hospitably opened the doors of the magazine to the stories of Howells, Mark Twain, and other promising new writers who were to be supported by superior illustrators.

Looking back over the long years of his editorship, Alden noted that

> the Harper establishment has been from the beginning a great workshop. The atmosphere of the place did not suggest any special aesthetic refinement. There was a corps of engravers who worked on a salary, meeting all requirements for the illustration of the books and periodicals of the house. Often in the engravings for the *Weekly,* and sometimes in those for the *Magazine,* different engravers would work on different portions of the same block. But the utmost possible attention was given to securing the most excellent workmanship.

Many of these illustrators, under the guidance of Charles Parsons, later became eminent artists in their own right. Alden remembered them in their studio in the Harper building, "seated at desks, drawing on wood and at times varying their work with riotous hilarity." They had no models, but many did work that found a place in the Academy exhibitions. E. A. Abbey, C. S. Reinhart, J. Alexander, A. B. Frost, and F. V. Du Mond were notable among those who worked under Charles Parsons in "that old workshop."

Howard Pyle, Frederic Remington, and William T. Smedley "formed a new group of later-day artists, with new methods and higher attainments. The studio and the model became necessary to the perfection of their work. The artist of this new school was not merely illustrating the writer's text; he stood for himself as an individual artist." Frederic Remington was not only one of the most prolific of the artists employed by Harper's, but, like Howard Pyle, he frequently illustrated his own essays and stories, supplying the reader with a lively example of the relationship of artist and writer. In a review of *Sundown Leflare,* written and illustrated by Remington, Howells concluded that it was because of his gifts as an artist rather than his talent as a writer that Remington would be remembered. The fact that Remington studied from life the rapidly disappearing "Wild Men of the West," however, gave both text and sketches a certain validity, for it was Remington's concern for truth that enabled him to put his figures before one "with such admirable, such almost absolute, detachment." [9] The artist thus teaches the writer the virtue of objectivity, of allowing the fact to speak for itself without further comment from the author.

One of Howells' most important novels, *The Landlord at Lion's Head,* is a further example of the happy collaboration of artist and writer. The first installment of this novel concerning a wayward youth and his older artist-friend, appeared in the July 4, 1896, issue of *Harper's Weekly.*[10] Filling the upper third of the large page of the *Weekly* was a pen-sketch, by W. T. Smedley, of the two chief characters, Mr. Westover, the artist, and twelve-year-old Jeff Durgin, the future landlord of his mother's summer boarding house in the mountains of New Hampshire. Smedley, in his many illustrations for the Howells' novel, showed his ability to seize the story sympathetically and convert it into drawings that preserved his individuality as an artist; Howells, for his part, caught in this novel the thoughts and character of an artist whose art is his life as well as his livelihood.

In a way, Howells' story is an exploration of the relation of the artist to society. For Westover, who went to a remote area of the White Mountains to paint the last fiery colors of a New England autumn, was soon drawn into the family circle of an impoverished farmer struggling for survival. The Durgins could no longer scrape a living from their rocky acres, nor fight the ravages of tuberculosis, nor control the one healthy child out of their unfortunate family. Westover's personality, felt largely through his painting, exerted a civilizing influence on the rough but intelligent Jeff and was a moral support to his plain, hardworking, staunchly strong mother. The symbolic significance of the Lion's Head, the mountain that loomed immediately before the Durgins' poor little house, is felt rather than fully understood in the opening sentence of this novel dealing with stubborn New England temperaments that are sometimes lost in snow or obliterated by mist.

> If you looked at the mountain from the west, the line of the summit was wandering and uncertain, like that of most mountain-tops; but seen from the east, the mass of granite showing above the dense forests of the lower slopes had the form of a sleeping lion.

This was the mountain that Westover had come to New Hampshire to paint, and he, therefore, began at once to search for the best angle and the right light. The other sleeping lion, Jeff Durgin, was, when the artist first arrived and asked for lodging, merely a cub; however, he was already the neighborhood bully, the untamed, selfish, almost savage young hunter and fisherman whom Westover attempted to study, first from this side, then from that, with the hope of bringing him within the scope of civilized man. Westover never succeeded. Nor did he succeed to his own satisfaction in painting the mountain itself, the outlines of which he endlessly contemplated: "The flanks and haunches were vaguely distinguished from the mass; but the mighty head, resting with its tossed mane upon the vast paws stretched before it, was boldly sculptured against the sky." The likeness of the mountain to a lion was perfect when seen in profile, as perfect as if "it had been the intention of art" to model a lion; however, "in winter the head was blotted by the snows," and the illusion was lost. Sometimes, at other seasons and unexpectedly, "the vagrant clouds caught upon it and deformed it, or hid it" entirely from the view of the gazer. "But commonly, after the last snow went in the spring until the first snow came in the fall, the Lion's Head was a part of the landscape."

Though Westover could no more successfully see all sides of Thomas Jefferson Durgin, either as a boy, or as a student at Harvard, or as the ruthless landlord of a flourishing summer hotel, his attempt to "compose" him into some sort of moral "form" did modify the "composition" of Jeff's character. Westover began the training of his wild young friend on the very evening of his arrival when he at least made Jeff "see" what otherwise he never would have been aware of, the shifting lights of evening.

Going to a nearby field after an early supper, with his pad and charcoal, to make "some tentative scrawl on his canvas," he noticed that the light on the mountainside was beginning to take the "rich tone of the afternoon deepening to evening." With a smothered exclamation, Westover grabbed his colors and began furiously to paint, forgetful of the boy behind him. "I don't think that looks very much like it," drawled Jeff while Westover continued to hunt for the right tints in dreamy oblivion of the sneering comment. "Perhaps you don't know," finally responded the artist happily lost in his painting. "I know what I see," replied the boy. "I doubt it," said Westover, and then he forgot the boy until he was roused from his dream by the screams of a small girl and her infant brother whom Jeff and his dog were holding at bay in the bushes. Westover dropped his paints, rushed to the rescue of the children, and soundly disciplined Jeff.

Westover's unconscious power as an artist to open the eyes of Jeff to the scene around him paralleled his overt effort to hammer into the boy's mind his moral obligation to the two crouching children. Like the mountain itself, the hard, granite foundation of Jeff's temperament was only modified by the changing lights in which it was viewed; it remained, throughout the novel, "as imperative and importune as the Great Stone Face itself." Stubborn though he was, there were other sides to Jeff's nature that could be seen in a variety of lights. Jeff, who had never before met his master, was quick to apprehend that the artist had a certain importance and brought his friends to admire the Durgins' prize boarder as he worked at his canvas under the face of Lion's Head day after day. The artist somehow maintained dominance over the unruly child of nature; Prospero controlled Caliban.

When, finally, his two weeks drew to a close, Jeff's mother, from whom the boy inherited his strength if not his harsh nature, astonished the painter by offering to return his board-money if he would let her have his canvas. But Westover, like most artists, had his own living to earn, and was forced gently to demur. Mrs. Durgin persisted: "I presume you'll think I'm foolish," she said in her stiff New England way. "But I do want that picture; I don't know when I've ever wanted a thing more. It's just like Lion's Head, the way I've seen it, day in and day out, every summer since I come here thirty-five years ago; it's beautiful!" When Westover again seemed to hesitate, Mrs. Durgin continued to plead, not in the least understanding that the $14 that she wished to return to him would not be enough to pay for any painting. "Why *don't* you let me have it then? If we ever had to go away from here—if anything happened to us—it's the one thing I should want to keep and take with me. There! That's the way I feel about it. I can't explain; but I do *wish* you'd let me have it." [11]

Mrs. Durgin finally was made to understand by this artist, who was of necessity a businessman, too, that he hoped to sell the painting in Boston for two or three hundred dollars, and she turned, with a sigh, to other matters. Could he possibly help her advertise her boarding house in a Boston paper? Did he think she could "do for boarders as well as some, if not better?" [12] Westover's position, as a person of insight in many areas, was established before he took his leave—under a rainstorm of apples hurled at his retreating figure by Jeff from behind the gravestones of his little brothers and sisters.

After five years in France "in the only air where he believed modern men were doing good things in the right way," [13] Westover returned to the Durgin boarding house, then called Lion's Head Hotel, to find the apple-pelter grown into a stocky, muscular young man whose daily duty it was to drive the "hack" from the station to his mother's prosperous hotel. Artistically, Westover "rejoiced in the fellow's young, manly beauty, which was very regular and sculpturesque"; [14] morally, he found him exactly as selfish and stubborn as he was as a child, and no more to be moved from the laws of his own character than the mountain itself. As a painter, however, Westover had learned patience and quietness; by then an old friend of the family, Westover let "the days go by in the swiftness of monotony. His excursions to the barn, his walks on the verandas, his work on his picture, filled up the few hours of the light, and when the dark came he contentedly joined the little group in Mrs.

Durgin's parlor." [15] In the mornings Westover had nothing to do, "for he worked at his picture only when the conditions renewed themselves with the sinking sun." Solitary walks in the open air, trips to the barn where he sometimes helped to look after the "cattle and the horses, whose subdued stamping and champing gave him a sort of animal pleasure," reading under the lamp in the evenings, put Westover in tune with a life that was quiet but never dull. At the same time, in a wordless fashion, he was able to understand and participate in the turbulent undercurrent of the lives of those around him.

The source of his power, both as an artist and a family friend, lay in the habit he had formed many years earlier of seeing things from his own angle and setting them down on canvas with no comment. As the weather grew colder, he found that he could paint for shorter periods out-of-doors; on that first cold day "he found that his own window gave him the best." With the stove at his back and the window thrown open, he spent his afternoons in his room with great contentment.

The snows kept off, and the clear sunsets burned behind the summit day after day. He painted frankly and faithfully, and made a picture which, he said to himself, no one would believe in, with that warm color tender upon the frozen hills. The soft suffusion of the winter scene was improbable to him when he had it in nature before his eyes; when he looked at it as he got it on his canvas it was simply impossible.[16]

The need Westover felt to see with his own eyes, through his own window, was akin to that which Howells as a realistic writer felt even as he was himself attempting to "paint" a picture of the frozen hills of New England temperaments softened by the light of a winter sun. The artist's vision of the mountain became the writer's symbol for the novel. What both artist and writer saw was a blend of the beautiful and the true, the aesthetic and the moral, through their contemplation of the mountain in various lights and from different angles. Both were absorbed by the strangeness of the actual scene before them. Moreover, their interpretation of "the real" was understandable to the ordinary person, whose life was altered by the insight of the artist. Mrs. Durgin, as well as the rest of the human race, loved the real because it was beautiful and would give all she possessed to own it, though she could not explain to herself why the painting was important to her. If this is "Philistine," Howells seemed to say, then that is the very nature of all art. Far from accepting the opprobrium with which Matthew Arnold surrounded the term "Philistine," Howells agreed rather with Leslie Stephen's ironic definition of the word as "a term of contempt applied by prigs to the rest of their species." [17]

In April, 1896—the month after he first proposed his "Philistine question" in "Life and Letters"—Howells reviewed for *Harper's Weekly* "the spring openings at the American Artists and the National Academy." [18] He hesitated to report quite candidly, he wrote, on his "many and varying impressions," which had been to him, for the most part, "very pleasant," for fear of the stern glance of the professional art critic. "That is the way with us Philistines," he remarked ironically; "we are shy of a real emotion from a painting or a statue, for fear it may be an ignorant emotion." Howells himself admitted that he liked to take his catalogue in hand, in true Philistine fashion, begin at the first painting and progress slowly around the gallery, marking with a star the pictures he had particularly enjoyed. He had learned, however, to keep to himself any joy he may have found in them until he had encountered someone who appeared to be sufficiently knowing to sanction his preferences. Such a person could be easily found, Howells had discovered, for artists frequent art shows in order to keep up with changing tastes, and they are seldom unwilling to express their views—such as they are.

> You have only to say, "Didn't you think that *The Splash in the Pool,* there in the first room, was rather interesting?" Or, "How did you like Boheme's *Clad in the Beauty of a Thousand Stars*"? Your artist friend will probably say of one, "Yes, that was rather nice—nice feeling," and of the other, "Oh, beastly thing," and there you have an emotion worth having. Sometimes your friend will volunteer an opinion, or take you to look at something he has liked very much. This is pure gain, and it breaks up the formality of your numerical progress round the rooms, and gives you the sense of seeing the thing in an original way.

In the light of the art critics' illuminating comments, Howells usually discovered that he had not gone far wrong in his likes and dislikes, and, of course, if by chance he had been led astray by his own impressions he could "instantly change them," and substitute those that he knew he would be "lastingly proud of." Surely it would be "terribly discouraging to the poor fellows who paint pictures" fully to realize, in the midst of all the other discouragements that they cannot avoid, "how deeply and enduringly ignorant of all they mean and wish in their work we Philistines are." Does art, indeed, speak a language that the ordinary person cannot learn? Perhaps only the professional art critic should utter his views. Howells, who enjoyed his visits to galleries as he valued his strolls through the streets and parks of New York, modestly claimed his right to speak in defiance of the critics: "I wish to express such ideas of mine, if they are ideas, very diffidently, and I should be sorry if anyone were influenced by them, even another Philistine." Characteristically, he declared,

> I do not see why one should not go to a picture show with a mind both empty and open; it is much better than to have it filled with a clutter of preoccupations. The effort to be critical, at first hand or at second hand, is very straining; it makes one cross, and keeps one from doing such small measure of justice as one ignorantly might to the pictures one has come to look at. After all, they are not there to be criticised, primarily; they are there to be enjoyed, and if you please, to be bought.[19]

Just as Howells encouraged and advised younger writers such as Garland, Crane, and many others, so he was ready to help young artists on their way if the opportunity offered itself. One such occasion was suggested by a letter he wrote to his brother-in-law, Larkin Mead, in behalf of a young sculptor, Bessie Potter, who hoped to be welcomed into Mead's studio in Florence. Miss Potter had worked under Lorado Taft at the Chicago Fair; she was also a friend of many writers such as Henry Fuller, Harriet Monroe, Hamlin Garland, Eugene Fields, and of many artists such as J. Q. A. Ward, Augustus Saint-Gaudens, D. C. French—all of whom looked upon her as a sculptor of promise. Having made an eight-foot figure of Art for the Illinois Building at the Chicago Fair, she was ready to be feted in London by Alma-Tadema, to be welcomed into the studio of Rodin in Paris, and to work with Larkin Mead in Florence.

Before she sailed from New York, early in 1897, Miss Potter wrote notes "to some of the critics who had been kindest, that I would be at the old St. Denis Hotel upon a certain date. A number of art critics came, among them Mr. Rupert Hughes—also Mr. Daniel Chester French, Mr. Robert Underwood Johnson, Mr. Richard Watson Gilder, and dear William Dean Howells bringing me letters of introduction to people in Italy." [20] Howells' letter was addressed to Larkin Mead, and this Miss Potter quoted in full, because, she said, it expressed better than she could herself what she was striving for in her statues. Howells wrote, in part, to his brother-in-law:

> I think she has put new life in your old dry bones of an art, and has given the Muse of sculpture (if there is one) a chance to become a fellow citizen, and to vote with the rest of us when her sex gets the suffrage. What I mean is that her work, while it is as Greek as the Tanagra figurines, is as utterly and inalienably American as you are, and perfectly modern. It is simply a joy to me, for it gets into sculpture the things I am always trying to get into fiction.[21]

Perhaps it was Miss Potter's little figures to which Howells referred in his review of the spring openings of 1896, when he remarked on his pleasure in "those little statues at the Artists, reflecting certain moods of modern life and fashion so charmingly." [22]

Almost forgotten in our day, Miss Potter was renowned at the end of the nineteenth century and well into the twentieth for statues, both large and small, that seemed to catch in stone the kind of realism expressed in paint by Brush, Chase, Twachtman, and others. Examples of her work may be sought out today in the Senate Chamber, Washington, in Fairmount Park, Philadelphia, in New York's Metropolitan Museum; no doubt one might even uncover in some storeroom in Paris a large statue of "The American Girl" which Miss Potter was invited to do for the Paris Exposition of 1900.[23] A study of that figure, indeed, might make clear the sympathetic understanding between the young sculptor and her older novelist friend!

In appreciation of her popular triumph, Miss Potter was invited, on her return from Europe, to become a member of the National Sculpture Society, the National Academy of Design, and the Society of American Artists. On May 15, 1900, Howells was asked to give "the main address" at a joint dinner of the National Sculpture Society and the Society of Mural Painters. He chose the subject, "Art and the True Principles of Art Criticism." As a newly elected member of the Sculpture Society, Miss Potter was perhaps seated with her husband, Robert Vonnoh, at one of the long tables at that important dinner.

Howells' speech, which was fully reported the following day in the *Evening Post* [24] and other papers,[25] suggests that the views Howells expressed on that occasion are those that he had come to believe in the course of his long experience with popular taste. As a literary artist, he fully realized that his interpretation of the reality of the American scene, in his many novels, had never achieved popularity and that they were by the end of the century losing ground against romanticism in its many forms. As an amateur in architecture, sculpture, and painting, all of which he enjoyed, he knew that, like the readers of his novels, he missed much of the artist's intent. The old question of the relation of the Philistine and the artist remained: can they communicate and, if so, how? Howells' lifelong habits of enjoying museums, art galleries, city streets, and public parks supplied him with an answer. What he had to say on the subject was of sufficient public interest to warrant the heading in the *Evening Post* of May 16, 1900, of "Mr. Howells on Judging Sculpture."

Since J. Q. A. Ward was President of the Sculpture Society at that time, Howells paid a tribute to the "Indian Hunter" in Central Park, as an example of American art that was appreciated by the "average man." "The true principle of art," Howells had learned, was that it must communicate with all classes. Writers, sculptors, artists, architects, when "they come honestly to rub their heads together," all know that the approval of "the ignorant, tasteless, uncritical multitude" is essential to their survival. Thinking of the current taste for romantic novels, Howells freely admitted that he might have failed the readers:

> When I see people reading the nine hundredth and ninety-ninth thousand of the latest historical romance, my heart sinks; but I do not lose my faith that, when some great novelist divines how to report human nature as truly as such romances report it falsely, people will read him too in the nine hundred and ninety-ninth thousand. I do not say that they will think his novel greater than those romances; probably they will not, just as the average man who enjoys the Indian hunter might not think it greater than the Robert Burns or the F. G. Halleck [statues in Central Park]. But happily that is not the artist's affair, in either art; his affair is to do a beautiful and true thing so simply and directly that the average man will not miss the meaning and the pleasure of it.

Though "the multitude admires many wretched and paltry things," said Howells, and though "it confuses the esthetical and ethical qualities" of works of art, nevertheless, it is the people who ultimately judge the value of art. Like all exponents of "progress" at the hopeful opening of the twentieth century, Howells believed that education would gradually improve popular taste: "We must in all these things rely upon education," he concluded. But, he warned, education must begin with the artists, "with those who write and paint and build," as well as with "those who model and carve."

"I should like to believe," said this "Novelist on Art," [26] in his address to the gathering of sculptors, painters, architects, and artists, "I should like to believe that as we simplify ourselves and get directly at the core of life, we find ourselves in a larger companionship than when we hold aloof from the elemental things which all can understand and feel." As "a literary man," in the presence of "a fine building, a beautiful picture, a noble statue," he usually found himself seeking for "a first cause of art." Since he was a writer, he had to "*deliterate* his mind, and somehow remand it to the origins of thought, to those primal sources in which *art* is really one." This "oneness" of art leads the simplest observer, as well as the artist, to "the heart of life." In this way art speaks to men, and is, indeed, the language of a democratic society. Perhaps the artist has something to learn from the Philistine; if he believes in equality and democracy he must be willing to address himself directly to the public.

"You do not make your statues for sculptors only, I suppose," Howells calmly remarked as he glanced at the throng of sculptors, artists, architects, writers, journalists, and city officials before him. "Therefore," he continued, "the interest of the non-sculptor is as much your concern as mine." But perhaps the sculptors in the audience disagreed with him, he mused aloud; perhaps they thought the statue in the park, for example, was "not there for criticism or analysis at all." Surely, when the artist in any field actually speaks to the ordinary person, he finds himself "in a larger companionship" than when he "holds himself aloof from the ordinary things that all can understand and feel." Indeed, the "uncritical multitude" renders his art "the highest tribute" in pausing before it and attempting to come to an understanding of its meaning. Paraphrasing Lincoln, Howells remarked that the average man, "is a terrible fellow," but "there are a great many of him." What he responds to and what he passes by is important for the artist to notice; "it is worth while trying to find out his secret if he has one." For the artist depends upon genuine communication, and at his own peril disdains the taste of the passer-by. "The difficulty is not to make him like the best, but to give him the best."

At the opening of the century, at the moment when the average man was in danger of betrayal, not only by the ivory-tower artist, but also by all the latent perils of mass production, Howells appealed to the leading artists of New York as the voice of conscience of the emerging society. An avowed Philistine, he believed that "there is a perfect democracy in the realm of the beautiful, and whatsoever pleases is equal to any other thing there, no matter how low its origin and humble its composition" [27]—a lesson he had learned many years earlier in the romantic city of Venice and that he now sought to apply to a rapidly growing New York.

NOTES

1. "Life and Letters," *Harper's Weekly,* XL (Mar. 21, 1896), 270.

2. "The What and How of Art" was the title given this essay when it was reprinted in *Literature and Life* (1902). It is to be noted that Howells' essay appeared before Tolstoy's "What Is Art?," which also deals with the question of democratic art.

3. Matthew Arnold discussed his interpretation of the term in *Culture and Anarchy* (1869) and again in his lectures in the United States in 1888. See Howells' comment in *Criticism and Fiction and Other Essays by W. D. Howells,* pp. 66–67. The term was given circulation at this time by Elbert Hubbard's little publication, *The Philistine,* which ran from June, 1895, to July, 1915. Both Hamlin Garland and Stephen Crane contributed to this periodical.

4. Discussed also in "New York Low Life in Fiction," New York *World,* Part II (July 28, 1896), p. 18.

5. October, 1895.

6. See "Toward a Theory of Aesthetics" in Part One of this book.

7. *Harper's Monthly,* C (May, 1900), 947–962. Alden was managing editor of *Harper's Weekly* from 1863 to 1869, and then became managing editor of *Harper's Monthly.* He held this position until his death in 1919. For another account of the Harper workshop, see Charles D. Abbott, "Fruitful Associations," *Howard Pyle, A Chronicle* (1925), Chapter III.

8. See also William A. Coffin, "American Illustration of Today," *Scribner's,* I (February, March, 1892), 196–205, 333–339.

9. "Mr. Remington's Wild Men," *Literature,* n.s. I (Feb. 17, 1899), 121–122.

10. Facing the opening page of *The Landlord at Lion's Head* is a handsome engraving of Howells by E. Schladitz, from a photograph by Cox. See Sister Mary Petrus Sullivan, "The Function of Setting in Howells's *The Landlord at Lion's Head,*" *American Literature,* XXXV (March, 1963), 38–52.

11. *The Landlord at Lion's Head* (1897), pp. 39–40.

12. *Ibid.,* p. 41.

13. *Ibid.,* p. 47.

14. *Ibid.,* 48.

15. *Ibid.,* 303.

16. *Ibid.,* 302.

17. "Philistinism," *Encyclopaedia Americana,* XXI (1962).

18. "Life and Letters," *Harper's Weekly,* XL (Apr. 18, 1896), p. 390.

19. *Ibid.*

20. By Bessie Potter Vonnoh, "Tears and Laughter Caught in Bronze," *Delineator,* CVII (October, 1925), 78. Miss Potter married the painter, Robert W. Vonnoh. They held a joint exhibition at the Montrose Gallery in December, 1913. In the *Delineator* article, a number of Mrs. Von-

noh's figurines appeared, and under one is a quotation from Howells' letter, "She has put new life into your old bones of an art," p. 8.

21. Feb. 5, 1897. *Life in Letters,* II, 74–75.

22. *Ibid.* "Life and Letters," *Harper's Weekly,* XL (Apr. 18, 1896), p. 390.

23. "Tears and Laughter Caught in Bronze." Miss Potter's bust of Vice-President Sherman is in the Senate Chamber; her statue of Major General S. W. Crawford is in Fairmount Park, Philadelphia; a mother and child group is in the Metropolitan. She also did the bird fountain, in memory of Theodore Roosevelt, at Oyster Bay, Long Island, and another such fountain at Ormond Beach, Florida. Miss Potter executed a statue of Maud Adams in solid gold. She was elected an Academician in 1921 and that same year received the Gold Medal award of the National Academy of Design.

24. *Evening Post,* May 16, 1900.

25. New York *Times,* May 19, 1900.

26. "A Novelist on Art" *The Literary Digest,* XX, No. 22 (June 2, 1900), 662–663. This article, reporting Howells' speech before the Sculpture Society, is largely quoted from the *Evening Post,* May 16, 1900.

27. *Venetian Life* (1886), p. 27.

· 4 ·

On Parnassus

"I generally go to the Century Club Saturday night," Howells wrote to Garland on March 14, 1898, "and for the rest I stay at home, and read to the family. In the afternoon I take long walks in the Park." [1]

Howells' name had been proposed for membership in the Century Club just before he left New York, in the spring of 1897, for a six-months' stay in Europe. By the time he returned in November to his apartment overlooking Central Park, he found himself a member of the Club to which he had been a frequent visitor for many years and to which he remained devoted until his death. "New York was the Athens of America and The Century was its Parnassus," one member later observed. To Howells the remark would have seemed valid, for "all the Muses were here. . . . The arts, the sciences, and scholarship were all so richly represented that the Century seemed to be a veritable Academy." [2]

While he was still living in Boston and editing the *Atlantic*

Monthly, Howells had made frequent trips to New York, in the course of which he came to know many members of the Century Club. When he moved to New York, he took an apartment on Stuyvesant Square, "in the vicinity of the Century Club," then at 109 East Fifteenth Street. "The society we saw," Howells later told a reporter from the New York *Times,*[3] "was mainly grouped then about Tenth and Eleventh Streets—intellectual, cultivated men and women." Society had not at that time "taken on an air of pluto-cratic fun-seeking"; it was still authentic, and had manners, and as far as the great world could, and had time, it appreciated literature and art." Though Howells was urged to join the Century Club more than once during these years, "the shadow cast" by the death of his elder daughter and his wife's invalidism prevented him from going out very much into the "great world." He preferred, instead, to join "a group of delightful people who meet at one house or another to hear a paper read which is worth while or to listen to a lecture." Those who appreciated such evenings belonged, said Howells, to "fashionable New York society,"—like and yet different from Boston society, "for, strictly speaking, Boston society was not so fashionable." [4]

Though Howells did not join the Century until he was an established novelist and editor of sixty years, his name was frequently listed in early accounts of the activities of the Club. James Herbert Morse, who kept a diary of the Club events, described a "grand dinner" given by the Centurians at Delmonico's in honor of How-ells' old friend, Bayard Taylor. In April, 1878, before Taylor set out as minister to Germany, two hundred and twenty-five guests were assembled, wearing "white neckties and dress coats as thick as yellow apples in an autumn orchard. Taylor, red-faced and rotund, stood, a giant in height and breadth, glowing and happy in his honors." [5] William Cullen Bryant, third president of the Club, as well as Howells and Mark Twain, spoke at the dinner. Clarence King, Whitelaw Reid, and Richard Watson Gilder were among the guests on this notable occasion described by Morse.

Howells remembered with particular pleasure the member whose diary has helped to keep alive the history of the Club. "One of the pleasantest homes to which we used to go was that of James Herbert Morse, school teacher as well as poet," said Howells to the

Times reporter. "There we enjoyed simple and charming evenings, meeting such friends as the Stocktons, Mrs. Dodge, Joe Jefferson, Sol Smith Russell, and others whom we all delighted to meet." Another name familiar to members of the Club came to Howells' mind as he thought back over the years. "For a long time, of course," he added, "the home of Gilder of the Century [Magazine] was a center, if not the center of literary hospitality."

The Century Club moved in 1891 to a beautiful Renaissance building just off Fifth Avenue on Forty-third Street,[6] and shortly thereafter Howells took an apartment at 40 West Fifty-ninth Street. The Century Club and Howells were merely a part of the movement of the city from the older squares of lower New York to the airy regions of upper Fifth Avenue and the Park. "Though we have no longer any literary circles," Howells wrote after the move, "we still have as much pleasure of our literary lives as ever." [7] Howells' reminiscences of Stuyvesant Square included the names of many literary and artistic friends whom he continued to meet at the Century Club before he actually became a member. Having only recently completed his social novel, *A Hazard of New Fortunes,* in 1890, Howells was already contemplating "A Traveller From Altruria," [8] a still more searching inquiry into the relationship between great fortunes and democratic art. He perhaps hesitated to become a member of the fashionable Century Club at this time, in spite of the fact that he there enjoyed meeting so many of his friends and associates. To understand why he overcame his scruples and finally joined the Club of artists, authors—and businessmen—one must glance back fifty years and consider the aims of the original organization.

The purpose of the Century Association,[9] established in 1847 as an outgrowth of the Sketch Club, was "to promote interest in literature and the fine arts" among its members, who according to its constitution, "shall be authors, artists, and amateurs of letters and the fine arts." The Association, familiarly called the Century Club, maintained from its earliest days a small library and art gallery in its house on Fifteenth Street. In 1891, however, the ranks of the membership included more businessmen than writers and artists. This was the time when vast fortunes were being amassed by John Jacob Astor, Cornelius Vanderbilt, J. Pierpont Morgan, all of whom were members of the Century Club; this was the period, too, when a few civic-minded men seriously considered the possibility of building not only a "Greater New York" but also a greater country by bringing together men from all walks of life. Those who gathered in their new Renaissance clubhouse were hopeful that unpredictable benefits might accrue when such members as Theodore Roosevelt, James Harvey Robinson, William Allen White, John Singer Sargent, and many other gifted men, mingled, as fellow Centurians, with lawyers, editors, architects, and businessmen.

Saint-Gaudens, for example, sitting with a brilliant group of architects and sculptors early in the decade when the Columbian Exposition was being planned, was said to have burst out with the remark, "Look here, old fellows, do you realize that this is the greatest meeting of artists since the fifteenth century?" [10] In the group were La Farge, Richard Morris Hunt, Frederick Law Olmsted, and other artists, city-planners, architects, and sculptors who not only contributed to the Exposition but were also building the mansions, the parks, the churches, the statues, the museums and the civic centers that, at the turn of the century, established the city we know today.[11] New York's two great cathedrals, St. Patrick's and St. John's, the Metropolitan Museum, Grace Church, the Vanderbilt Mansion, the Public Library, Pennsylvania Station, Columbia University, as well as Central Park and Washington Square—all bear the stamp of those who met and talked at the Century Club. The names of the painter, Albert Bierstadt; the actor, Lawrence Barrett; Brander Matthews, critic, novelist, and professor; Nicholas Murray Butler, the new president of Columbia University; Bishop Henry C. Potter, then beginning the great Cathedral on Morningside Heights—these names alone suggest the position the Club held at this extraordinary period in the growth of the city and the country. Howells, as the most eminent writer of his day in the eyes of these men, found himself perfectly at home in an organization established for the purpose of bringing together artists and writers for the refreshment to be found in the free exchange of ideas.[12]

A greatly enlarged art gallery and library, which formed part of the new home of the Century Club, played their part in the liberalizing of the program of the Club in 1891. Augustus R. Macdonough, who had been secretary of the Club in 1868, remarked in his first report that "in order to make the Club a genuine reflection of certain intellectual elements in the life of this city" a separate library and a gallery for paintings were essential. "With the advance of population, the classes of men who love art and profess letters and seek general culture enlarge in ever increasing ratio; and if the Century would keep up with the times, it must often widen its portals to welcome more men of mark." [13]

When the new Club on Forty-third Street was finally achieved, Macdonough wrote an article for *Century Magazine* [14] in which he made it clear that the same aims were followed in 1891 when the Association became officially the Century Club, and a greatly increased membership moved into "palatial quarters," which were supported by higher membership fees. Significantly, Macdonough recorded that "at the present time the artists, still, as always, the flower and crown of the Century, represent one-seventh of the club," merchants and financiers holding the controlling vote among the seven hundred members. Macdonough grouped clergymen, journalists, physicians, professors, and writers with the artists as "really the salt of the Club." The two "main piers of the Century's edifice—Literature and Art," wrote Macdonough, were from the early days of the Association supported by "practical men of action"; thus "ideas and knowledge mingled from different spheres, criticism of both art and life grew broad and practical, and innumerable outlets for impulse upon the community were opened."

Writers frequently contributed their books to the growing library; artists often left their paintings as permanent exhibits in the art gallery.[15] Most rewarding, however, was "the mutual enlightenment among men knowing the worth of one another's work," which necessarily brought with it an atmosphere of "absolute equality" among authorities in so many diverse fields, stifling sham, pretension, and pedantry. On Saturday evenings, when members were apt to gather for sociability over dinner and conversation afterwards, "the strain of driving the business and social machinery of this great city unbent," and men of all professions found "rest in interchange of fresh thoughts." From this "friction of minds," wrote Macdonough, "flashed incessant currents, conveying force and light. Art, seeking the ideal in life, and practice, working with its realities, instructed and invigorated each other." Conversation ranged over "boundless fields," from Michelangelo to the latest issue of *Punch,* from "the newest guess of science" to the Decalogue; from Gladstone's speech in Parliament to a current Broadway play. No one ever left a gathering of the Century after one of these spirited evenings without carrying away "some new fact, or impression, or conviction to spread in ever widening circles among his associates in the outer community," wrote Macdonough at this high point in the history of the Club. "The artist learned the artistic needs of the lay public; the author absorbed the passing spirit of the time; the politician rose to broader views; the scientist found his limitations; the divine came in touch with liberal inquiry; the editor caught the tone of living convictions."

Howells was undoubtedly one of the authors who "absorbed the passing spirit of the times" by his contact with the Century Club both before and after he became a member. His sensitive response to changing taste in art and architecture, his interest in science and experimentation of all kinds, the reflection of the religious and social issues of his day, the natural, conversational quality of his prose—all suggest the mind of a writer who enjoyed the varied experiences of evenings at the Century.

The new range of subjects opening before the realistic novelist, as described by Howells in *Criticism and Fiction* (1891) in the same year in which Macdonough wrote his essay on the Century Club, show that Howells shared the enthusiasm for the flood of new ideas and attitudes discussed by the extraordinary group of men whom he had come to know in New York. "The whole field of human experience was never so nearly covered by imaginative literature in any age as in this," wrote Howells, "and American life especially is getting represented with unexampled fulness." [16] No one writer, no one book reflects the multiplicity of new ideas, he believed, but a great many very good writers are "striving to make each part of the country and each phase of our civilization known to all the other parts . . . The world was once very little, and it is now very large." The classics no longer suffice, for they do not put us in touch with new ideas; "we could no more turn back and be of the literary fashions of any age before this than we could turn back and be of its social, economical, or political conditions." Furthermore, formerly, all science could be grasped by a single mind; but now the man who hopes to become great or useful in science must devote himself to a single department. It is so in everything—all arts, all trades; and the novelist is not superior to the universal rule against universality. He contributes his share to a thorough knowledge of groups of the human race under conditions which are full of inspiring novelty and interest. He works more fearlessly, frankly, and faithfully than the novelist ever worked before.

Though the novelist's work "may be destined never to be reprinted from the monthly magazines," it nevertheless makes its own contribution to the rapidly evolving civilization, the goals of which are being defined by writers, artists, scientists, politicians, ministers—all of whom have a part to play in our progress toward a genuine democracy. The hope for a better society that Howells thought he saw in the Chicago Exposition in 1893 and the possibilities lying ahead for "plutocratic New York" in the years that followed had already been foreshadowed in *Criticism and Fiction*.

The Club was, no doubt, a sustaining interest to Howells after his return from Chicago, for many of its members had contributed to the triumphant effectiveness of the White City. J. Alden Wier, the well-known painter, at this time lectured at the Club on the architecture of the Exposition, and the chairman, Daniel H. Burnham, with whom Howells had stayed in Chicago, visited the Century as an honored guest and became a nonresident member. Among the gala occasions of 1895 was the celebration of Twelfth Night, for forty years a festive evening for Centurians, when tableaux of Trilby, Pygmalion and Galatea, and St. Anthony's Temptation were presented with accompanying music. Early the next year Howells attended a dinner to honor John S. Billings, the new librarian of the Astor-Lenox-Tilden Foundation. On this occasion he met Edward Eggleston, E. C. Stedman, C. D. Warner, Henry van Dyke, John Burroughs, Brander Matthews, and other congenial spirits.[17] Here, at the Century Club, one associated with men who, according to Howells, "were the liveliest in prose and the loveliest in verse" to be found in New York. In a pleasant bit of doggerel, Howells referred to the group he met at the Club as

This frank and hearty brotherhood,
This league of lasting amities,
This commonwealth of worth and wit,
With all things that pertain to it— [18]

When Howells joined this "commonwealth of worth and wit" in 1897, it must, indeed, have seemed to him a brotherhood of "lasting amities." Not only had he been nominated by J. Q. A. Ward, whom he had known from the old Ohio days, but his name had been seconded by Edmund C. Stedman, whom Howells had first met in Washington before he left for Venice and had come to know more intimately in the eighties. The list of members of the period reads like a list of Howells' personal friends of many years' standing —Saint-Gaudens, who had just completed a plaque of Howells and his daughter; Rutherford Mead, Howells' brother-in-law and a member of the architectural firm that had recently completed the new building for the Century Club; Richard Henry Stoddard, whose hospitality Howells had particularly enjoyed when he first came to live in New York; George Watson Gilder, George William Curtis, John Brisben Walker, and many other editors and publishers with whom Howells' relationship was both professional and personal. All these men and many others—George Fuller, Henry James, John Hay, Edward Eggleston, F. Hopkinson Smith, John La Farge, Henry Adams, to mention only a few—were associated with the Club, which for years had been a focal point in Howells' life.

The year 1897, when Howells became a member, marked the fiftieth anniversary of the Century Club, which was duly celebrated by another dinner. Bishop Potter welcomed the new members, among whom were the artist, Edwin A. Abbey, the actor, Joseph Jefferson, and the historian, James Harvey Robinson, as well as President Charles C. Hall of Union Theological Seminary and the literary critic, Hamilton Mabie. William Allen Butler, Edmund C. Stedman, and Richard H. Stoddard read poems, and the history of the Club from its beginning as the Sketch Club was traced by Parke Godwin and Daniel Huntington, the former president. The fact that the ancestor of the Sketch Club was the New York Academy of the Fine Arts, founded in 1802, and that this, in turn, became the National Academy of the Arts of Design in 1826 accounts for the sustained interest of the Club in painting as well as in literature. One is tempted to linger over the names of the artists, John Trumbull, Samuel F. B. Morse, Thomas Cole, A. B. Durand, and the writers, from Halleck to Bryant to George William Curtis, whom Howells heard praised, during the evening, for their contributions to the honor of the Club. The long list included also "distinguished personages from abroad," such as Charles Dickens, W. M. Thackeray, Matthew Arnold, among the writers; Benjamin Constance and Hubert Herkomer among the artists; and, among the men of science, Tyndall, Huxley, and Herbert Spencer—who had, from time to time, been the guests of the Century Club.[19]

From such "diversity of seeds" sown in the "strong soil" of the Century Club sprang other groups, such as the Authors' Club, the University Club, and a number of artists' clubs, as well as clubs of engineers and architects.[20] Members of the Century Club were prominent among those who, in 1898, organized the National Institute of Arts and Letters. The Brooklyn *Daily Eagle* [21] gave its "First Public Meeting" large headlines. "In the absence of Charles Dudley Warner," the article reported, "William Dean Howells presided." Hamilton W. Mabie read Warner's paper on the copyright bill, and Henry van Dyke spoke on the subject of the relation of the people to literature and of the publisher to the author.

The following day Howells wrote to Warner to tell him that his absence was "regretted by everyone the other night at the Institute meeting, the more so because I had to preside in your place." Mabie read the paper excellently, Howells assured Warner, "and none of your good points were lost. I liked so much what you said of perpetual copyright that I wanted to reinforce it from the fount of my internal socialism with the suggestion that *all* property should be held for 42 years; but on my legs I am such a dumb dog that I cannot even snarl, and so your claim rested unimpaired with the audience." After Warner's paper and another on music by Horatio William Parker, "Van Dyke followed with a hearty and heady talk about books and the people." When the public proceedings were over, "the members of the Institute went into a side room and smoke-talked till I went home with my underclothes full of tobacco fumes. We seemed to all to have a lot of courage, and a lot of hope." [22]

Since the program of this opening meeting in New York of the newly founded Institute was made up entirely of members of the Century Club, one wonders whether the gathering in the smoke-filled side room afterwards was not very like a meeting of the Club. The long account of the meeting that appeared in the Brooklyn *Daily Eagle* fortunately included a list of the members of the Institute, which reads like a roll call of the Century, with the addition of outstanding names associated with the Saturday Club of Boston, such as those of Charles Eliot Norton, Thomas Sergeant Perry, Josiah Royce, and Barrett Wendell. It is possible that some of these old friends and associates of Howells came down to New York especially for the occasion.

The Institute, which was "founded for the advancement of art, music, and literature," decided, after six years of deliberation, to select from its membership thirty men to organize a section of the Institute to be known as an Academy. Seven names were selected by ballot as sponsors of the new Academy. Five of the men chosen were members of the Century Club—Howells, Saint-Gaudens, Stedman, La Farge and Hay [23]—and the first meeting of the Committee was held at the Club. The original seven were empowered to choose the next eight—Henry Adams, Thomas Bailey Aldrich, Henry James, Thomas Lounsbury, Charles Follen McKim, Charles Eliot Norton, Theodore Roosevelt, and J. Q. A. Ward—and they, in turn, chose the succeeding group of names, until the Academy list of fifty names was complete.

The Academy soon became a separate organization and held a meeting on November 7, 1908, when Howells was elected president.[24] One year later in December, 1909, the first Public Meeting of the Academy was held in Washington, D.C. In his opening address, Howells referred to "the love of such beauty as the American condition of the universal arts has fostered," adding that

> to relate itself to the esthetic life of the nation, which in the last analysis is its ethical life, will be the instinctive impulse, and will become the conscious purpose of an association which through its experience has been constructive, and from its condition is critical.[25]

Howells meant by these somewhat vague words that every member of the Academy was elected because he himself was a "constructive" artist, and, as such, was in a position to render a "critical" account of his own technique. The gathering together of creative artists in all fields enabled Howells, he said,

> to entertain with a livelier hospitality the hope that what I have imagined one of our literary sections doing for some signal performance each year in literature, some member of our several artistic sections will do for what he thinks the best work in painting or sculpture or architecture or music.

Critical comment, Howells hoped, would be offered "freely, and gladly, in payment of a debt of delight"; thus, fostering a spirit of generosity and freedom, the Academy would be saved "from the last and sharpest reproach of academies; it would not be academic." The work of all artists must be judged in relation to "the American conditions" and with as "fresh an ardor as stimulated the poet or novelist or historian, the painter or sculptor or composer who created it." Perhaps, Howells admitted, this might prove "too fond a fancy"; "I am aware," he continued, "of speaking rather for myself than for all my fellow-Academicians or for any of them. But this feeling liberates me, as I hope its expression will liberate them, to any bolder prevision of our duty to the esthetic life of our nation."

The program of the meeting in Washington, which included addresses on modern architecture, music, and art, as well as poems by Richard Watson Gilder and Julia Ward Howe, reflected Howells' awareness of our cultural needs. Of particular interest, because so indicative of the range of Howells' concept of "American conditions," were papers by James Ford Rhodes on "The Molly Maguires in the Anthracite Region of Pennsylvania" and by T. W. Higginson on "Ruskin and Norton." Howells' "prevision" saw the interrelation of social and aesthetic issues in this country and noted as well the relevance of the thought of an older generation and an older culture—as reflected in the letters exchanged between Ruskin and Norton—to the cultural life of our nation.

For this breadth of understanding of our national life, as well as for the "delicate precision" of his powers as an artist, Howells was in 1915 awarded the Gold Medal of the Institute of Arts and Let-

ters.[26] He was the seventh to receive the Medal in the list that included Augustus Saint-Gaudens, William Rutherford Mead, and
John Singer Sargent.[27] At a joint meeting of the Academy and the
Institute in Boston, Hamilton Wright Mabie made the presentation
with the remark that Howells, arriving on the literary scene "in the
closing hours of the first day of creative work in American literature" as seen in Cooper and Hawthorne, gave it new "elevation of
thought and dignity of form." His knowledge of languages, his four
years in Venice, as well as his experiences as editor of the *Atlantic
Monthly* and *Harper's,* added depth to his picture of his countrymen. "Under such influences the realist who had the Tolstoyan passion for his kind became the sensitive artist whose tools have the
delicate precision of a Benvenuto Cellini." Howells' sense of art,
said Mabie, underlay all that he accomplished:

> A man of the modern temper, undismayed by the newest
> method and the latest radicalism, Mr. Howells is always the art-
> ist. However advanced his doctrine, his speech never misses the
> charm which has made art the universal language. In Altruria,
> as in Venice, one hears the accent which survives all changes
> of time and place and taste. A journalist at times, Mr. Howells
> never ceased to be a man of letters; a patient and courteous
> editor, he never lost the artist's sense of responsibility for the
> casual line as for the carefully executed work.

Since he could not be present, Howells replied to these words by
letter, saying that he supposed the Medal had been bestowed on
him as much for longevity as for literary merit, for he had been
writing novels for nearly fifty years. "The fashion of this world
passes away," he remarked, "and I have seen it come and go in my
art, or phases of it." Howells closed his brief letter with a reference
to Burke's aesthetics, on which he had, in a sense, based his *Criticism and Fiction* twenty-five years earlier and for which he had
found further support in the Institute and the Academy. "But if I
could believe the vital things were not the same in your esteem, I
could not prize your medal as I do. As it is," he added,

> with my belief that you have peculiarly in your keeping the
> standard of the arts which Burke says every man has by mere

fidelity to nature, and that you will have it increasingly as you welcome to your number whoever is striking in any art, I prize your award more than all the words of my many books could say.

A year after the death of Howells a Memorial Meeting was held in the New York Public Library [28] at which messages were read by Hamlin Garland from people all over the world. Various aspects of Howells' writing were discussed by Henry Van Dyke, Brander Matthews, Jesse Lynch Williams, Robert Grant, and Augustus Thomas—all but one of whom were members of the Century Club, as well as members of the Academy, for the essential ideals of the two clubs were the same in regard to the relationship of art and literature. "In literature and art," said Augustus Thomas, the dramatist, "some observers have thought that the worker's choice of his department was a matter of differing intensity of mental vision, a draughtsman seeing objects in a plane presentation; the painter seeing them with the added relief and distinction of color; the sculptor seeing them detached and 'in the round.'" Howells, the speaker pointed out, "saw his people with the sculptor's stereoscopic clearness and detachment"; hence his characters remain "as fresh and modern" today as at the time he conceived them. At the close of the meeting the announcement was made that funds for the Howells Medal of the American Academy of Arts and Letters had been anonymously presented. The object of the Howells Medal, which is still given every five years, is "to commemorate the name of our great American novelist" by honoring "the most distinguished work of American fiction during that period." [29]

A year after Howells' death, the cornerstone was laid for the building at 633 West 156th Street, which houses the Academy and the Institute. The architects were three well-known Centurians, McKim, Mead, and White, and the handsome Renaissance structure is a reminder today of the architectural ideals of the generation of writers, artists, and architects who built into their productions a clear statement of their philosophy of art and society, based on the belief that the values of the past may be made available to the present.

This faith shone forth in glory at the Chicago Exposition of

1893; it was the inspiration of most of the public buildings of New York at the turn of the century; it is the despair of the 1960's, when another generation is expressing in glass and steel the aspirations of the twentieth century. The meaning of the endeavors of the earlier group is well symbolized by the home built for J. P. Morgan, a member of the Century Club, by the same three architect-members of the Club; to it was later added a library and art gallery. Here the Academy, including Howells, had assembled on November 20, 1915, to examine the treasures soon to be handed over to the public.[30]

In 1922, under the presidency of William Milligan Sloane, the "Names, Records, and Portraits of Former Members in the Order of Their Election to the Academy" was issued by the Academy in a small volume entitled *In Memoriam*. In his introductory remarks, the president attempted to analyze the "distinctive feature" of the American idea of an Academy; he found it in the fact that the American Academy "imperiously forbids all specialization tending toward narrowness and aridity, demanding that the fine arts acknowledge their interdependence, that they draw life and succulence one from the other and so keep the central current of their evolution in our soil united and unobstructed." A Centurian himself from 1878, Sloane was reflecting the sense of the interrelation of the arts for which the Club had stood for many years; his speech showed that the Academy had made these same beliefs a permanent part of its program. Sloane concluded his introduction by saying that "the individual achievements of those who compose the membership of our association" was proof enough of "how fertile the American soil is, how vigorous the American spirit in the fine arts."

Howells' photograph, as first president of the Academy, appeared immediately after Sloane's introduction and the one-page *vita* following the picture provided perfect illustration of the thought of Sloane's introduction. As one turns the pages of this little book and studies the photographs of La Farge, Henry Adams, Kenyon Cox, Mark Twain, Charles Eliot Norton, Augustus Saint-Gaudens, Henry James, and Augustus Thomas, to mention only a few of the thirty men first chosen to form the nucleus of the Academy, one begins to realize something of their united effect on our present society. In spite of shifts in tastes and changes in political, economic, and social forces, their influence is not lost. The philosophy of the interrelation of art and society in a democracy that they, in their various ways, expressed had within it the seeds of further growth.

NOTES

1. *Life in Letters,* II, 88.
2. Henry Steele Commager, "The Century, 1887–1906," *The Century, 1847–1946* (1947), pp. 57–58.
3. "W. D. Howells, at 75, Talks of Old Literary New York," New York *Times,* Sunday, Feb. 25, 1912. See also Howells' two "Papers" on the *Reminiscences of Justine McCarthy.* Appendix III of this book.
4. See "Writers, Artists, and Publishers," Part One, Chapter 2 of this book.
5. Henry Irving Brook, "The Century, 1867–1886," *The Century, 1847–1946,* p. 45.
6. See "New Home of the Century Club in New York," *Harper's Weekly,* XXXIII (Nov. 2, 1889), 876.
7. "Some Suggestions from Mr. McCarthy," *Literature,* n.s. II (July 21, 1899), 33.
8. "A Traveller From Altruria" began to appear in the *Cosmopolitan* in November, 1892, and was completed in that magazine in October, 1893.
9. For a full and interesting account of the first hundred years of the Century Association, see *The Century, 1847–1946.* The various chapters of this book were written by eminent members of the Century Club, which is owned and directed by the Century Association.
10. *The Century, 1847–1946,* p. 59.
11. See Franklin Matthews, "The Greater New York," *Harper's Weekly,* XLI (Apr. 17, 1897), 385–391.
12. See Leonard Bacon, "Poets and The Century," *The Century, 1847–1946,* pp. 184–204. See also Frank Jewett Mather, Jr., "The Century and American Art," *ibid.,* pp. 102–154.
13. *The Century, 1847–1946,* p. 31.
14. "The Century Club," *Century Magazine,* XLI (March, 1891), 673–689.
15. Among the artists who belonged to the Century at the time were George Inness, J. Q. A. Ward, Augustus Saint-Gaudens, Olin Warner, Winslow Homer, Edwin Austin Abbey, John La Farge, Albert Bierstadt, Elihu Vedder, Edwin Blashfield, Howard Pyle, and John Sargent. Many of the paintings of these artists hang on the walls of the Club today.
16. *Criticism and Fiction,* pp. 68–69.
17. *The Century Club, 1847–1946,* p. 70.
18. *Ibid.,* p. 57.

19. *The Fiftieth Anniversary of the Founding of the Century* (1897), pp. 47–48.

20. "The Century Club," *Century Magazine*, XLI (March, 1891), 689.

21. Brooklyn *Daily Eagle*, (Jan. 31, 1900), p. 9.

22. *Life in Letters*, II, 125–126.

23. The other two members of the Committee were Samuel Langhorne Clemens and Edward MacDowell. See *In Memoriam, A Book of Record* (1922). See also Brander Matthews, "The American Academy of Arts and Letters," *Outlook*, XCIII (December, 1909), 685–693, and Robert Underwood Johnson, "A Growing Force in Art and Letters," *The Art World*, I (October, 1916), 48–50. At the time he wrote the above essay, Matthews was president of the Institute and Johnson was secretary of the Academy. Both men were members of the Century Club.

24. "Sketch of the Academy and List of Members," *Proceedings*, I, No. 1 (June 10, 1910), 44–45. Howells was second vice-president of the Century Club at that time (1909–1911).

25. *Ibid.*, 7–12.

26. *Proceedings*, II, No. 3 (November, 1916), 51–53. On April 17, 1916, Congress granted a national charter to the Academy. *Ibid.*, p. 68.

27. Others who received the Gold Medal before Howells were James Ford Rhodes in history, James Whitcomb Riley in poetry, and Augustus Thomas in drama.

28. The meeting was held in the Stuart Gallery of the New York Public Library, on Mar. 1, 1921. It is fully reported in the *Proceedings*, II, No. 11 (July, 1921), 4–21.

29. *Proceedings*, II, No. 3 (November, 1916), 51–53.

30. *Ibid.*, No. 2 (September, 1915), 4.

Epilogue

Howells, as friend and associate of many artists, had an ironic understanding of his role in American society. "Have you ever noticed," he asked an interviewer in the early twentieth century, "that in our civilization, the artist, who is the only person in the right, is apparently the only person in the wrong?" [1]

Howells perhaps had in mind the stand he had publicly taken against the Spanish-American War,[2] which had brought down upon his head a barrage of newspaper editorials and articles. That Mr. Howells' "delicate fancy" is disturbed when confronted by "the grim spectre of war" commands, of course "our universal sympathy," declared the New York *Times* of May 13, 1899, in a three-column article entitled "War, Art and Mr. Howells." However, the writer continued sententiously, "when Mr. Howells declared with more emphasis than discretion that war had never inspired anything beautiful in art, he erected interrogation points in many minds." The artist—in this case Howells himself—was the person in the right in the newspaper furor that followed, though to most of the newspapers and journals of the time he was "apparently the only person in the wrong."

A staunch belief in the insight of the artist, in the larger sense, had been borne in upon Howells during his early days in Ohio, when he had studied with fascinated attention the great traveling canvas, "Adam and Eve in a State of Innocence." This belief had been tested during his four years in Venice, where he learned to apply the techniques of painters and dramatists to his early sketches of "Venetian Life." There he laid the foundations for a particular kind of realistic writing, which was not impaired but rather enriched by years of editorial work on the *Atlantic Monthly* and *Harper's Magazine*. His daily contact with artists in all fields encouraged him to transfer to his own novels the insights of the men who were, like himself, aware of the movements in science, social thought, and religion as well as in art and literature. At the height of his enormously creative life as novelist, critic, and essayist, Howells at last joined the Century Club, where he found himself in contact with many of the artists, writers, sculptors, architects he had, for years, known in other relationships. In an essay entitled "The Century and American Art," [3] Frank Jewett Mather, Jr., gives us a glimpse of Howells passing in and out of the doorway of the Club. After discussing the artists who from the early days of the Club had added luster to its name, Mather observes that one of the striking characteristics of these men was that though they might actually be great celebrities, they frequently were not "personages" in the Club sense. To illustrate his point, Mather adds, "W. D. Howells was perhaps the most celebrated member I have known. But nothing much happened when the quiet and somewhat reserved little gentleman entered the Club." [4]

Perhaps it was because of the quiet and reserved temperament of this artist among novelists, that Howells not only studied the ways and methods of his fellow artists but was accepted by them as one who was peculiarly aware of the intent of their work. From the days when as a young reporter in Columbus, Ohio, Howells used to watch J. Q. A. Ward, chisel in hand, before one of his sculptured figures, to the afternoons he spent in Saint-Gaudens' New York studio, from his early association with Augustus Hoppin, the illustrator of his first novel, to his fruitful collaboration with W. T. Smedley, the artist of *The Landlord at Lion's Head,* Howells was aware of the fact that he, as a novelist, had something to learn from artists in other fields, and, indeed, that he in turn had something to impart to them. For example, after watching George Fuller bending over his canvases in his studio on Tremont Street, Howells suggested the titles for Fuller's finished paintings; when the temperamental Pennell was sent to Italy by Gilder to draw the etchings for *Tuscan Cities,* he and Howells were able to sustain a humorously sympathetic partnership described in Pennell's letters to his wife and enlarged upon in Howells' *Indian Summer.* Having been drawn into the orbit of the young men, such as George Bancroft, William and Henry James, and Thomas Sergeant Perry, who read *Le Révue des Deux Mondes* together and attempted to paint in W. M. Hunt's studio on the rocks of Newport, Howells came to know more clearly some of the problems of modern art. During his frequent periods in New York in the 1880's, Howells watched La Farge at work on the magnificent altar painting in the Church of the Ascension on lower Fifth Avenue; he also listened to, and no doubt shared in, the discussions of the Washington Square Arch, for his brother-in-law, William Rutherford Mead, was a member of the famous firm that designed and erected the monument.

During these same years, Howells was working on *Harper's,* under the editorship of Henry Mills Alden, and was traveling back and forth to London, visiting and talking with Henry James. James, like Howells, was deeply concerned, not only with the relationship of writing and painting, but also with the question of *The Art of Fiction,* to borrow the title James gave his essay on the subject in 1884; both men were critics as well as novelists, and were the first writers in this country seriously to consider the relationship between *Criticism and Fiction,* to make use of the title of Howells' small volume of 1891. Howells and James evolved their ideas on these interrelations over a period of many years during which they worked out their theories in conversations and in letters. The writing of fiction they assumed to be "an art" related to the other arts but following its own laws as well. James, in his own novels, approached the impressionistic painter more closely than did Howells; Howells' objectivity suggests perhaps more nearly the technique of the sculptor. When asked whether he ever lost himself in his work, Howells replied, "Never. The essence of achievement is to keep outside, to be entirely dispassionate, as a sculptor must be, in molding his clay." [5]

Both James and Howells felt themselves to be artists, and both followed with interest the movements of their day in the work of their friends among the artists—Vedder, Chase, Abbey, Sargent and others—as well as among critics and teachers, such as W. C. Brownell, Clarence King, Brander Matthews, and their fellow novelists, Henry Adams, John Hay, Hamlin Garland and F. Hopkinson Smith. All of the men enumerated in this brief summary of Howells' many-sided relationships with the writers and artists of his day were members of the Century Club either before or after Howells' entrance into this organization.[6] Many of these names are to be found among the thirty founders of the Academy. However, other important friends of Howells, who were not members of the Century Club, were also among the founders of the Academy. Charles Eliot Norton, Edward Everett Hale, and Thomas Wentworth Higginson, for example, first helped organize the Institute of Arts and Letters as a branch of the American Social Science Association, and thus became members of the Academy. These New Englanders had been friends and associates of like-minded New Yorkers for many years.

Their very names are reminders of Norton's summer gatherings at Ashfield, Massachusetts, where they and many other men and women came together to discuss the social implications of the post-Civil War era in our country. Howells made it a practice in the seventies and eighties to join in the Ashfield discussions of topics, which ranged from the preservation of the beauties of Niagara Falls to the problem of labor legislation, from the need of a copyright law to the beautification of American cities and towns. These mid-summer meetings in a New England country town were attended by editors of *Harper's, Scribner's,* the *North American Review,* as well as the *Atlantic Monthly,* and undoubtedly tinged those magazines and others with the wide-ranging thought of those who spoke in Ashfield's town hall. George W. Curtis, Howells' predecessor in *Harper's* "Easy Chair," was one of the most constant visitors to these forums, and he, as well as Howells, learned to consider aesthetic problems in the larger framework of their social implications.[7] Born a generation after Curtis, Howells came under the influence of the social attitudes of the 1880's, which turned his thought to serious consideration of the place of art in an ideal commonwealth. The origins of his belief in the importance to society of the new movements in art and literature, however, Howells himself traced to the post-Civil War period. To a reporter from the New York *Times* [8] he observed when he was almost seventy that after the War, many thought "The time had come for repose, for taking inventory of the inherent qualites of art that might be expected of a young country that had outgrown its first restless action of youth." In painting, literature, and all the other arts, men looked for great changes. Howells paused here, the reporter said, "and sighed a bit wearily for the lost ideals," remembering, perhaps, the Spanish-American War, during which he had also witnessed the destruction of art values in war hysteria. Thinking back over his own disillusionment of the 1890's, Howells then resumed: "There came a great wave of prosperity over the country, and in the sweep of its oncoming it swallowed the sculptor, the painter, the writer. They turned their talents to commercial interests, and neglected the self-sacrificing spirit of doing the things they liked the best." The thing the artist likes best to do, Howells felt, always turns out to be the artist's real contribution to a society slowly progressing toward "the conditions" described by a Traveler from Altruria.[9]

In October, 1916, at the outbreak of another war, a new and ambitious magazine was launched. It was entitled *The Art World,* and in its Foreword many of the concepts popularized by Howells a generation earlier found grandiloquent expression. "The Editors" wrote,

In this hour of calamity and of growing intellectual and aesthetic bewilderment, there is need of a Magazine which will discuss with frankness and Common-sense every phase of the Right Arts: Architecture, Drama, Landscape-Architecture, Belles-Lettres, Music, Painting, Poetry and Sculpture, and will prove that Life and Art act and react, dynamically upon each other.

Since Howells had become known as a social critic who believed in the unity of the arts,[10] one is not surprised to find in the March, 1917, issue of the *Art World,* a handsome, full-page portrait of Howells accompanying an essay by Hamlin Garland, entitled "William Dean Howells, Master Craftsman." Howells' belief in the social importance of the interacting arts in our country deeply influenced American culture up to and beyond the outbreak of World War I. Garland and many other young writers shared Howells' aesthetic beliefs and profited by the guidance of this "Master Craftsman."

NOTES

1. Quoted by Francis Whiting Halsey, *American Authors and Their Homes* (1902), p. 109.

2. "A Charming Spanish Novel," *Literature,* n.s. 1 (May 12, 1899), 409–410. "Arms and the Man," *Literature,* n.s. 1 (May 19, 1899), 433–434. "Poetry, War, and Mr. Howells," *Literary Digest,* XVIII (May 27, 1899), 607–608. See also "Life and Letters," *Harper's Weekly,* XL (Jan. 4, 1896), 6–7.

   In 1900 Howells became vice-president of the Anti-Imperialist League. Letter to E. W. Orway, Jan. 2, 1900. Manuscript Room, New York Public Library.

3. *The Century, 1847–1946,* pp. 154–177.

4. *Ibid.,* p. 2.

5. An unsigned statement, written on the reverse of a photograph of Howells, briefly summarizes a conversation with Howells and quotes him as making the remark cited in the text. Print Room, New York Public Library.

6. Frank Jewett Mather, Jr., "The Century and American Art," *The Century, 1847–1946,* pp. 154–177.

7. "Prof. Norton and Ashfield," New York *Evening Post,* Saturday, Nov. 30, 1907. See Appendix V of this book. For an amusing example of Howells' social views in relation to art, see Bliss Perry, "Recollections of the Saturday Club," in Edward W. Forbes and John H. Finley, Jr. (eds.), *The Saturday Club, A Century Completed, 1920–1955* (1958), pp. 5–6. Appendix IV of this book.

8. "Mr. Howells Talks About Fiction and Fiction Writers," New York *Times,* Sunday, April 30, 1905, Sec. III, p. 2.

9. See "Mr. Howells' Socialism," *American Fabian,* IV, No. 2 (February, 1898), for a reflection of how the social views of Howells were looked upon in his day. This two-page lead article ends with a defense of Howells "as a man" from an essay by Harry Thurston Peck, who became a member of the Century Club in 1893. See also the "Report of

the Board of Management of the Century Club," *Reports, Constitutions, By-laws of the Century Club,* 1921, for Howells' obituary, by Alexander D. Noyes, in which Howells' socialism is commented upon. Appendix VI of this book.

10. Howells constantly used artists as illustrations of the creative process in other fields. See "The Easy Chair," *Harper's Monthly,* CXIV (February, 1907), 480–481; "Eighty Years and After," *ibid.,* CXL (December, 1919), 21–28.

Appendix I

Howells on the French and Italian
Notebooks of Nathaniel Hawthorne
(in *"Recent Literature,"* Atlantic Monthly, *XXIX*
[*May, 1872*], *624–626)*

It would be hard to say what chiefly delights the reader of Hawthorne's Italian Note-Books, unless it is the simple charm of good writing. There is very little of that wonderful suggestiveness which the American Note-Books had, with their revelations of the inventive resource and the habitual operation of the romancer's genius, and rarely that sympathy with which the descriptions in the English journals were filled. To the last, Hawthorne confessedly remained an alien in Italy, afflicted throughout by her squalor, her shameless beggary, her climate, her early art, her grimy picture-frames, and the disheartening absence of varnish in her galleries. We suppose that his doubt whether he was not bamboozling himself when he admired an old master, is one which has occurred, more or less remotely, to most honest men under like conditions; but it is odd that his humor did not help him to be more amused by the droll rascality and mendicancy with which a foreigner's life in Italy is enveloped. His nature, however, was peculiarly New-Englandish;

the moral disrepair, like the physical decay, continually offended him beyond retrieval by his sense of its absurdity. He abhorred an intrusive beggar as he did a Giotto or a Cimabue, and a vile street was as bad to him as a fresco of the thirteenth century. But even the limitations of such a man are infinitely interesting, and, as one reads, one thanks him from the bottom of his soul for his frankness. Most of us are, by the will of heaven, utterly ignorant of art, and it is vastly wholesome to have this exquisite genius proclaim his identity with us, and in our presence to look with simple liking or dislike upon the works he sees, untouched by the traditional admiration of all ages and nations. The affectation of sympathy or knowledge is far more natural to our fallen humanity, and the old masters send back to us every year hordes of tiresome hypocrites, to whom we recommend Hawthorne's healing sincerity. It is not that we think him right in all his judgments, or many of them; but that if any one finds in the varnish and bright frames of the English galleries greater pleasure than in the sacredly dingy pictures of Italian churches and palaces, or thinks Mr. Brown finer than Claude, his truth in saying so is of as good quality as in his declaration that he loves Gothic better than classic architecture.

At times Hawthorne's feeling about art seems capable of education, but he appears himself to remain nearly always in doubt about it, and to find this misgiving a kind of refuge. It is true that in regard to sculpture he has not so much hesitation as he has about different paintings. The belief that it is an obsolete art, hinted in "The Marble Faun," is several times advanced in these journals, and he affirms again and again his horror of nudity in modern sculpture, —a matter in which, we think, he has the better of the sculptors, though it is not easy to see how the representation of the nude is to be forbid without abolishing the whole art. It is a fact, which tells in favor of such critics as believe sculpture to be properly an accessory of architecture and nothing more, that though Hawthorne's sympathies with other forms of art were slight and uncertain, he instinctively delighted in good and noble architecture. This is probably the case also with most other refined people who have no artistic training, and it is doubtful if either painting or sculpture can have any success among us except in union with architecture,—the first of the arts in appealing to the natural sense of beauty.

The reader of these Notes will not learn more of Italian life than of Italian art; it is Hawthorne's life in Italy, and often without contact with Italy, that is here painted. But it is not his most intimate

life; it is his life as an author, his intellectual life; and one often
fancies that the record must have been kept with a belief that it
would some day be published; for with respect to his literary self,
Hawthorne was always on confidential terms with the world, as his
frank prefaces show. It has nothing of carelessness, though nothing
of constraint in the mental attitude, while in the midst of its grace
and delightfulness there is frequent self-criticism. He says after a
somewhat florid passage, "I hate what I have written," and he considers and reconsiders his ideas throughout, like a man conscious of
daily growth. Sometimes, but quite rarely, there is a glance of *personal* self-examination, as where, with a half-humorous air, he gives
his impression that Miss Bremer thinks him unamiable: "I am
sorry if it be so, because such a good, kindly, clear-sighted, and
delicate person is very apt to have reason at the bottom of her harsh
thoughts when, in rare cases, she allows them to harbor with her."

An amusing trait of the literary consciousness with which the
journal is written is the author's habit of introducing his quaint or
subtile reflections with that unnatural, characteristic "methinks" of
his, which, like Mr. Emerson's prose " 'tis," is almost a bit of personal property. But if Hawthorne tells little of himself, he atones
for it as far as may be by so sketching ever so many other interesting people, and the queer at-odds life foreigners lead in Italy. There
is a precious little picture of a tea-drinking with Miss Bremer in her
lodging near the Tarpeian Rock, which precedes the passage we
have just quoted, and the account of a ride with Mrs. Jameson,
which we would fain transfer hither, but must leave where they are.
Story, Browning, Mrs. Browning, Powers, and a host of minor
celebrities are all painted with that firm, delicate touch, and that
certain parsimony of color which impart their pale charm to the
people of Hawthorne's romances. Most prominent is the sculptor
Powers, for whom the author conceived a strong personal liking,
and by whose universal inventiveness and practical many-minded-
ness his imagination was greatly impressed. He listened with so
much respect and conviction to all the sculptor's opinions upon art,
that the dismay into which he falls when Mr. Powers picks the
Venus de' Medici to pieces, just after Hawthorne has taught himself
to adore her, is little less than tragical, and there is something
pathetically amusing in his subsequent efforts to rehabilitate her
perfection. At the same time the reader's sense of Hawthorne's own
modesty and sincerity is indefinitely deepened. In the whole range
of art he is confident of but one or two things,—that modern nude

sculptures are foolish and repulsive, and that the works of Giotto and Cimabue are hideous, and had better be burnt. Yet we think that his journals might be read with greater instruction upon art than many critical works.

The life at Florence, with its poetical and artistic neighborhood, its local delightfulness, its ease, its cheapness, is temptingly sketched; but perhaps the reader of "The Marble Faun" will not be quite content to find Donatello's Tower in the Villa Montauta on Bello-Sguardo. Not that the place is not beautiful enough for any romance, but that most will have conceived of a wilder and remoter Monte Beni. It is interesting, by the way, to note that it is not till Hawthorne's fourth or fifth visit to the Capitol that he seems to have observed the statue which suggested his romance. Then at last he says: "I looked at the Faun of Praxiteles, and was sensible of a peculiar charm in it; a sylvan beauty and homeliness, friendly and wild at once. The lengthened, but not preposterous ears, and the little tail, which we infer, have an exquisite effect. . . . A story, with all sorts of fun and pathos in it, might be contrived on the idea of one of their species having become intermingled with the human race. . . . The tail might have disappeared by dint of constant intermarriages with ordinary mortals; but the pretty hairy ears should occasionally reappear, . . . and the moral and intellectual characteristics of the faun might be most picturesquely brought out, without detriment to the human interest of the story. Fancy," he concludes, "this combination in the person of a young lady!" Here it is evident that he thinks merely of a short story, with no shadow of tragedy in it. Afterwards how the idea expanded and deepened and darkened! And is it not curious to reflect that Donatello *might* have been a girl?

At times, in reading these journals, the romance seems the essence not only of what was profound in Hawthorne's observation in Italy, but also his notice of external matters, such as the envy and mutual criticisms of artists; all the roots of the book are here, and the contrast of them with their growth above ground is a valuable instruction.

It belongs to criticism of "The Marble Faun," rather than these Note-Books, to remark how the strictly Italian material of Hawthorne's experience scarcely sufficed for the purposes of the romancer; but it is true that he remained Gothic and Northern to the last moment in the classicistic South, even to the misspelling of nearly all Italian words. We believe, however, that he describes not only himself in Italy when he says: "I soon grew so weary of admirable things that I could neither enjoy nor understand them. My receptive faculty is very limited; and when the utmost of its small capacity is full, I become perfectly miserable, and the more so the better worth seeing are the objects I am forced to see." This is the picture of our whole race in that land.

Appendix II

Howells' Essay,
"A Sennight of the Centennial"
(in Atlantic Monthly, XXXVIII [July, 1876],
92–107)

The Centennial is what every one calls the great fair now open at
Philadelphia. "Have you been at the Centennial?" "How do you
like the Centennial?" Some politer and more anxious few struggle
for logical precision, reflecting that you cannot go to a Centennial,
any more than you can go to a Millennial. These entangle themselves in International Exhibition, or talk of the Exposition. The
English, who invented it, and have a genius for simplicity (in some
things), called the first international exhibition the World's Fair.
But this simple and noble name does not quite serve for us, since
our World's Fair means the commemoration of our hundredth national anniversary; and so, at last, Centennial is the best name, in
spite of its being no name at all.

The Centennial is so far peculiar in other ways that one may
fitly give one's self the benefit of a doubt whether it is wholly ad-
vantageous to have seen other world's fairs in order to the intelligent appreciation of this; whether, in fact, it were not better never

to have seen anything of the sort before. We will assume, for the present writer's purpose, that this is so. We may even go a step further and suppose that one's acquaintance with the Centennial is to be most fortunately formed upon a dull drizzling day, somewhat cold and thoroughly unpleasant, like the 17th of May, for example. On that day, a week after the opening of the show, the first impression was certainly that of disorder and incompleteness, and the Centennial had nothing to do but to grow upon the visitor's liking. The paths were broken and unfinished, and the tough, red mud of the roads was tracked over the soft asphalt into all the buildings. Carts employed in the construction came and went everywhere, on easy terms alike with the trains of the circular railway whose engines hissed and hooted at points above the confusion, and with the wheeled-chairs in which ladies, huddling their skirts under their umbrellas, were trundled back and forth among the freight cars of the Pennsylvania Railroad. At many points laborers were digging over the slopes of the grounds and vigorously slapping the sides of the clayey embankments with the flat of their spades; and ironical sign-boards in all directions ordered you to keep off the grass on spaces apparently dedicated to the ceramic arts forever. Even if these grassless spots had been covered with tender herbage, there seemed not enough people present to justify the vigilance that guarded them; but I think this was an illusion, to which the vastness of the whole area and its irregular shape and surface contributed. There were probably fifteen thousand visitors that day, but many thousands more dispersed over the grounds and scattered through the different buildings would have given nowhere the impression of a crowd. With my simple Bostonian experiences as ground of comparison, I had been diffidently thinking that Mr. Gilmore's jubilees possibly afforded some likeness to the appearance of the spectators at the Centennial; I am bound to say now that the Centennial at no time and in no place gave any such notion of multitude. From day to day the crowd sensibly increased, but it never struck one as a crowd, and it hardly ever incommoded one, except perhaps in the narrow corridors of the Art Hall, and the like passages of the Annex to that building; these were at times really thronged.

If we had been the most methodical of sight-seers we could hardly have systematized our observations on a first day. It was enough if we could form a clear idea of the general character of the principal features and their position. Even this we did not at all do. We wandered quite aimlessly about from one building to another, and, if we ever had anything definite in view, gave ourselves the agreeable surprise of arriving at something altogether different. Nevertheless from these desultory adventures some distinct impressions remained,—such, namely, as that of a great deal of beauty in the architecture. The Agricultural Hall we did not see till next day, and we therefore did not see what I believe is considered the best of the temporary structures; but the Main Building has a lightness, in spite of its huge extent, which is as near grace as it might hope to come; and the Machinery Hall has the beauty of a most admirable fitness for its purpose. The prospect of the interior is very striking, and much more effective than that of the Main Building, where the view, from the floor at least, is more broken. The Art Hall, which is otherwise conventionally well enough, is disfigured by the colossal bronzes at the entrance:—

"Non ragioniam di lor, ma guarda e passa."

The show of sculpture within seems to have been almost entirely left to the countrymen of Michelangelo, who are here reposing, for the most part, upon his laurels. One of them has posted in the most conspicuous place in the rotunda his conception of Washington,—Washington perched on an eagle much too small for him. The group is in plaster; the eagle life-size and the Washington some six feet high from the middle up; having no occasion for legs in the attitude chosen, Washington thriftily dispenses with them. The poor man who made this thing is so besotted with it as to have placarded his other works, "By the sculptor of the Washington." This is not his fault, perhaps, and I am not so sure after all that his Washington is as bad as the bronze statue of Emancipation (I suppose), a most offensively Frenchy negro, who has broken his chain, and spreading both his arms and legs abroad is rioting in a declamation of something (I should say) from Victor Hugo; one longs to clap him back into hopeless bondage. Then there is the wax Cleopatra in the Annex: an image to bring tears to the eyes of the legislative gentleman who lately proposed to abolish the study of the nude in our State drawing-schools. It will not do to describe the extreme dishabille of this figure; it is enough to say that it is Cleopatra coming to meet Antony (the delightful printed explanation handed you by the attendant says Caesar) in her barge, fanned by a black slave, and attended by a single Cupid, whose ruff, as he moves his head, shows the jointure of his neck; a weary parrot on her finger opens and shuts its wings, and she rolls her head alluringly from side to side and faintly lifts her right arm and lets it drop again—for twelve hours every day. Unlike many sculptures this has no vagueness of sentiment, and it explicitly advertises a museum of anatomy in Philadelphia. For the last reason it might be fitly expelled, but a large number of visitors of every age and sex would miss it; certainly it has a popularity which the other two Disgraces of the Art Hall have not.

After the three objects I have mentioned, I think the room devoted to the German paintings is most disagreeable. The pictures are indifferent good and bad; the taste, the gross and boastful vanity, the exultant snobbishness, of the show is intolerable. Of course portraits of the imperial family, in all attitudes of triumphant warfare, abound, but there is one picture, the Surrender of Sedan, which ought not to have been admitted except for extraordinary artistic merits; and these it has not. On the brow of a hill stand Wilhelm, Bismarck, and the other Chiefs of Police, swollen with prodigious majesty and self-satisfaction, while a poor little Frenchman, with his hat in one hand and a paper in the other, comes creeping abjectly up the slope, half bowed to the earth and not daring to lift his eyes to the imperial presence. It is a picture to make any Frenchman "bound" with rage, if he happens not to laugh, and I do not see how we are to escape our share of the outrage offered in it, by the singularly offensive despotism from which it comes, to our ancient friend and sister (or say step-sister) republic. When I think of it, I am ready to justify the enormous charges at the restaurant of the Trois Frères Provençaux (so called because each of the Brothers makes out his bill of Three Prices, and you pay the sum total), as a proper reprisal upon us; but I would fain whisper in the ears of those avengers that not all Americans are guilty. There is nothing else among the works of art that I can recollect, calculated to wound any one's national sensibilities. To be sure, Mr. Rothermel does not spare a huge slaughter of rebels in his Battle of Gettysburg, but I heard it said that this picture was not a work of art. I do not know about such things myself. I had a horrific interest in the spectacle, almost as large as the canvas, which covers the whole end of one room; and I thought the rebels were fighting hard, and, if they were dying, were dying bravely.

The rooms devoted to the English pictures were most delightful. There were many works of their masters; they had sent us of their best, and not of their second-best, as the French had done, and there was a kindliness of intent and a manifest good feeling toward our fair, if not toward our nation, to which every generous American must at once respond. Not only had they sent us of their best, but their best pictures are for our pleasure and not their profit; they are owned by Englishmen who risk everything that may happen to their treasures in the voyage over-seas, and gain nothing but the satisfaction of doing a gracious and graceful thing. To courtesy of which we cannot be too sensible we owe the sight not only of famous Gainesboroughs, Reynoldses, Wests, and Lawrences, but also the works of the great modern painters, Landseer, Leighton, Millais, Alma Tadema, and the rest. I may be wrong in stating that no other nation has done anything like this, but I certainly recollect nothing else of the kind; and the English have added to the favor done us by having distinctly lettered on the frame of each picture the name of the painter and the owner, as well as the subject of it, thus sparing the spectator the fatigue and trouble of referring to the catalogue. By all odds theirs is the most satisfactory department of the Art Hall; and they have not only done us a great pleasure, but have done themselves great honor. Here, if nowhere else, one is conscious of modern mastership in painting; here is the sense of a strong and definite impulse which in all its variety has a unity expressed in every work; one would know these strikingly characteristic pictures for English art anywhere and everywhere; one might like them or not, but one could not mistake them; and with any refinement of literary taste, one quite ignorant of the technicalities of art may enjoy them. It may be a fault in painting to be so literary; nevertheless it is pleasant to see pictures painted by poets—by men who have evidently had ideas to express, and have thought and felt and wrought poetically. These great Englishmen have not merely painted well, but they have painted about something; their pictures tell stories, and suggest stories when they do not tell them. I leave to skilled criticism the discussion of their comparative artistic merits, and speak as one of the confessedly unlearned in art, when I say that their pictures interested me far beyond any others. We had certainly no cause, considering all things, to be ashamed of the show of American paintings in comparison even with many of the English, and still less with those of other nations. There were not many positively poor, and there were many strikingly good, especially landscapes painted with sympathy, and portraits painted with character; but they showed a distracting variety of influence, and they did not detain you and call you back again and again to tell you something more, and to add yet this suggestion and that. Some

did so, but most did not; a perception of their merely artistic qualities exhausted them—the point at which the English pictures began
more deeply to delight. They were too often unstoried like our scenery, without our scenery's excuse. You felt that American art had
made vast advances on the technical side, but that it lacked what
English art has got from its intimate association with literature; that
it was not poetical; that generally its subjects were seen, not deeply
felt and thought; it wanted charm.

Of the French pictures the most striking were the horribly fascinating Rispah defending her dead Sons from the Vulture,—a powerful achievement of ghastly fancy, painted with prodigious realism
and knowledge,—and Carolus Duran's deliciously fascinating portrait of Mademoiselle Croisette (of the Théâtre Française) on horse-
back. Comparatively few of the pictures were yet in position, and
the display had nothing of the strongly distinctive quality of the
English. Whole rooms devoted to the French were barred against
the public, but enough was visible to emphasize the national taste
for the nude. When one caught sight of this in paintings just un-
packed and standing against the wall, it was as if the subjects had
been surprised before they had time to dress for the Centennial, so
strongly is the habit of being clothed expressed in the modern face.
In the Austrian room were some needless exposures, for which the
vast and rather cumbrous gorgeousness of the Homage of Venice
to Queen Catharine Cornaro hardly atoned, with all its overdress-
ing. But that is an interesting picture.

The Belgian rooms were very incomplete, and not very characteristic. Among the Swedish pictures were some beautiful landscapes, full of the cold northern sentiment, with the dark water
and the birchen shade. From Mexico and South America there were
curious specimens of the theatrico-historical, such as used to please
us fifty years ago, and some portraits of national statesmen, interesting for their evident faithfulness. Italy had sent no pictures that
commended themselves to special remembrance. Her strength—or
her weakness—was her sculpture, which had at its best the character of illustration. I believe there were few things ideal, and with
all the exquisite execution and pleasing fancifulness of conception,
the capricious and the absurd intolerably superabounded. Indeed,
England alone of all the foreign countries had sent of her best art
to the Centennial. At almost any sale of French pictures in Boston
you see the work of more famous painters; here there was not one
first-rate name; and this was true of the Continent generally. The

show impressed one as that of pictures that had not succeeded at home.

The Horticultural Hall, whither we went from the Art Gallery, is one of the buildings which are to remain, and its lovely architecture, in which the light arabesque forms express themselves in material of charming colors, merits permanence. It is extremely pleasing, and is chiefly pleasing as architecture; for the show of plants is not very striking to the unbotanized observer, who soon wearies of palms and cactuses and unattainable bananas, and who may not have an abiding joy in an organ played by electricity, with a full orchestral accompaniment similarly operated. Far more beautiful than anything in the hall was the great bed of English azaleas near it, as delicate and tender and rare in color as the lovely English pictures. At the fact that these and a houseful of rhododendrons could be safely brought so far and made to bloom so richly in our alien air, one may fitly wonder not a little.

We had time that first day for hardly more than a glance at the different buildings. We went next to the Machinery Hall, through the far extent of which we walked, looking merely to the right and left as we passed down the great aisle. Of that first impression the majesty of the great Corliss engine, which drives the infinitely varied machinery, remains most distinct. After that is the sense of too many sewing-machines. The Corliss engine does not lend itself to description; its personal acquaintance must be sought by those who would understand its vast and almost silent grandeur. It rises loftily in the centre of the huge structure, an athlete of steel and iron with not a superfluous ounce of metal on it; the mighty walking-beams plunge their pistons downward, the enormous fly-wheel revolves with a hoarded power that makes all tremble, the hundred life-like details do their office with unerring intelligence. In the midst of this ineffably strong mechanism is a chair where the engineer sits reading his newspaper, as in a peaceful bower. Now and then he lays down his paper and clambers up one of the stairways that cover the framework, and touches some irritated spot on the giant's body with a drop of oil, and goes down again and takes up his newspaper; he is like some potent enchanter there, and this prodigious Afreet is his slave who could crush him past all semblance of humanity with his lightest touch. It is, alas! what the Afreet has done to humanity too often, where his strength has superseded men's industry; but of such things the Machinery Hall is no place to speak, and to be honest, one never thinks of such things there. One thinks only of the glorious triumphs of skill and invention; and wherever else the national bird is mute in one's breast, here he cannot fail to utter his pride and content. It would be a barren place without the American machinery. All that Great Britain and Germany have sent is insignificant in amount when compared with our own contributions; the superior elegance, aptness, and ingenuity of our machinery is observable at a glance. Yes, it is still in these things of iron and steel that the national genius most freely speaks; by and by the inspired marbles, the breathing canvases, the great literature; for the present America is voluble in the strong metals and their infinite uses. I have hinted already that I think she talks too much in sewing-machines, but I dare say that each of these patents has its reason for being, and that the world would go mostly unclad without it. At least I would not like to try to prove the contrary to any of those alert agents or quick young lady attendants. Nevertheless, a whole half-mile of sewing-machines seems a good deal; and *is* there so very much difference between them?

Our first general impressions of the different buildings were little changed by close acquaintance. What we found interesting in the beginning, that we found interesting at the end, and this is an advantage to those whose time is short at the Centennial. You know and see continually more and more, but it is the line of your first enjoyment. This is peculiarly the case in the Main Building, where the contrasts are sharpest, and the better and worse most obvious. In the case of some of the nations (notably Russia, Turkey, and Spain) no judgment could be formed, for there was as yet nothing to look at, when we first came, in the spaces allotted to them. A few amiable young Spanish workmen loitered smiling about, but neither Turk nor Russ was visible. Before the end of the week the Muscovite had developed a single malachite table, but the Ottoman had still done nothing. But by this time the vigor of Spain was surprising: her space was littered with unpacking goods, and already many things were in place, though the display had not yet the order that could make it easily enjoyed. The people who had been most forward were the Norwegians, the Swedes, the Danes, the Egyptians; and to the last I found pleasure in this superior readiness of their departments. The Chinese, whom we found in disorder and unreadiness, pushed rapidly forward during our stay, and before we left, the rich grotesquery of their industries had satisfactorily unfolded itself. We were none the less satisfied that there should be

still a half-score of their carpenters busy about the showcases; their
looks, their motions, their speech, their dress, amidst the fantastic
forms of those bedeviled arts of theirs, affected one like the things
of a capricious dream. It would be interesting to know what they
thought of us spectators. We saw but one Jap in his national costume; a small, lady-handed carpenter, who wrought with tools of
eccentric uses upon one of the showcases, and now and then darted
a disgusted look through his narrow eye-slits at the observer; he
had his name neatly lettered on the back of his coat, and it is the
fault of my ignorance that I cannot give it here. The other Japanese
were in our modification of the English dress; they all had that gen-
tlemanly air of incurious languor which we know in students of
their nation at the Cambridge law-school, and that unease in our
dress, which they had evidently but half subdued to their use. It is
a great pity not to see them in their own outlandish gear, for picturesqueness' sake; the show loses vastly by it; and if it is true that the
annoyances they suffered from the street crowds forced them to
abandon it, we are all disgraced by the fact. It would have been
better to give each Jap a squad of soldiers for his protection everywhere, than lose his costume from our fair for such a reason. There
is a lamentable lack of foreignness in the dress at the Centennial.
The costumed peoples have all put on European wear. To be sure,
the still, sphinx-eyed young Egyptian whom we saw scorning our
recentness from a remote antiquity in his department wore a fez,
but a fez is very little; at the Hungarian wine-booth the waiters
wore the superb Hungarian dress, but this seemed somehow in the
way of trade, and I suspect their name was Schulze, they spoke
German so well. One Turk we did indeed see, in most consoling
bagginess of trousers, crimson jacket, and white stockings, but we
liked quite as well the effect that so many Quaker bonnets on dear
old Quaker ladies gave the crowd. One hears that you find nothing
characteristically Quaker at Philadelphia, any more, and perhaps
these ladies were from the country. At any rate they were frequently
to be seen in their quaint bonnets and dresses of drab, often with
quiet old gentlemen in broad-brims and shad-bellied coats, who
would have been perfect if their cloth was drab instead of black,
though one must still thank them for the cut of it.

We saw them not only at the Centennial, but also on the trains
going to and from the lovely country-place in which our favored
lines were cast during our sojourn. New England has so many other
advantages that one may freely own she is but a barren stock in

comparison with the fertile Pennsylvanian country. With us, even Nature is too conscientious to waste anything, and after our meagreness the frolic abundance of that landscape was not less than astonishing. The density of the foliage, the heavy succulent richness of the herbage, the look of solid comfort and content about the farms, spoke of both pleasure and profit in the country life; whereas our farmers seem (and with reason) to hate their thankless and grudging acres. There were great barns and substantial homesteads of brick and stone, kept with a scrupulous neatness; the pretty, tasteful stations were of stone, and all day long and all night long the incessant trains came and went upon that wonderful Pennsylvania Railroad, bearing the prosperity of the most prosperous commonwealth to and fro. From the passenger's point of view it is the best managed road in the country. I have heard Mr. Scott spoken of as a railroad despot, and I have felt it my duty to hate him. I now make him my apology—if it is he who has been able to teach all those amiable and efficient young men in charge of his trains to treat the public not only with civility but respect; to be polite, to be prompt, to call out intelligibly the name of the next station after that you have just left; to be cleanly uniformed, and to be a joy instead of an abomination to travel. I say from a conscience blameless of free passes that such a man has a right to enslave the public, and I wish that all the conductors and brakemen throughout the land might go and sit at the feet of his employees, and learn their kindness and quickness. Perhaps, however, they must all be Pennsylvanians to do this. Nothing at the Centennial strikes you more agreeably than the good manners of the public functionaries of every grade and service. They listen patiently and answer clearly (in that Philadelphian accent which has its charm), and one may accost them without the least fear of being snubbed out of countenance. They might not improve on acquaintance, but I came away friends with all the Philadelphians I saw in any sort of office. When one thinks of how many officials in other parts of the country he has (in imagination) lain in wait to destroy, this seems a good deal to say.

Our second day at the Centennial began in the Main Building, where after a glance at the not very satisfactory Italian department we found ourselves presently amid the delicate silver-work, the rich furs, the precious and useful metals, the artistic representations of national life of Norway. It was by far the completest department in the building, and for that little country, winter-bound in paralyzing cold and dark for so great a part of the year, the display of tasteful and industrial results was amazing.

The Viking race is not extinct, but the huge energies are so re-fined and directed by the modern spirit to the production of things that may take the mighty West and the delicate South equally with surprise. The silver jewelry was as airily pretty and elegant in de-vice and workmanship as the famous filigree of Genoa, which it so much resembled; and the iron-workers had indulged their stalwart poetry in an iron ship, fashioned like the old Viking craft, and all equipped with iron, at whose prow stood the effigy of Leif Ericsson:—

> "His helmet was of iron, and his gloves
> Of iron, and his breastplate and his greaves
> And tassets were of iron, and his shield;
> In his left hand he hald an iron spear."

And his ship, with a touch of that sentiment painfully lacking in so many of the foreign departments, was called the Vinland. The show of furs and feathers, of luxurious wraps and quilts of eider-down, was surpassingly rich, and the mark of an artistic taste was observ-able in the preparation and arrangement of these, as in everything else. The most interesting things in this and the Swedish depart-ments were, of course, the life-size figures illustrative of present cos-tumes and usages, the work, I believe, of a distinguished Norwegian sculptor. It was like reading one of Björnson's charming stories, to look at these vividly characteristic groups, all of which were full of curious instruction. In one place an old peasant and his wife sit reading in a cottage room; in another a bereaved family surround the cradle of a dead child; here is a group of Laps; there some Swedish peasants stand over a stag which one of the hunters has shot; yonder are a Norwegian bride and groom in their wedding-gear, the bride wearing a crown of ornaments of barbaric gold,—which in this case were actual heirlooms descended from mother to daughter in one peasant family through three hundred years. All was for sale. "We will even separate husband and wife, and sell the bride away from the groom," laughingly explained the commis-sioner. The very pavilion itself, built of Norse pines, and orna-mented in the forms of the old Norse architecture was to be sold; yet there was nothing of the offensiveness of a mere mart in this, as there was in other departments, notably in the extremely shoppy show of the Austrians. The Norwegians had not merely contributed their wares, but had done us an honor and a pleasure by the thoroughly artistic character of their exhibition. So had the Swedes; so had in less degree the Danes, who showed some interesting figures illustrative of the Danish military service, actual and historic, and whose display of exquisite pottery, shaped and colored in the most delicate spirit of antique art, Greek and Egyptian, was certainly one of the most charming features of the fair. So had the Khedive of Egypt, whose section was in perfect order, and who has superbly commanded, it is said, that nothing shall be returned to him and nothing shall be sold, but that all his contributions shall be appropriately given away in this country: despotic splendor that one could more admire if one did not know that the Khedive's march of improvement has been through the blood and tears of his subjects, and that his prosperity is in reality the pomp of a successful slave-driver.

The Italian department, to any one who knows what Italy's wealth in objects of art is, seems—with some signal exceptions—a rather poverty-stricken effort of bric-à-brackishness. It presents a huddled, confused appearance; it is a shop where the prices asked are worthy of the Trois Frères themselves. The spirit of the Brazilian exhibition is pleasant in contrast. The things shown are sincere evidences of the national industry and illustrative of the national civilization; moreover, they are displayed in a Saracenic pavilion that pleases the eye, and are tastefully and intelligibly ordered.

It was not possible, when we saw it, to judge the French department as a whole, and I ought not perhaps to speak of it at all, since so much of it was incompletely arranged. Yet, with all the richness and infinite variety of material the general effect was of shoppiness. The British show was in a more generous spirit, and it was far more interesting. It represented, of course, in English and colonial exhibits, a whole world of varied arts and industries, among which the aesthetic observer would be most taken with the contributions from the Indian empire, and with that wide and beautiful expression of the artistic feeling in household decoration in which England is now leading the world. We Americans could long ago show machinery whose ingenuity and perfection surpassed anything the insular brain had conceived, and now we show in the utilitarian application of the metals, as in tools, and the like, an easy equality, but we cannot yet approach the English in the subjection of material to the higher purposes of both use and pleasure. Their show of tiles, of brasses, of artistically wrought steel and iron, of pottery, of painted glass, was wonderful. We ought, however, to take credit where it is due; in artificial teeth and all the amiable apparatus of dentistry, nothing could approach us; and I must except from a sweeping confession of inferiority the style and workmanship of several large American displays of gas-fixtures: as the most gas-burning people in the world, we were here fitly first; and we were first too, I thought, in the working of silver. The shapes and ornamentations by the different great silver-working houses did justice to the nation which owns the Nevada mines; it proved our capacity for rising equal to an advantage. In glass, however, after the rich colors and manifold lovely forms of the foreign exhibits, we were cold and gray, and in all manufactured stuffs dull and uninteresting; we may have been honest, but we looked poor. I say nothing of our supremacy in a thousand merely ingenious applications and adaptations; that goes without saying; and I say nothing of the display of the publishing houses: books were the last things I cared to see at the Centennial. But I heard from persons less disdainful of literature that the show of book-making did us great honor.

The Main Building is provided with many fountains of the soda sort, and one large fountain for the unsophisticated element, all of which were pretty, and contributed to that brightness of effect which was so largely owing to the handsomeness of the show-cases and pavilions. The finest of these were American. We were thought to have sometimes dimmed the lustre of our jewels by the brilliancy of the casket, but the general display gained by this error. In the middle of the building a band played many hours every day, and over all, with his *bâton* and both arms extended, perpetually triumphed the familiar person of Mr. Gilmore, whom one fancied partially consoled for his lost Coliseums by the bigness of the edifice and the occasion, though, as I said before, the multitude was in nowise comparable to that of our Jubilees. The sparseness of the visitors was more apparent than real, as seen from the organ loft at the end of the building or from the galleries overlooking the central space, but it was worth while to suffer the illusory regret produced by this appearance in order to enjoy the magnificent *coup d'œil* which was to be gained only from those heights.

In the afternoon we made the tour of the State buildings, of which, generally speaking, it is hard to detect at once the beauty or occasion. Doubtless the use could be discovered by public or representative bodies from the various States. The most picturesque building is that of New Jersey; that of Massachusetts was comfortable and complete, which most of the others were not. The Michigan building promises to be handsome; the Ohio building has some meaning in being of Ohio stones, and it is substantially and gracefully designed; the West Virginia building is observable for its exterior display of native woods. But really the most interesting of these not apparently well-reasoned structures is the Mississippi house, which is wholly built of Mississippi woods, the rough bark logs showing without, and the gables and porch decked with gray streamers of Spanish mosses. A typical Mississippian, young in years but venerable in alligator-like calm, sits on this porch (or did there sit on the afternoon of our visit), with his boots on the railing and his hat drawn down over his eyes and sheltering his slowly moving jaws as they ruminate the Virginia weed. He had probably been overquestioned, for he answered all queries without looking up or betraying the smallest curiosity as to the age, sex, or condition of the questioner. Being tormented (I will not name the sex of his tormentress), concerning the uses of a little hole or pouch (it was for letters, really) in the wall near the door, he said that it was to receive contributions for a poor orphan. "I," he added, "am the orphan"; and then at last he looked up, with a faint gleam in his lazy eye which instantly won the heart. This Mississippian was white; another, black, showed us civilly and intelligently through the house, which was very creditable every way to the State, and told us that it was built of seventy different kinds of Mississippi wood. We came away applauding the taste and sense shown in the only State building that seemed to have anything characteristic to say for itself. But in a country where for the most part every State is only more unrepresentative in its architecture than another, it is very difficult for the buildings to be representative.

In their neighborhood were the foreign buildings, the most noticeable of which were the English, Japanese, and Canadian. The English were stuccoed without, showing the wooden anatomy of the building to some extent, and suggesting the comfort of country or suburban homes; the Japanese was like the pictures of all Japanese houses; the Canadian was a sturdy stroke of poetry. It was all built of Canadian timber and lumber. Rough saw-logs formed the stalwart pillars of the portico; boards and planks piled upon each other defined the shape of the building, which had something immensely gratifying and impressive. To be sure, no Canadian could go there for entertainment, but no Canadian could look at this great lumber lodge without thinking of home, which the profuse tiles of the New Jersey house or the many-shingled sides of the Massachusetts building could never suggest to a native of those States.

Massachusetts, through the poetic thoughtfulness of one of her women, had done far better in the erection of the Old Colony House of logs, which we found thronged by pleased and curious visitors. Without, it looks much like the log-cabins with which any dweller in the Middle West is familiar, but it is of three rooms instead of one; and within it aims at the accurate commemoration of Plymouth in its arrangement and furnishing. There are many actual relics of the Pilgrim days, all of which the crowd examined with the keenest interest; there was among other things the writing-desk of John Alden, and at the corner of the deep and wide fire-place sat Priscilla spinning—or some young lady in a quaint, old-fashioned dress, who served the same purpose. I thought nothing could be better than this, till a lovely old Quakeress, who had stood by, peering critically at the work through her glasses, asked the fair spinster to let her take the wheel. She sat down beside it, caught some strands of tow from the spindle, and with her long-unwonted fingers tried to splice the broken thread; but she got the thread entangled on the iron points of the card, and there was a breathless interval in which we all hung silent about her, fearing for her success. In another moment the thread was set free and spliced, the good old dame bowed herself to the work, and the wheel went round with a soft triumphant burr, while the crowd heaved a sigh of relief. That was altogether the prettiest thing I saw at the Centennial.

It was not till our third day that we went to the Woman's Pavilion. Those accustomed to think of women as the wives, mothers, and sisters of men will be puzzled to know why the ladies wished to separate their work from that of the rest of the human race, and those who imagine an antagonism between the sexes must regret, in the interest of what is called the cause of woman, that the Pavilion is so inadequately representative of her distinctive achievement. The show is chiefly saved to the visitor's respect by the carved wood-work done by ladies of the Cincinnati Art School. Even this, compared with great wood-carving, lacks richness of effect; it is rather the ornamentation of the surface of wood in the lowest relief; but it is very good of its kind, full of charming sentiment; it is well intentioned, and executed with signal delicacy and refined skill. It is a thing that one may be glad of as American art, and then, if one cares, as women's work, though there seems no more reason why it should be considered more characteristic of the sex than the less successful features of the exhibition. We did not test the cuisine of the School of Cooking attached to the Woman's Pavilion; the School of Second Work was apparently not yet in operation: if it had been a Man's Pavilion, I should have thought it the dustiest building on the grounds. It seems not yet the moment for the better half of our species to take their stand apart from the worse upon any distinct performance in art or industry; even when they have a building of their own, some organizing force to get their best work into it is lacking; many of those pictures and pincushions were no better than if men had made them; but some paintings by women in the Art Hall, where they belonged, suffered nothing by comparison with the work of their brothers. Woman's skill was better represented in the Machinery Hall than in her own Pavilion; there she was everywhere seen in the operation and superintendence of the most complicated mechanisms, and showed herself in the character of a worker of unsurpassed intelligence.

I sometimes fancied that the Agricultural Hall might reclaim the long-sojourning visitor rather oftener than any other building, if he were of a very patriotic mind. It seems the most exclusively American, and it is absorbingly interesting in traits of its display. There are almost as many attractive show-cases and pavilions as in the Main Building, and they are somehow seen to better advantage. Then there is obviously a freer expression of individual tastes and whims. It was delightful, for example, to walk down the long avenue of mowing and reaping machines, and see those imperfectly surviving forms of "dragons of the prime," resplendent in varnished fine woods and burnished steel, and reposing upon spaces of Brussels carpeting, attended by agents each more firmly zealous than another in the dissemination of advertisements and in the faith that his machine was the last triumph of invention. Their fond pride in their machines was admirable; you could not but sympathize with it, and on a morning after it had rained through the roof upon the carpet and shining metals of one reaperman, who went about mopping and retouching in an amiable desolation, we partook almost insupportably of his despair. We railed bitterly at the culpable negligence of the management, and were not restored to our habitual mood of uncritical enjoyment till we came to our favorite case of sugar-cured hams: a glass case in which hung three or four hams richly canvased, not in the ordinary yellow linen, but in silk of crimson, white, and gold. These were of course from Cincinnati, and the same pork-packer had otherwise shown a humorous fancy in the management of material which does not lend itself readily to the plastic arts in their serious tempers.

The most artistic use of any material was undoubtedly made by some Louisville tobacco dealers, who had arranged the varieties and colors of their product with an eye to agreeable effect which I never saw surpassed in any Italian market, and who had added a final touch by showing different sorts of tobacco growing in pots. It would be interesting to know whether this most tasteful display was the work of an American. Vastly and more simply impressive was a wholly different exhibition from Iowa, to some of whose citizens the happy thought of showing the depth and quality of the soil in several counties of the State had occurred. Accordingly there it was in huge glass cylinders, in which it rose to a height of four, five, and six feet—a boast of inexhaustible fertility which New England eyes could hardly credit. This was one of the inspirations which gave a shock of agreeable astonishment, and revived the beholder even after a day of sight-seeing.

There were fanciful and effective arrangements of farm implements; exhibitions of farm products both foreign and domestic; shows of the manufactured and raw material—literally without number. To remember one was to forget a thousand, and yet each was worthy to be seen. I remember the cotton from India with its satisfying Hindoo names; the pavilion of Brazilian cotton, and the whole array of Brazilian products; the pavilions of American wines and the bacchanal show of Rhine wines, where the vine in leaf and cluster wreathed pillar and cornice, and a little maid sat making more vine-leaves out of paper. The finest of the pavilions seemed to me that of an Oswego starch manufacturer, where an artistic use of the corn and its stalk had been made in the carved ornamentation of the structure. But there were many and many cases and pavilions which were tasteful and original in high degree; and when one looked about on the work of preparation still going forward over the whole territory of the building,—as large, almost, as a German principality,—one felt that the tale was but half told.

A beneficent Sunday in our country retreat interrupted our sightseeing; a Sunday of rural scenes and sounds, when the trains forbore to chuckle to and fro on the Pennsylvania Railroad in exultation at Pennsylvanian prosperity, and the rich landscape throbbed under the gathering heat. The meadow-lark sang everywhere; the redbird's voice was mellow in the dense woods; the masses of the dogwood blossoms whitened through all the heavy foliage. It was a land of blossoms and of waving grass, and a driver over the country roads in the afternoon, past thriving farms and thrifty villages, showed it a land of Sabbath-keeping best clothes, clean faces, neat hair, and domestic peace on innumerable front steps and porches, where children sat with their elders, and young girls feigned to read books while they waited for the young men who were to come later.

Monday was hot and abated our zeal for the Philadelphian spring by giving us a foretaste of what the Philadelphian summer must be. The sun fried the asphalt pavements of the Centennial grounds, and a burning heat reverberated from them, charged with the sickening odor of the cement. That was a day for the stone interior of the Art Hall, but to tell the truth we found none of the buildings so hot as we feared they would be. It was very tolerable indeed both in the Main Building and the Machinery Hall, and in the United States Building we should not have lost patience with the heat if it had not been for the luxurious indifference of that glass case full of frozen fishes there, which, as they reposed in their comfortable boxes of snow, with their thermometer at 30°, did certainly appeal to some of the most vindictive passions of our nature; and I say that during the hot months it will be cruelty to let them remain. There are persons who would go down from Massachusetts to join a mob in smashing that case on the 4th of July, and tearing those fish to pieces. There are also people of culture in this region who would sign a petition asking the government to change the language of the placard on the clothes of the Father of his Country, which now reads, "Coat, Vest, and Pants of George Washington," whereas it is his honored waistcoat which is meant, and his buckskin breeches; pantaloons were then unknown, and "pants" were undreamt of by a generation which had time to be decent and comely in its speech. This placard is a real drawback to one's enjoyment of the clothes, which are so familiarly like, from pictures, that one is startled not to find Washington's face looking out of the coat-collar. The government had been well advised in putting on view these and other personal relics, like his camp-bed, his table furniture, his sword, his pistols, and so forth. There are also similar relics of other heroes, and in the satisfaction of thus drawing nearer to the past in the realization of those historic lives, one's passion for heroic wardrobes mounts so that it stays at nothing. In one of the cases were an ordinary frock-coat of black diagonal, and a silk hat such as is worn in our own epoch, objects which it is difficult to revere in actual life, but for which in their character of relics we severely summoned what veneration we could, while he searched our mind for association of them with some memorable statesmen. We were mortified to think of no modern worthy thus to hand down a coat and hat to the admiration of posterity, and in another moment we should have asked whose they were, if we had not caught sight of a busy attendant in his shirt-sleeves and bare head, just in time to save us from this shame.

We passed on to the interesting exhibition of Indian costumes and architecture, and to those curiously instructive photographs and plaster models of the ancient and modern towns of the Moquis. These rehabilitate to the fancy the material aspect of the old Aztec civilization in a wonderful manner, and throw a vivid light upon whatever one has read of the race whose empire the Spaniards overthrew, but which still lingers, a feeble remnant, in the Pueblos of New Mexico. If the extermination of the red savages of the plains should take place soon enough to save this peaceful and industrious people whom they have harassed for hundreds of years, one could hardly regret the loss of any number of Apaches and Comanches. The red man, as he appears in effigy and in photograph in this collection, is a hideous demon, whose malign traits can hardly inspire any emotion softer than abhorrence. In blaming our Indian agents for malfeasance in office, perhaps we do not sufficiently account for the demoralizing influence of merely beholding those false and pitiless savage faces; moldy flour and corrupt beef must seem altogether too good for them.

I have to leave in despair all details of the government show of army and navy equipments, the varied ingenuity and beautiful murderousness of the weapons of all kinds, the torpedoes with which alone one could pass hours of satisfaction, fancifully attaching them to the ships of enemies and defending our coasts in the most effectual manner; the exquisite models of marine architecture; the figures of soldiers of all arms—not nearly so good as the Danish, but dearer, being our own. Every branch of the administrative service was illustrated, so far as it could be, and the bribes almost sprang from one's pocket at sight of the neat perfection with which the revenue department was represented. There was manufacture of Centennial stamped envelopes, which constantly drew a large crowd, and there were a thousand and one other things which every one must view with advantage to himself and with applause of the government for making this impressive display in the eyes of other nations.

After paying our duty to these objects, we took our first ride on the narrow-gauge railroad, of which the locomotive with its train of gay open cars coughs and writhes about the grounds in every direction, with a station at each of the great buildings. I believe this railroad has awakened loathing in some breasts, and that there has been talk of trying to have it abolished. But I venture to say this will never be done, and in fact I do not see how the public could get on without it. The fare is five cents for the whole tour or from any one point to another; the ride is luxuriously refreshing, and commands a hundred charming prospects. To be sure, the cars go too fast, but that saves time; and I am not certain that the flagmen at the crossings are sufficiently vigilant to avert the accidents whose possibility forms a greater objection to the railroad than mere taste can urge against it. As we whirled along, a gentleman next us on the transverse seat entered into an agreeable monologue, from which we learned, among many other things, that they had in the Agricultural Building the famous war-eagle, Old Abe, whom a Wisconsin regiment carried through the war; and the next morning we made haste to see him. We found him in charge of one of the sergeants who had borne him through thirty battles, and who had once been shot down with the eagle on his perch, and left for dead on the field. The sergeant was a slim young fellow, with gray eyes enough like the eagle's to make them brothers, and he softly turned his tobacco from one cheek to the other while he discoursed upon the bird—his honors from the State government of Wisconsin, which keeps him and a man to care for him at the public charge; his preference for a diet of live chicken; his objection to new acquaintance, which he had shown a few days before by plunging his beak into the cheek of a gentleman who had offered him some endearments. We could not see that Old Abe looked different from other bald eagles (which we had seen in pictures): he had a striking repose of manner, and his pale, fierce eye had that uninterested, remote regard said to characterize all sovereign personages. The sergeant tossed him up and down on his standard, and the eagle threw open his great vans; but otherwise he had no entertainment to offer except the record of his public services,—which we bought for fifty cents.

We were early on the ground that morning, and saw the Centennial in some aspects which I suppose the later visitor misses, when the crowd becomes too great for social ease. The young ladies in charge of pavilions or quiescent machinery, and the various young men in uniforms who superabounded at nine o'clock, gave the Machinery Hall the effect of a vast *conversazione,* amidst which no one could wander unconscious of a poetic charm. I am sure this was blamelessly pleasant, and if the Centennial did nothing but promote all that multitudinous acquaintance, it could not be considered other than a most enormous success. These happy young people neglected no duty to the public; there never was on this continent such civility and patience as that of the guards and policemen and officials of the Centennial, and the young ladies would leave a word half-breathed, half-heard, at the slightest demand of curiosity concerning anything they had in charge. In the midst, the Corliss engine set an example of unwearying application to business, and even while one gazed in fond approval, innumerable spindles began to whirr and shuttles to clack, and a thousand *tête-à-têtes* were broken up as by magic.

It was very pleasing to see the enthusiasm of inventors or agents concerning their wares, and the eagerness with which they met curiosity. I do not now speak so much of young ladies like her in charge of a perfumery stand in the Main Building, who would leave her company with both elbows on the counter and his chin in his hands, to spring away and atomize with odorous extracts any passer who showed signs of loitering near; rather I sing such geniuses as he of the Carriage Hall, who illustrated his cradle attachment to the parental bedstead, and his automaton baby-tender. From how much getting up at night, and how much weary care by day, these inventions had sprung, one could only conjecture; but I am sure that the most profound domestic experience inspired them. The inventor was never weary showing how, with his cradle hung by springs to your bedside, you had but to roll over and rock the most refractory baby to sleep, without losing your temper or your rest; how on simply inserting an infant into the aperture of his wheeled stool, the child walked about all day in perpetual content, a blessing to himself and his parents. The terms of confidence which he established with admiring mothers, the winks he gave, the nudges which I am sure he aspired to give, were all charming, and came from nothing less than a sense of having benefited the whole human race. Almost as serenely confident was the young lady who operated the Radiant Flat Iron in the Machinery Hall, an implement in whose hollow frame burnt a gas-flame blown hotter by a draft of air, the two elements being conveyed thither by India-rubber tubes from reservoirs under the ironing-table. "But what makes the pressure of the gas and air?" "Oh, you see I stand on a sort of bellows, which I work by resting from one foot to the other as one always does in ironing." The world is perhaps not yet prepared for the intricate virtues of the Radiant Flat Iron, but in the mean time we venerated its ingenuity. It is, doubtless, as promising of general usefulness as that beautiful ice-boat which our chair-boy hurried us away to see, and which seems peculiarly popular with the wheelers of chairs; they perhaps envy its capacity for getting over space at the rate of a mile a minute, though this need not be, as it is time they should rather desire to annihilate. They are an obliging race, and the chairs are a great help to the enjoyment of the Centennial. They are to be found in each of the principal buildings, and it is best to take them anew in each hall, instead of hiring one for a tour of the whole. If you do that, much time is lost, and in getting out to climb steps and cross broken spaces and railroad tracks, the occupant of the chair shares too actively in the enterprise. The chairs are mainly for ladies; very few men have the self-respect requisite for being publicly trundled about in that manner.

To any one who knows the different American types, the attendants and operatives in the Machinery and Agricultural Halls would afford curious study. The Western face distinguishes itself very easily from that of the Middle States, but in its eagerness is not so readily told from that of New England, which shows how largely New England has characterized the appearance, while Pennsylvania has prevailed in the accent, of the younger States. Where New England came out with most startling evidence was in the visages of the Waltham watch-makers, who, whether pure Yankees or Yankeeized foreigners, had looks that no one could mistake. They were at work there all day with their life-like machinery, and on every side the thousand creations of American inventive genius were in operation, with an exhilaration and impressiveness in the whole effect which can in no wise be described. Of the huger machinery, the working of some pumps that drove their streams of water far over and across a great tank was the gayest and most strenuous sight. I should hardly know how to justify to the inexperienced the joy I knew in putting my hand over an air-blast, that flung it into the air like a leaf. Nevertheless, such things are.

I have left the Carriage Hall to the last, though it was one of the first things we saw. I am not a connoisseur of wheeled vehicles, and I dare say I admired not too wisely. The American shapes seemed to me the most elegant; there was a queerness, a grotesqueness, an eccentricity, about the English, when they were not too heavy. But what most seizes the spectator is some one's ghastly fancy of a white hearse. It shows that a black hearse is not the most repulsive thing that can be. There are some exquisite specimens of car-architecture for a Brazilian railroad; a buggy from Indiana is kept—I do not know why—in a glass case; and there is a very resplendent Pullman car through which we walked, for no reason that I can give—probably the mere overmastering habit of sight-seeing.

We thought it well during our week at the Centennial to lunch as variously as possible, and I can speak by the card concerning the German Restaurant, the two French Restaurants, and the Vienna Bakery; the native art in cooking we did not test. The German Restaurant and the Lafayette Restaurant are very reasonable in their charges, less expensive, indeed, than most first-class city restaurants. The Trois Frères Provençaux is impudently extortionate. Not that dishes cooked with so much more sentiment than any you can find elsewhere are not worth more, but that there are absurd charges for what Americans ordinarily pay nothing for: bread, butter, and service at double and quadruple the Parisian rates. But it is even worse at the Vienna Bakery, where they have twenty-five cents for a cup of coffee, and not good coffee at that—not at all the coffee of Vienna. Happily, no one is obliged to go to these places for sustenance. There are a hundred others within the grounds where you may lunch cheaply and well, or cheaply and ill, which most of our nation like better. There is, for instance, a large pavilion where one may surcharge the stomach with pie and milk at a very low price. There is an American Restaurant, there is a Southern Restaurant (served by lustrous citizens of color), there is a restaurant attached to the Old Colony House; there is no end to them; and I am very glad to say of them, and of all other American enterprises for the public comfort, that their opportunity has not been improved to the public ruin. The extortion seems to be all by the foreigners,—unless sixty cents an hour is too much for a wheeled chair. I think it is; but the chairs will doubtless be cheaper when the cars of the circular railroad have run over two or three. All stories of the plundering of strangers by the Philadelphians may be safely distrusted. Probably never before in the history of world's fairs has the attitude of the local city towards its guests been so honest, so conscientious, so generous.

The grounds of the Centennial are open twelve hours every day, and your payment of fifty cents admits you for all that time to everything there. No account, however close, however graphic, can give a just conception of the variety and interest of the things to be seen. The whole season would not exhaust them; a week or a month enables you to study a point here and there. Yet if you have but a single day to spend, it is well to go. You can never spend a day with richer return.

A very pleasant thing about the exhibition is your perfect freedom there. There are innumerable officials to direct you, to help you, to care for you, but none of them bothers you. If you will keep off those clay slopes and expanses which are placarded Grass, there will be no interference with any caprice of your personal liberty. This is the right American management of a public pleasure.

The muse at all minded to sing the humors of a great holiday affair could find endless inspiration at the Centennial; but there are space and the reader to be regarded. Yet I must not leave the theme without speaking of the gayety of the approaches and surroundings; the side shows are outside here, and the capacity for amusement which the Centennial fails to fill need not go hungering amid the provision made for it by private enterprise. It is curious to see the great new hotels of solid and flimsy construction near the grounds, and the strange city which has sprung up in answer to the necessities of the world's fair. From every front and top stream the innumerable flags, with which during a day in town we found all Philadelphia also decked. Yet it is an honest and well-behaved liveliness. There is no disorder of any sort; nowhere in or about the Centennial did I see any one who had overdrunk the health of his country.

Not the least prodigious of the outside appurtenances of the Centennial is that space allotted on a neighboring ground to the empty boxes and packing cases of the goods sent to the fair. Their multitude is truly astonishing, and they have a wild desolation amidst which I should think the gentlemen of the Centennial Commission, in case of a very disastrous failure of the enterprise, would find it convenient to come and rend their garments. But no one expects failure now. Every day of our week there saw an increase of visitors, and the reader of the newspapers knows how the concourse has grown since. The undertaking merits all possible prosperity, and whatever were the various minds in regard to celebrating the Centennial by an international fair, no one can now see the fair without a thrill of patriotic pride.

W. D. Howells.

Appendix III

Howells and Justine McCarthy
on the Tavern Club

(*in* Reminiscences by McCarthy [*1899*], *Vol. I,*
pp. 208–209)

Justine McCarthy, the prolific journalist and politician made two
visits to this country in the interest of Irish Home Rule, the first in
1870 and the second in 1886. In his *Reminiscences* (1899) he included (pp. 208–209) "the following kindly and genial letter" from
a man "famous through all the reading world" and described his
evening with Howells at the Tavern Club.

'302 BEACON STREET, BOSTON, September 21, 1886.

'DEAR MR. MCCARTHY,—I hope you have not forgotten
me, who vividly remember the pleasure of meeting you at Mr.
Lowell's when you were in the country before, for I have
boasted to the members of the Tavern Club, of which I am
unworthily president, that I knew you personally, and that I
could use the influence of an old acquaintance in getting you
to accept a dinner from them. The Tavern Club is made up of
all the best and nicest young lawyers, doctors, artists, and

littérateurs here, and we have entertained Lowell, Salvini, Irving, and others, at the simple dinners which our Italian artist makes for us; and now we want you, whom we love for yourself and your cause. You are to be in Boston early in October; won't you name some evening—*not* Friday, Saturday, or Sunday—when you will dine with us? Speeches brief, and no reporters.

'Yours sincerely,
'W. D. HOWELLS.'

The dinner-party came off, and was not by any means the only pleasant gathering to which I was introduced by the courteous attentions of Mr. Howells. I have a grateful recollection of that Tavern Club dinner. The fare was good, the wines were good, the speeches were short, crisp, and sparkling, and there was an air of friendly comradeship throughout the whole evening which reminded me of some of the dead, unforgotten days of that better and artistic Bohemia which we once used to have in London. There was a keen cross-fire of conversational wit and humour at the Tavern Club dinner; and I remember that we got into an animated discussion on Mr. Howells's favourite theory as to the sphere of the novel writer. I am not going to discuss the theory here; we have all considered it and argued about it, and made up our minds concerning it, and unmade them again many times since that day; and Mr. Howells's theory has at all events the advantage over many other theories, that its author was able himself to put it into practice and to make it a success. Perhaps Mr. Howells was inspired by his genius to take a certain course in the first instance, and then unconsciously developed the theory to suit the conditions of the achievement; but, anyhow, I know we had a charming argument, and passed a most delightful evening. Dixie, the clever American comedian, was there, and gave us some wonderful imitations of Henry Irving and other leaders of the drama—imitations that were not mere mimicries, but which positively created new parts for the performer, and showed us precisely how he would be sure to play them if they came within the range of his study. I have had many evenings of social and intellectual enjoyment in Boston, none more full of enjoyment than that evening at the Tavern Club dinner.

On the basis of *Reminiscences,* Howells wrote two "Papers" for *Literature* entitled "Some Suggestions from Mr. McCarthy" (July 14, 1899, No. 27 n.s., p. 9; July 21, 1899, No. 28 n.s., p. 33). In these two "Papers" Howells describes the *salons* of 1870, which had almost disappeared in 1886 and had entirely gone by 1899. See also H. M. Alden, "Fifty Years of Harper's," *Harper's Magazine,* C (May, 1900), 955, for comment on McCarthy's relationship to the magazine as a contributor.

Appendix IV

Howells' View of Arrogance
Toward Workmen

*(in The Saturday Club, A Century Com-
pleted, 1920–1956*
Edward W. Forbes and John H. Finley, Jr.
[eds.]
[Houghton, Mifflin, 1958])

In "Recollections of the Saturday Club," Bliss Perry tells us that

. . . by 1903 the men of letters had shrunk to a single un-
questioned representative, Mr. Howells, and he had long since
removed to New York. Aldrich had been elected, but apparently came only once. Robert Grant would, I think, have been
considered the "runner-up," on the strength of his *Unleavened
Bread*.

Mr. Howells, however, continued to appear occasionally at
the Saturday Club and also at the Tavern Club, where he had
been much beloved. I believe that he was never as happy in
New York as he had been in Cambridge. "No one ever drops
in any more to talk about books," he said to me once in the
1890's in New York, "no one except once in a while Brander
Matthews." There was one side of that gentle nature of his,
lying down and scarcely revealed in his books except perhaps

in his *Hazard of New Fortunes,* which startled me once by its fierce Tolstoyan passion. We had been lunching with Mrs. Fields at Manchester, to meet Charles Dudley Warner. The only other guest, except Miss Jewett, was Mrs. "Jack" Gardner. That lady was then building Fenway Court, now known as the Isabella Stewart Gardner Museum. She gave a most entertaining account of her struggles with the Italian workmen; how she had mounted a shaky platform herself, adze in hand, to show them how to bevel some ceiling beams, how she had fought the workmen and contractor down on the matter of wages, and bluffed them out of a threatened strike. She had a keen sense of humor, and there was in truth something exhilarating in this picture of a lone Yankee woman subduing the insurgent sons of Italy by sheer pluck and will power. Mr. Howells laughed a little with the rest of us, but as we got into the cab to be driven back to the railroad station, this former consul in Venice, who admired and loved Italian workmen and was himself none too rich in worldly goods, broke out in bitter denunciation of the arrogance of wealth and its hardheartedness in grinding the faces of the poor. I had known Mr. Howells very pleasantly for years, but in that blazing instant I discovered that I had known him only on the surface.[1]

A note from Howells to Mrs. Gardner suggests that he had been invited to Fenway Court the year before but had been unable to attend. The note reads:

> 48 West 59th St.,
> Dec. 10, 1902.

My dear Mrs. Gardner:

   I am just home from a week's absence, and find your kind note. You may be sure I will not forget your leave to come and see your wonder-house the next time I am in Boston. I wish I could promise myself would be soon; ma non vedo l'ora!

> Yours sincerely
> W. D. Howells.[2]

The next year, on February 24, 1903, a dinner was given at the Tavern Club in honor of Howells.[3] At this time, perhaps, Howells made the visit to the Saturday Club remembered by Bliss Perry, and also took occasion to pay his deferred respects to Mrs. Gardner at Fenway Court.

NOTES

1. In *The Saturday Club, A Century Completed, 1920–1956,* edited by Edward W. Forbes and John H. Finley, Jr. (Houghton, Mifflin, 1958), pp. 5–6.
2. This letter is in the Gardner Museum in Boston and was photostated for me by the permission of the Director, Dr. George Stout.
3. See T. B. Aldrich's letter to Howells, Jan. 22, 1903. The Ballinger Collection, Vol. I. Houghton Library, Harvard.

Appendix V

Professor Charles Eliot Norton's
Annual Ashfield Dinner of 1907

(*in New York* Evening Post, *November 30, 1907*)

PROF. NORTON AND ASHFIELD

Elevation of a Little Town by a Big Man

The Famous "Annual Dinners" He Established—A Summer
Resident For Forty Years, He Has Been a Powerful Influence
in the Place
[Special Correspondence of The Evening Post.]

ASHFIELD, Mass., November 23.—This little hilltop village has a
unique title to interest in the eightieth birthday observances of Prof.
Charles Eliot Norton, who has been a summer resident here for
forty years. The personality of the famous man is often seen most
intimately through the freer self-revelation in the life of some remote community. This is true of Professor Norton's relations to
Ashfield, not because he could be otherwise than himself in any
surroundings, but because the great needs of an isolated village so

appealed to his sympathy as to make the heaviest possible drafts upon his social and civic activity.

Professor Norton's Ashfield work is generally known only so far as concerns the famous "Ashfield dinners," but other aspects of his life here illustrate his character quite as clearly. He did pioneer work in the "village beautiful idea," and was exceedingly plain spoken in a long campaign against ugliness. If some one's lawn was weedy and shaggy, if a house needed painting, he would administer a personal reproof at some public meeting. He was not careful whom he hit. The creamery association erected a building, in which it combined the workrooms and apartments of the manager in an awkward and ungainly fashion. Professor Norton talked about it at one of the Ashfield dinners, and as he spoke he caught the eye of the president of the creamery association, one of his best friends, and one who had often smoothed the ruffled plumage of victims of previous castigations. But the professor went right on.

"Perhaps you think," he said, "that I am treading on some one's toes. I want to tread on some one's toes, and I want to tread on them hard."

The magnificent row of maples on the main street is a monument to the day of carnage when the telephone company encountered Professor Norton. He organized a corps of workers for lining turf, mowing grass, and killing weeds, and for years the entire village turned out, from a veteran of nearly ninety years down to the children. At noon the party would repair to the town hall for a jolly luncheon hour, followed by a talk by Professor Norton on village improvement.

An angry growl went up from all over western Massachusetts at the suggestion made at some public meeting that the country people should make more use of the tooth brush and bath tub. "But it did good," said an Ashfield man the other day. "Most of the farmers put in bath tubs now when they build anew. You can see what he has done with the young people, too. Look at those little fellows touching their hats."

FRIEND OF THE CHILDREN

The Ashfield young people have indeed been close to Professor Norton, trooping to his house with their birds' nests and butterfly collections, and finding him ready to talk by the hour about anything that interested them. Conversing with the boy who was collecting specimens of wood, he would maintain that a piece of beech was chestnut, in order to get the boy to put his knowledge into definite statement. For a long time he sent from his Cambridge home all the stamps from his large foreign mail to the boy who was making a collection. Until a short time ago he used to wield the axe in his wood lot, and his intimacy with the youngsters was indicated one day when an urchin was criticising him because he did not hold his axe after the truly bucolic manner. There were stormy days for the Ashfield boys when their ball team used to meet a nine from a neighboring manufacturing village of head-punching proclivities. Professor Norton was commonly near the base line when the first ball was pitched, and his counsel was an anchor in some of these days of the tempest.

If Professor Norton heard of a boy that wanted an education, but was discouraged by unpropitious circumstances, he would seek him out and talk it all over with him—sometimes lending him money if it seemed best. That these protégés came close to his heart, is suggested by the time he took at one of the last Ashfield dinners to tell the progress of one of the Ashfield boys who was working his way through college. He started an annual children's exhibit, with prizes for winners in garden cultivation, mechanical contrivances, and other original lines. One of the boys whose ambition was stimulated by contact with Professor Norton studied electricity to such good purpose that at fifteen he was able to wire and light his father's house.

Professor Norton, soon after his arrival here, induced George William Curtis to establish a summer home in this town, and a considerable colony has followed. In spite of its declining population, this little village of less than a thousand people, ten miles from a railroad station and isolated by its hill-top position, has all the trimness of a smart city suburb. Mr. Curtis, seconded by Professor Norton, undertook the reform of the library, once a little collection of persistently vagrant habits, entertained now at a house and now at a shop, but always transient in its stay. Now with about 5,000 volumes it has a permanent home.

THE ACADEMY'S FOUNDER

The academy is principally Professor Norton's achievement. The older people remember it as a limbo of rag-stuffed windows, the wood piles in the front yard suggested a saw-mill. To-day it has a modern building, well-equipped, and a fund of $20,000. This property came from the dinners and from fairs, and from gifts that would never have been received but for Professor Norton and Mr. Curtis.

The annual dinners were instituted by Professor Norton to build up the academy fund and to give a remote village personal contact with great men. As the result of his efforts, probably no American town of its type has entertained so many famous personalities. The community that through these occasions has heard utterances of such historic import as that of Curtis, when he gave his reasons for revolting from Blaine; as that of Lowell, when first after his return from the court of St. James he justified himself to the American people. It has listened year after year to the idealism of Norton, the rollicking humor and charming sentiment of John White Chadwick, to the originality and erudition of Stanley Hall. It has wrestled with Edward Atkinson and the Aladdin oven. It has heard Gov. W. E. Russell, Moorfield Storey, MacVeagh, Choate, and Phelps. It treasures the fancies of Charles Dudley Warner, suggested impromptu by the figures upon a paper napkin. It looks upon Howells as almost an Ashfield boy, for did he not speak here in days of diffidence, when his manuscript trembled as the youth addressed his audience?

The homeliness of background deepened the impression of the feasts. Here was a low studded hall, its whitewashed walls of severest simplicity, in size and equipment inadequate for anything more exciting than a church social, so crowded that reserve of room for passage between tables would almost push the diners under the heavily laden boards. The mountain of Yankee eatables was heaped upon the tables, and the guests ate all courses from one plate, the sturdy Yankees showing a certain dignified scorn of company manners in thus adhering to the habit of farm and grange.

No time was allowed for elaborate service, for the audience proved the supremacy of the mental over the fleshly by the haste of the onslaught upon the crowning triumph of apple pie, that the speech-making might begin. The food, sometimes defended from insects by long strips of netting, remained on the tables for economy of time. The old-fashioned settees of non-reversible backs whirled through the air in the hands of lusty hay-makers, with possibilities of scraping the low ceiling, that all might face the speakers. To guests used to elaboration in service and table furniture as preliminary to oratory, this Puritan simplicity etched into strongest relief the eloquence that followed, with its wide outlook and tonic quality. Most delightful of all was the courtly grace of Professor Norton as toastmaster, seeming to combine the charm of the old Southern aristocracy, Gallic deftness of reporter, and the spiritual atmosphere of Puritanism.

There were stormy days at the dinners when Professor Norton used to express his anti-imperialistic sentiment, which became so pronounced as to offend the rock-ribbed Republicanism of the hills, so that a partial boycott of the feasts followed. Partly on this account, partly from advancing age, Professor Norton resigned his task as master of the feast in 1903, and no one was willing to undertake to succeed him.

The dignity of country life was a foremost note at these gatherings. The interests of Ashfield were treated as worthy of consideration in the presence of national leaders and alongside of national problems. Thus Professor Norton cast his influence to counteract the self-depreciating spirit so usual in the country town. Rural decline worried him long before the "decadent hill town" figured in the magazines. He often referred to the independent life of old Ashfield, with eighty home industries then flourishing here. By the time the hill town disputants had begun to bite and devour one another, Professor Norton and Mr. Curtis had accomplished the salvation of Ashfield.

Appendix VI

Howells' Obituary
by Alexander D. Noyes

(*in* "Report of the Board of Management of the Century Club 1921," *Reports, Constitutions, By-laws of the Century Club, 1921*)

It is evidence of the changing popular conceptions from one generation to another that WILLIAM DEAN HOWELLS, who in his earlier days was himself deemed an innovator and iconoclast in the field of fiction, should nowadays seem to the new public all but old-fashioned. He had his bout with the Thackeray and Dickens worshipers, to whom what the public of thirty or forty years ago called Howells's realism was an undoubted grievance; but to disciples of the present-day innovators who have learned to consider literary nakedness as the genuine realism, Howells may well seem mid-Victorian. Nevertheless, Howells had what is rather pitifully lacking in the Wellses and Bennetts, and what will make his best stories live as neither the best nor the worst of theirs are at all likely to do; clear insight into human nature, extraordinary grasp of the actual working of the human mind in those bewildering dilemmas which arise in everyday life, real though wholly unostentatious culture, the art of outlining personal characteristics so that the subject lives, and a style which, with all its easy and unaffected grace, had the distinction of never intruding between the reader and the story.

Howells, in his polemical days, had a good deal to say of the unnatural theories of human nature and the unwarranted strain on circumstance to which the older novelists resorted; yet the longer he wrote, the more frequently he was himself drawn by the exigencies of his plot into the very pitfalls against which he had warned his readers. The dramatic moment in the *Hazard of New Fortunes* when the old German Radical, the dreamy young worker among the poor, and the editor of the magazine on which both are employed, are all brought by chance at once to the spot where two of them are killed, is only one of them. But Howells was too good an artist not to let his story lead him, regardless of his theories.

His literary theories and his literary art were in fact very largely independent of one another. As a critic, Howells was one of the foremost admirers and literary promoters of the Russian novelists; yet he himself has nothing of the savage realism of Dostoyeffsky and little of the harsh touch of Tolstoy; his own art resembling far more closely the very un-Russian method of the expatriated Russian Turguenieff. Howells had his hobbies and sometimes tried them in his novels; but even with such somewhat rare experiments as the introducing of current slang in the language of his narrative —presumably on the theory that it might some day be good English—the only consequence was to create in the contemporary reader's mind the mild surprise with which he would have listened to the same phrase from the lips of a cultured acquaintance, and to give a curiously archaic touch to the passage when read again in later years.

It was so with Howells's half-avowed Socialist proclivities. One rarely took them quite seriously even in the *Easy Chair,* and never in the novels; he seemed to be analyzing Socialism as he analyzed the mind of the dreamy unpractical young philanthropists in his stories. But his books are very human books; his gallery of human types is a delight to which we perpetually return. He did not hesitate to draw the eccentric, even the coarse and selfish character, and his pictures are convincing. But neither by the mid-Victorians nor by the present-day apostles of human dulness are we ever admitted also to such genial and well-bred company, sketched with such truth and touched with such gentle humor, as in Howells's novels.

It has been said that the highest possession of the Century is its traditions and its memories. Both are embodied in this notable list of comrades who have left us this past year. Yet what they were to the Century, the Century was to them and will continue to be to those of us who remain in its genial circle. As the years go on, and one after another of the familiar names drops from the roll, the feeling comes all the more strongly home to the rest of us that the Club's traditions, which have such deep root in the character and achievement of the past, are equally sure of living into the long future.

ALEXANDER D. NOYES
Secretary

THE CENTURY HOUSE
January 8, 1921

Index